Robert Feather is a chartered metallurgist, an experienced journalist/ broadcaster/lecturer, and has written a number of books and numerous articles and appeared in TV documentaries on archaeology, ancient history and religion.

His book, *The Mystery of the Copper Scroll of Qumran*, was published by Inner Traditions, of America, in June 2003. A previous book, *The Copper Scroll Decoded*, published by HarperCollins in 1999, has been translated into Dutch, Italian, Japanese, and Portuguese, and talks are in progress for a version in Russian. He recently appeared in Discovery Channel and National Geographic documentaries on the Copper Scroll and Egypt. A BBC TV documentary, entitled *The Pharaoh's Holy Treasure*, based on the book, was first screened in March 2002 and the author participated in a BBC/Discovery documentary entitled *The Spear of Jesus* in 2003. A sequel to the documentary, co-presented by Robert Feather, was screened by National Geographic at Christmas 2010 in America and will shortly be shown in Europe and the rest of the world.

His latest book *The Secret Initiation of Jesus at Qumran* was published in America by Inner Traditions and in the UK by Watkins.

Previous books by Robert Feather

The Copper Scroll Decoded
The Mystery of the Copper Scroll of Qumran
The Secret Initiation of Jesus at Qumran
Doyen of the Dead Sea Scrolls

A Clash of Steel (fiction)

Black Holes in the Dead Sea Scrolls

The Conspiracy • The History • The Meaning • The Truth

Robert Feather

Foreword by

J. Harold Ellens, PhD

WATKINS PUBLISHING

LONDON

This edition first published in the UK and USA 2012 by
Watkins Publishing, Sixth Floor, Castle House,
75–76 Wells Street, London W1T 3QH

Design and typography copyright © Watkins Publishing 2012

1 3 5 7 9 10 8 6 4 2

Designed and typeset by Donald Sommerville

Printed and bound in China by Imago

British Library Cataloguing-in-Publication Data Available

Library of Congress Cataloging-in-Publication Data Available

ISBN: 978-1-78028-377-7

www.watkinspublishing.co.uk

Distributed in the USA and Canada by Sterling Publishing Co., Inc.
387 Park Avenue South, New York, NY 10016-8810

For information about custom editions, special sales,
premium and corporate purchases, please contact
Sterling Special Sales Department at 800-805-5489
or specialsales@sterlingpub.com

The book is dedicated to the blessed memory of Robert Shrager, who proof-read and offered constructive criticism to my previous books. His input is sorely missed, and I hope there are not too many commas in the wrong place!

Contents

Acknowledgements

This book has been in gestation for about three years and nine months and many midwives and nurses have assisted in its birth. They are listed in alphabetical order which does not relate to the invaluable degree of help each person has contributed.

Ruth Abraham: critic and supporter; Tony Abraham: artist, critic, cover-design consultant; Vivien Ansell: critic and advisor; George Brooke: Professor at Manchester University, scholar and critic; Tom Conway: Elmbridge Multi-faith Forum; Sarah Feather: proofreader and critic; Tuvia Fogle: literary agent, Il Caduceo srl., Milan, Italy; David Freeman: rabbi, consultant; Helen Freeman: rabbi, consultant; Deborah Hercun, managing editor, Watkins Publishing; Adrian Korsner: photographer, jazz aficionado, cover designer; Michael Mann: publisher, Watkins Publishing; Józef Milik: former leader of the Dead Sea Scrolls translation team, Ecole Biblique; Yolanta Zaluska Milik: art historian, Paris; Irene Morley: University College, London; Nabil M. Mustapha: Chairman, Elmbridge Multi-faith Forum; Ahmed Osman: author, consultant; Donald Sommerville, copyeditor and typesetter; Geza Vermes: Professor Emeritus at Oxford University, Dead Sea Scrolls doyen; Mark Winer: rabbi, consultant.

Plates

Fresco of King Akhenaton riding his royal chariot, in the Tomb of Panehesy, Amarna. Footholds have been carved out in the wall for pilgrims to climb up and place prayers in niches. *(R. Feather)*

Line drawing of a relief on the wall of the Tomb of Apy at Amarna, showing twelve loaves of bread on the table in front of the altar. *(Courtesy Egypt Exploration Society)*

Images of Queen Nefertiti and King Akhenaton marked with the early Christian symbols of the alpha and omega, in the Tomb of Panaehesy at Amarna. The faint figure of an infant with a yellow halo in the arms of Neferetiti is almost certainly that of Jesus, To the left is the baptismal font carved out by early followers of Jesus. *(R. Feather)*

Examples of clay jars and containers found at Amarna and now in the Petrie Museum, London. Similar-shaped jars have been found at Qumran and its sister site at Ain Feshka. *(R. Feather)*

Plan of the city of Akhetaton showing the Temple storage magazines. *(Adapted from J. D. S.Pendlebury,* The City of Akhenaton Part III, The Central City and The Official Quarters, *Egypt Exploration Society, 1951)*

Professor George Brooke, Professor Hanan Eshel and Dr Lutz Doering at the Brown University conference 'Qumran – The Site of the Dead Sea Scrolls', in November 2002. *(R. Feather)*

Excavations at Qumran by the Magen/Peleg team in 2002, during which they claimed to have found evidence the site was a pottery factory. *(R. Feather)*

Elephantine Island viewed from the directions of Aswan, showing huge boulders shaped like elephants that made the Greeks change its name from Yeb to Elephantine. *(R. Feather)*

Geza Vermes, Emeritus Professor of Oxford University. *(R. Feather)*

John Franks, the man who freed up publication of the Scrolls. *(R. Feather)*

Professor Emanuel Tov, the last editor-in-chief of the Dead Sea Scrolls publication team, at a lecture in Manchester. *(R.Feather)*

Examples of *shabtis* carrying mattocks, on display in the Metropolitan Museum, New York. *(R.Feather)*

John Marco Allegro with a mattock he excavated at Khirbet Qumran. *(Courtesy Mrs Joan Allegro)*

Pottery fragment with lettering identical to that used by a scribe who wrote one of the Dead Sea Scrolls. *(Courtesy Professor André Lemaire)*

Scene from the window of appearances, showing mattocks on the end of the Aton rays. *(Courtesy Egypt Exploration Society)*

Józef Milik with Robert Feather in Paris, 2001. *(R.Feather)*

Robert Feather with Professor Harold Ellens. *(R.Feather)*

Foreword

Robert Feather takes the Bible seriously. Therefore, he has an insatiable interest in the Dead Sea Scrolls (DSS). He is a remarkably creative scholar who sees the significant relationship between these two sets of ancient writings. He has published a dozen books on the Dead Sea Scrolls, in five different languages. In this volume he presents the comprehensive picture of his understanding of all these ancient documents. He wants to clarify what the DSS really say and how they illumine a sound interpretation of the Bible.

When I say Feather takes the Bible seriously, I mean that he has a great literary appreciation for this ancient set of Jewish writings that have become sacred scriptures for Jews and Christians, as well as being highly honoured by many Muslims. In the same way he esteems the DSS as ancient Jewish documents that can tell us a great deal about how to read and understand the Bible as well as how to understand the intellectual, theological and historical origins of the literary and philosophical traditions of the Western World. He believes that making the DSS speak the language of the people and making sure that they are interpreted correctly is the urgent duty of the scholarly world.

It is for these reasons that Feather raises many critical questions about the archaeological methods, the political complexities and the obscure procedures of the scholarly community through which the scrolls came to light, were made available to us or, in some cases, were delayed from reaching the interested community. I was personally present with James M. Robinson when he was working day and night for a week collating and preparing for publication two volumes of DSS fragments which had been kept from scholarly attention for nearly 30 years. The Huntington Library made the relevant photographs available to Robinson, unofficially and some say illegally. At the same time Robert Eisenman obtained access to another set of photographs of these long unpublished fragments. That was 40 years after the discovery of the DSS in 1947. When Hershel Shanks of the Biblical Archaeology Society published those two huge folio volumes, all the scrolls were finally available for scholarly analysis for the first time. Robinson and I and Shanks and a few others gathered in the NY Press Club auditorium for a spectacular announcement of this signal moment in DSS history.

Since that rather awesome day, an immense scholarly endeavour has produced a massive critical literature explicating the scrolls. James C. VanderKam, Peter Flint, Lawrence Schiffman and Geza Vermes are just a few of the recent stellar lights that have presented the history, literature, and interpretation of the DSS to the public. They joined such earlier notables as Józef Milik, Millar Burrows, Frank Cross, Michael Wise, Martin Abegg and Hartmut Stegemann in making these ancient documents available in scholarly and popular publications. Together, these scholars and their numerous colleagues have produced virtually uncountable translations, descriptions, analyses, dictionaries, glossaries, commentaries and archaeological studies of the DSS. The analysis and interpretation of these scrolls, from the desert caves between the Judaean village of Qumran and Jericho on the Jordan River, will surely continue for at least another century before all the possibilities are exhausted.

However, Robert Feather is concerned about what has been missed in all this process. Sometimes he thinks that much of this was sound and fury signifying far less than it should have. Some leading scholars like Józef Milik and Geza Vermes do not altogether disagree with him. There are many unanswered questions. Why were the scrolls found in desert caves in clay jars? Why was the Qumran Community isolated from the rest of society? What did it mean that they were at odds with the temple elite? What temple? Where did the scrolls come from, particularly the peculiar Copper Scroll with its strange ancient 'Egyptian' markings? What is the meaning of all the references to Egypt in the scrolls? Why were many of the scrolls and especially the two volumes of important fragments delayed for a couple of scholarly generations before they were finally clandestinely published by Robinson, Eisenman and Shanks?

Feather abhors conspiracy theories, but he is willing to ask the tough questions, on these and numerous other counts, that have left the DSS in a shroud of mystery even to this day. He thinks it is time for some courageous truth-telling. He has launched a very controversial project with this book. That makes it all the more interesting and important, of course. The author is a skilful writer and narrator. Once you begin to read his work, it is impossible to put it down. You will notice that he is convinced that the answers to all the mysterious questions are plain and forthright. Some scholars will agree with him with a great sense of illumination, while others will as vigorously disagree. In any case, Feather's perspective must be published and taken into serious consideration.

He implies that there are really three reasons why the essential questions that must be answered in order to get a thorough understanding the DSS have not been answered by the scholarly community so far. First, many of the questions have not been asked the right way around. Second, some have not been asked at all because traditional interpretations have been assumed, and alternatives were not sought or wanted. Third, scholars have not taken a wide enough view of the world behind these texts, the world in these texts, and the world in front of these texts. The world in front of the text has mainly to do with our own present perspective on life and the world in this post-modern era. That tends to shift the way we ask the important questions; this shifts the perspective toward a set of assumptions that has to do with *our* biases and obscures our vision of how *ancient people* viewed the world from which the DSS came.

Robert Feather has done a distinct favour for the world of popular readers, as well as the world of those scholars who will take note.

J. Harold Ellens, PhD
Holy Week, 2011

Preface

Observing the contentious state of the Dead Sea Scrolls milieu is like looking into a bird cage full of squawking, cackling turkeys, ducks and headless chickens, preening peacocks and ostriches with their heads buried in the sand. An occasional proud swan struts by, completely oblivious to its surroundings.

The kind of obscuration that clouds the present understanding of the Dead Sea Scrolls and Qumran is aptly described by a rabbi of the Middle Ages, Azariah Figo (1579–1647 AD).[1] He gives his interpretation of the rabbinic distinction between Moses and other prophets, in that Moses saw God through a polished glass, while others saw Him through a dim glass.

In the study of the books of the first part of the Hebrew Bible, known as the Torah, the process is sometimes referred to by the acronym 'PaRDeS',[2] where:

P stands for the Hebrew word *p'shat* – literal reading of the texts;
R stands for the Hebrew word *remez* – a hint the text gives towards its hidden meaning;
D stands for the Hebrew word *d'rash* – the moral message behind the text;
S stands for the Hebrew word *sod* – the secret meaning.

For scholars looking at the Dead Sea Scrolls the first three processes are accessible and generally agreed, although sometimes with serious disputes occurring. For the fourth process there is almost complete incomprehension, and scholars are faced with black holes that they studiously try and avoid, or try to bury in the sands of time.

Whilst examining the inadequacies of present-day scholastic comprehension of the Scrolls, this book falls into two parts:

1 The four basic types of problems of delays in translation: misconceptions, prejudices, jealousies and incompetence that have dogged Dead Sea Scrolls scholarship since the earliest days of their discovery and still do.
2 Revelations that try and explain these problems and new proposals that offer solutions to many of today's black holes and controversies.

There are also problems external to the texts that have added to delays in understanding the scrolls that commenced immediately they were discovered.

1 Disagreements over the origins of the scrolls and the role of Khirbet Qumran as the hub from which the scrolls were hidden.
2 Delays in publication and restricted access to the scrolls.

Numerous contentious passages in the scrolls, which are effectively huge black holes, defy any agreed understanding and remain to be resolved.

So what is a black hole? At the centre of our galaxy something lurks that acts as if it had 4.5 million times the mass of the sun. It sucks in light and every type of radiation that crosses its event horizon. Black holes are areas to be avoided at all costs. This provides a useful analogy for the numerous unanswered questions in biblical and Dead Sea Scrolls studies, where no one has much idea of a reasonable explanation. Avoidance is how most scholars treat them. Those who try to cross the event horizon and shine light into such a hole find they are dissipating their energies on unprovable guesses, and suppositions, which few of their peers accept as credible.

Many of my contemporaries give scant attention to the possible explanations that I have put forward to help illumine these black holes. A common reaction is: 'You don't belong to a recognized Biblical Studies department of a university and therefore don't have the right qualifications.' This almost reduces me to laughter. Not only do they often not even bother to examine my work in any detail, they are throwing stones from inside a glass case. The disagreements amongst scholars in the field of Dead Sea Scrolls studies are probably more acrimonious than in almost any other discipline. Insults and contradictions fly back and forth, and some have even resorted to potentially criminal acts of character impersonation, as I explain later in the book. To accusations that I am merely an amateur I usually respond that I am a chartered engineer and professional metallurgist, and, if given a chance, relate anecdotes about marginalized scholars and amateurs from different disciplines who have been proved right and made major scientific breakthroughs. One example is particularly relevant to the subject of black holes.

Saul Perlmutter and Carl Pennypacker, at Berkeley Observatory, altered our entire understanding of the Universe. Astronomers in the 1980s were eager to find examples of a particular type of supernova, but they were hard to detect. Perlmutter and his partner wanted to search for these using a new technique, but their colleagues were sceptical about their proposals and refused them time on the radio-telescope facilities. Finally granted the access he needed in 1992, Perlmutter found a supernova. During 1992–3 Perlmutter and Pennypacker located five supernovae, which was almost unprecedented in previous searches by others,

Other astronomers got very excited and went 'supernova hunting' – this was a vital field because the type of supernova they were seeking would help them discover if and how fast the universe was expanding, and if and when it might start to contract again. It now appears, contrary to what was once believed, that the expansion of the Universe is accelerating. Alhough they began as comparative outsiders, Perlmutter and his partner altered our entire conception of the universe and the forces operating within it. For his work, Perlmutter shared in the 2011 Nobel Prize for Physics.

Another case of the outsider solving a problem the professionals could not occurred in relation to a collection of *talatat* recovered from Karnak, in Egypt. *Talatat* are rectangular building bricks,[3] originally developed around 1350 BC, in the period of the revolutionary Pharaoh Akhenaton, and used in the construction of his holy city of Akhetaton, at a place now known as El-Amarna. When Akhetaton was destroyed, some twenty to thirty years after Akhenaton's death, these building blocks were carted off to Karnak and Luxor, in southern Egypt, for re-use as infill in newly restored temples to the gods. Vast numbers of these *talatat* (approximately 90,000) were rediscovered in the early 20th century, during excavations at

Karnak and Luxor, and some of them still carried inscribed images from scenes at Akhetaton and other locations. Because of the huge numbers involved, Egyptologists and archaeologists were unable to reassemble more than a tiny fraction of the larger pictures. The *talatat* were therefore put into storage and there they lay for years, awaiting a solution. Then, in 1966, along came the amateur outsider, Ray Winfield Smith, a retired naval computer expert, who addressed the problem using lateral thinking, and decided to input photographs of individually labelled *talatat* into a computer, and classify them by shape, colour and style of inscribed image.[4] He was then able to move the images around on his computer screen and recover the original positioning of the bricks. The results were astonishing and by 1972 he had re-assembled 800 images of large sections of walls with detailed scenes of activities at Akhetaton. Some of these show everyday pursuits and ceremonies within the city temples, including celebration of the Jubilees Festival. One of the most remarkable can be seen at the Luxor Museum, where a procession of temple priests is seen carrying what can only be a scroll rolled on to what is called in Judaism an *Etz Hayim* (Tree of Life) pole, looking almost exactly like the scrolls carried around synagogues of today.

In addition to the inter-scholar disputes and the failure of scholarship to deliver believable answers to a vast number of 'problem' texts in the Dead Sea Scrolls, there are other factors that have been, and are still, working against a resolution of what I term the black holes.

The first has been an almost continuous sniping from the wings by people challenging the authenticity of the Dead Sea Scrolls as being authored and collected by a religious community located at Khirbet Qumran, by the Dead Sea. These fractious attacks have side-tracked serious study and helped dissipate objective interpretation.

The second is an 'elephant in the room' syndrome, a subject which few people like to talk about or understand fully, but which has contributed to, and probably been the most powerful influence on, the ongoing delays in release and publication of the texts, since the very earliest findings in the 1950s right up until today. This 'elephant', which will be fully exposed later in this book, has also added to distortions in the understanding of the scrolls through the biased perspectives it has engendered.

I will examine the various serious hindrances to a clear understanding of the Dead Sea Scrolls and then present proposals that illuminate the darkness and provide comprehensive explanations for almost all of the obscurities and black holes dogging Dead Sea Scrolls studies. The presentation of a revolutionary inter-dependent, fact-based set of confirmable evidence will throw light on the Dead Sea Scrolls, and also help to resolve many of the anomalies and misunderstandings in the Bible itself. This evidence encompasses a refutation of the minimalist position that downgrades many records in the Bible to mere myth and legend and finds little historicity in the pre-exodus period of the Hebrews. The conflict between minimalists and maximalists is what Hans Barstad, amongst others, terms 'the crisis of history in biblical studies' and what William Dever refers to as 'non-specialists who cannot control the data' and 'new nihilists' in the Sheffield and Copenhagen schools, like Niels P. Lemche and Philip Davies, whose use of archaeology is a travesty.[5] For Professor Robert Eisenman the situation is even worse: 'because they contradict the "internal evidence" of what the Scrolls themselves actually say – they made the Scrolls impossible to interpret, in effect, rendered them mute . . . No sense has still really been made of the documents at Qumran.'

The views of numerous scholars, academic and otherwise, will be cited, commencing with those of Professor Geza Vermes, one of the United Kingdom's most learned commentators on the Dead Sea Scrolls, who first visited Qumran and mixed with the resident team at the Ecole Biblique, in 1952. He has been closely involved with the Qumran texts for over 60 years and made their study his life's work . . . and yet there are many critically important questions to which he, like others, has no ready answers.

Interview with
Professor Geza Vermes

Part I

Undoubtedly one of the foremost Dead Sea Scrolls scholars in the United Kingdom, Professor Vermes is also famous for his books on the role of Jesus,[1] especially in relation to Judaism. I was privileged to be able to discuss a wide range of topics with him at his Oxfordshire home, in the early part of March 2010.

We began by discussing some of the problems and misunderstandings affecting Dead Sea Scrolls scholarship.

RF: In relation to the *Discoveries in the Judaean Desert* series of official publications on the Dead Sea Scrolls, you have said the publication work has now been largely completed, 'but we have only just started to scratch the surface of understanding'.

GV: The final volumes have been published. And there will be some revisions, but, yes, Emanuel Tov has finished his work on the official volumes.

RF: What about the questions that are unanswered, what I think of as the 'black holes', the things that don't have a consensus understanding?

GV: If you want consensus, everyone to say the same thing, it will not happen. I think that to imagine the supposition that there is no connection between the scrolls and the site and that the scrolls came from somewhere else, that's the basis of the dissension. It doesn't strike me as in any way likely, so I think the basic supposition should be that there is a link between the writings

1

and the archaeological findings at Qumran. To deny the link is to destroy the hub of the evidence.

RF: I fully agree with you, and what seems to be the general approach of the dissenters is that they look at some of the evidence, but not all of the evidence; they don't look at the carbon datings, or they don't look at the cemetery . . .

GV: In the last 30 years or so we have had a constant flow of theories that deny the religious character of the site, deny the connection of the scrolls to the site.

RF: The problem is we are being diverted by a plethora of ill-thought-out theories claiming Qumran was something other than a religious centre – that the main activity was making perfume, pots, growing crops; it was a trading post, rustic villa, and so on. We even have the incredible claim that it was a fortress from Norman Golb! Certainly they were making honey, and scroll material and many other things, but that was not their main raison d'être.

GV: I call it the Qumran Hilton! Yes, of course they are making honey, and probably they were making balsam, curative medicines . . .

RF: Yes, and who builds a fortress at the bottom of an overhanging cliff?

GV: Who builds a fortress with no proper walls? Who builds a fortress without safe water supplies? Also the idea that the cemetery is full of defenders, all buried individually, very nicely, very carefully. By whom? By the Romans?

RF: Aside from what I call all these distraction theories, there are a lot of unanswered questions, which I think are much more important to solve. Like who was the Teacher of Righteousness, who was the Wicked Priest, who was the Plant of Righteousness? Who was Melchizedek to the Qumran Community? Do we have any consensus answers to those questions?

GV: We have numbers of answers [to] all the various theories. My theory is we don't know.

RF: OK, so we have unknowns. Do you think Onias IV was the Teacher of Righteousness; Menelaus may be the Wicked Priest?

GV: Possibly . . . Menelaus, maybe.

RF: I think it was Onias IV, because he was a high priest, he is deposed by someone who becomes a high priest, and he flees to Egypt, and he builds a temple there, which is a very odd thing to do. And he doesn't put the traditional *menorah* as the central piece; he has a golden globe as the main decorative furnishing in his Temple, at Leontopolis. Excavations there have shown there were some similar features in the cemetery at Leontopolis and the cemetery at Qumran, in the styles of burial – which indicates he had an influence at both places.

GV: Possible.

RF: OK, more awkward questions. What are they talking about when they mention the Plant of Righteousness?

GV: I can't say.

RF: All right, so who are the messiahs they are waiting for?

GV: Suppose a king and a priest.

RF: Yes, but everyone talks about the king being in the line of David, a Davidic king, but how can it be? In the sense that David is no example for a Messiah: he has Uriah killed; 70,000 Hebrews are slain because of his misdemeanours; he is roundly condemned by the prophets for his evil ways. It's not a good example for a messiah. In fact one of the prophets, Nathan, says his line will never be blessed because of his misdeeds. So if it's not David, who is it?

GV: I know of no other.

RF: And the priestly messiah? That's unprecedented. I don't think there is any mention in biblical texts of a priest who is going to be messiah?

GV: We have got funny ideas about messiah.

RF: These are the sort of things, I think, that need to be answered, rather more than just the nuances of the texts. When it says the first task of the messiah, when he returns, is to smite Seth. What do you make of that?

GV: I suppose he is quoting Numbers. It happens to be there.

RF: But they must have had some character in mind when they say the first task is actually not to deal with the Romans, which you would expect, but with the Assyrians, and to deal with Seth. The only explanation I have heard is that the Seth mentioned was the son of Adam. Is that possible? Would the messiah be worried about a minor character like the son of Adam?

3

GV: I don't believe they were working that way. If they had been, they would have developed the idea.

RF: Can I suggest some radical ideas for you.

GV: All right. Why not?

RF: The king as the messiah who would come back, that they are figuring would come back and restore the boundaries of his kingdom and smite Seth, was, I believe, related to the Seth of Egypt, the traditional god of evil.

GV: Ummm.

RF: So what do you think about the kingly messiah as a memory of Akhenaton? So the priestly messiah has to be his high priest. Guess what the name of the high priest is. It was the same as the leader of the forces described in the War Scroll.

GV: We knew about him?

RF: Well, we know about the high priest at Amarna, from inscriptions. His name was Meryre. There's a tomb in the northern hills at Amarna. Have you ever been to Amarna?

GV: No.

RF: It's a vast open plain where Akhenaton built a virgin city. He disassociated himself and the country, or at least the priestly ruling classes, from pagan idolatry and instituted a form of what was really a very pure form of monotheism. So if there is any king that is going to have any influence all the way down to the Hebrews, it has to be him. Freud made a similar connection.

GV: Sounds Chinese to me! Could the Hebrew patriarchs have been part of this?

RF: [Freud connected Moses to Akhenaton.] He was the first to make a connection between the Hebrew patriarchs and Akhenaton.

GV: The Hebrew patriarchs – were they connected or were they just Jews?

RF: If Psalm 104 gets down from a wall inscribed at Amarna, around 1350 BC into the Hebrew bible, how did that happen?

GV: . . . words are words.

RF: It's a certain fact that an inscription in the tomb of Ay, in Amarna, the Great Hymn gets paraphrased into Psalm 104.

GV: Your belief is stronger.

RF: Well, there is a lot of evidence, Geza: the name of the high priest at Amarna is Meryre; the leader who is going to carry the banner in the final war of the forces of light against the forces of evil is Merire, same name. And if you look in the Bible at the description of the high priest, you're not going to accept this, but the description of the high priest is exactly the same as the *shabti* that we have in the Metropolitan Museum, in New York, of Meryre. If you look at that little statue, his dress, his robe, what he is wearing are exactly the same.

A second part to the conversation with Professor Vermes is included later in the book as a postscript to the discussion on the reasons for the delays in publications of the Scrolls and to help identify the 'elephant in the room'.

Timeline from Amarna to Qumran

BC

c1350   Akhenaton dies. The Hebrews flee from Akhetaton taking their knowledge and important possessions with them.

c1210   Exodus of Israelites/Hebrews from Egypt led by Moses. Ten Commandments received in Sinai, Tabernacle built. Rebellions of Korah priests, and Dathan, Abiram and On.

1170   Joshua leads entry into Canaan. Tabernacle at Mount Gerezim, administered by Shiloh priests.

1150   Period of Judges.

1050   King Saul rules Israel.

1020   King David rules Israel.

c970   King Solomon builds First Temple at Jerusalem. Banishes Shilonite priests in favour of Aaronite priests.

940   Period of Divided kingdom.

320   Greek Ptolemy rule.

140   Essenes settle at Qumran.

198   Greek Seleucid rule.

175   Zadokite High Priest Onias III deposed and replaced by his brother Jason.

172   High Priest Onias IV flees to Egypt and is replaced by Hellenist High Priest Menelaus.

171   Onias III murdered at instigation of High Priest Menelaus.

167   Hellenization increases. Temple at Jerusalem transformed into sanctuary for Olympian god Zeus. Judaism proscribed.

166   Jewish uprising under Judas Maccabee.

164   Maccabees re-establish Jewish rule, beginning of Hasmonean rule. Re-dedication of Jerusalem Temple.

161   Judas Maccabee killed in battle. His brother Jonathan becomes rebel leader.

152   Jonathan Maccabee appointed High Priest.

143   Simon Maccabee appointed High Priest and ethnarch.

142   Jonathan Maccabee executed in prison.

135   High Priest Simon Maccabee murdered by his son-in-law.

135   John Hyrcanus I appointed High Priest and ethnarch.

104   Aristobulus I appointed High Priest and king.

103   Alexander Jannaeus becomes High Priest and king.

88   Plot to overthrow Jannaeus by Pharisees in league with Seleucid King Demterius III. 800 Pharisees crucified.

76   King Alexander Jannaeus dies. His widow Salome Alexandra becomes queen. Their son, Hyrcanus II, becomes High Priest.

67   Hyrcanus II becomes king. Deposed in same year by his brother

Aristobulus, who becomes High Priest and King Aristobulus II.

63   Romans under Pompey conquer Jewish state. King Aristobulus II deposed. Hyrcanus II reinstated as High Priest. Antipater, an Idumean convert to Judaism, made overseer of Judaea.

42   Antipater assassinated.

40   Antigonus, son of Aristobulus II, made king and High Priest, ousting Romans from control of Jerusalem region, with Parthian support. Hyrcanus II maimed and exiled.

37   Rome appoints Herod the Great, son of Antipater, as king. He reconquers Jerusalem for Rome. Second Temple restored. Hasmonean dynasty ends.

30   Hyrcanus II executed.

27   Augustus (63 BC–14 CE) made Emperor of Rome.

14   Augustus succeeded by Emperor Tiberius (42 BC–37 AD).

4   King Herod the Great dies. Jesus born.* King Herod's three sons share power. Herod Archelaus appointed ruler of Judaea and Samaria. Galilee and Peraea ruled by his brother Herod Antipas. North-east of Galilee ruled by Herod Philip.

AD

6   Herod Archelaus deposed by Augustus. Direct Roman rule of Judaea by the prefect Coponius. Census leads to Zealot uprising.

26   Pontius Pilate appointed prefect of Judaea. Jesus commences ministry.

35   John the Baptist beheaded at Machaerus by Herod Antipas.

c36   Jesus crucified.

36   Pontius Pilate (dies?) removed from office. High Priest Caiaphas removed from office.

37   Emperor Tiberius dies, Caligula (12–41 CE) becomes emperor.

39   Herodian ruler of Galilee Prince Agrippa replaces Prince Antipas.

41   Agrippa I appointed King of Judaea by Emperor Claudius.

44   King Agrippa I dies and Roman procurator appointed.

66   Zealot uprisings commence.

68   Qumran destroyed by Romans.

70   Second Temple destroyed by Romans under Titus.

73   Zealot stronghold at Masada captured by Roman 10th Legion under Lucius Flavius Silva.

132   Revolt against Romans led by Bar-Kochba.

* The conventional date for Jesus' birth is the year 0. Another plausible date, suggested by Hugh Schonfield (*The Passover Plot*, Element, 1993) and others, is 6 or 7 CE, based on the works of Josephus and the Gospels of John and Luke.

Chapter 1

Persistent Textual Problems

The introductory interview with Professor Geza Vermes records aspects of the present thinking of the premier Dead Sea Scrolls expert in the United Kingdom and one of the most respected authorities on the subject in the world. He has no particular axe to grind and responded to some rather searching questions with a refreshing openness, and wherever he had no satisfactory answer he simply said 'we just don't know'. Although few academics and scholars are prepared to admit the parlous state of Dead Sea Scrolls scholarship and the many 'don't knows' that exists today, it cannot be concealed that many fierce battles are going on across the pages of blogs, learned journals and on conference floors. Many controversies remain unresolved and, if anything, are growing in intensity.

The earliest controversies on interpretation of the Dead Sea Scrolls arose in the early 1950s when André Dupont Sommer, Professor at the Sorbonne, Paris, and Edmund Wilson, a writer on the *New Yorker*, together with John Allegro, a recruit to the Jerusalem team from Oxford and Manchester University, thought they saw Jesus as being prefigured in some of the scrolls. All of these early writers were heavily criticized by the Ecole Biblique group, based in East Jerusalem, who claimed authority for their view of the scrolls' interpretation. In the case of John Allegro, they publicly castigated him in a letter to *The Times* newspaper of London in 1956.[1]

One would have thought that in the years between 1956 and now an amicable consensus would have been reached. Unhappily, matters have actually got worse. So what is today's understanding of the meaning of the scrolls and the origins of the Qumran community? The simple answer is there is barely any consensus.

Here a few examples. In a recent radio interview, Robert Cargill of the University of California, Los Angeles, who has done a lot of work on 3D analysis of the site of Qumran, said he was warned by his colleagues to 'get in and get out' of the field of Qumran studies as it was too contentious.[2]

There are hardly more than two senior scholars who agree on any major issue involving the understanding of controversial Dead Sea Scrolls texts. Here are some examples:

- Professor Robert Eisenman (California State University) believes that James, the brother of Jesus, was the Teacher of Righteousness – he is virtually alone in this stance.
- The late Professor Carsten Thiede, Basel University, and Jose O'Callaghan, Director of Seminari de Papirologia, Sant Cugat del Valles, Barcelona, thought that some of the Greek fragments found in Cave 7 were New Testament texts – hardly anyone agrees with this claim.
- Barbara Thiering, University of Sydney, Australia, contends that the Teacher of Righteousness was John the Baptist and Jesus was the Wicked Priest – few people agree with this view.
- Professor Lawrence Schiffman, New York University, contends the scrolls are not Essenic but basically Sadducean – there is little support for this theory.

There are many other examples of serious disagreements between scholars, which will be cited as we proceed through the book, culminating in an incredible case of character impersonation that some so-called scholars have descended to.

All this does not mean that the general body of scholars is hostile. On the contrary, the vast majority are very welcoming of new comers and generally an amiable, amusing fraternity. When I first walked into a conference on the Copper Scroll at Manchester University, in 1996, I was a complete outsider, but was rapidly made to feel part of the attendee family. Subsequently, I have made many friends within the community, even though my views differ substantially from those many of them hold.

With finalization of the 44th and latest volume of *Discoveries in the Judaean Desert*, the official version of the editorial team's translations, Professor Emanuel Tov, former editor-in-chief, has said that the main task of translating the 85,000 or so scrolls and fragments found in the

11 caves near Qumran is virtually completed.[3] We have apparently entered the tidying-up phase and the impression given is that everything is nicely under control.

Nothing could be further from the truth!

What we have may be superficial agreement on literal translations of many of the texts, but as Carolyn Osiek points out in a recent paper in the *Journal of Biblical Literature*, that does not mean there is agreement on the deeper understanding and meaning of a text. Geza Vermes has said, 'We have merely scratched the surface of understanding the texts. We need more time.' Yet here we are some 60 years on from the finding of the first of the scrolls, and at least 30 years on from the translation of some of the more controversial texts, and they still defy an agreed interpretation.

In a radio interview in August 2010, Professor Lawrence Schiffman talked about the next steps to be taken in Dead Sea Scrolls studies. He specified a requirement for the study of the role of the priesthood and the role of women in the scrolls. However, he also said, 'we need to work on understanding the scrolls in a wider context. That's the new generation of what we need next.'[4]

The question has to be asked. Why is there still such enormous disagreement amongst Dead Sea Scrolls scholars? Why are there so few agreed conclusions on the sobriquets that appear in the Scrolls? Is some deeper, critical factor being missed? I believe the answer to the last question is yes.

Such is the depth of disagreement in the understanding of the meaning of certain scrolls that recently three eminently respected scholars, Michael Wise, Martin Abegg and Edward M. Cook, have decided to ditch the standard model of hostility between the Qumran-Essenes and the Hasmonean authorities, built up over generations, mainly on the evidence of one Dead Sea Scrolls scrap of leather, 4Q448 (the so-called King Jonathan Fragment). They now conclude that, at least in the time of King Jannaeus, there were cordial relations between the two parties.[5]

A main problem with such controversial theories is that they make it that much more difficult to arrive at a sensible interpretation of the meaning of many of the difficult Qumran texts when the setting for their origins is so widely disputed.

The Dead Sea Scrolls collection of some 85,000 separate items, representing some 850 different texts, falls into three distinct groups: biblical texts; apocrypha and pseudepigraphic texts; and sectarian material dealing with the Qumran community's concerns.

In terms of understanding the meaning of the Dead Sea Scrolls, particularly the sectarian material, the so-called consensus is largely a myth!

Chapter 2

Confusion in the Role of Qumran

Before we get to grips with the really important issues of failures in the current understanding of the scrolls, commencing in Chapter 3, we need to traverse the quagmire that challenges the origins and purpose of Qumran and has diverted the energies of so many scholars and wasted so much valuable time. I can only imagine that the shoals of red herrings have been dredged up by dissident scholars, because they have little else to say on the essential elements of the scrolls themselves.

When it comes to the question of what were the origins and the main function of activities at Qumran, the 'experts' will respond with silence, equivocal answers or varying explanations. There is certainly a consensus that the main function was as a religious centre, but there are numerous highly qualified, vociferous objectors, who have their own pet theories. These are the many lone voices crying in the wilderness. It is not unusual to witness academics shouting across conference venues as they vehemently pursue their own personal agendas.

As Magen Broshi likes to say, 'If there are ten different theories about what was going at Qumran, by definition nine of them are wrong.' More recently, Professor George Brooke of Manchester University has identified at least 15 different theories emanating from respected scholars around the world.

Apart from the 15 or so different theories about what was going at Qumran, each propagated by one or two individuals, even the so-called mainstream scholars, who believe Qumran was a religious site, disagree on fundamental issues relating to Qumran.

Before even getting to questions of what was the purpose of the Qumran site there is another, not insignificant issue that needs to be addressed. The table illustrates a few opinions of leading scholars:

Date of Founding of Qumran

James Charlesworth (Princeton Theological Seminary); Ben Stevens[1]	c150 BC
Roland de Vaux and J. Milik (Ecole Biblique, Jerusalem)	c140 BC
June Austin[2]	c130 BC
Theodor H. Gaster (University of London)	c125 BC
Jodi Magness (University of North Carolina); Hartmut Stegemann (University of Göttingen)	c100 BC
George Brooke	c80 BC

There has thus been little agreement on the date the community actually came into existence, religious or otherwise. This question is intimately coupled to the challenge of identifying the founder of the community, the so-called 'Teacher of Righteousness', and the likely date when he led his followers to the site. These issues will be confronted later on in this book. My own view is that the dates given by Roland de Vaux and others are the most probable.

Here are some of the many minority opinions about the purpose of activities at Qumran. All of those listed here have, at most, limited support.

- Yizhar Hirschfeld (Professor at Hebrew University, Jerusalem) believes Qumran was a farm with a manor house.
- Professor Norman Golb, Chicago University, like Hershel Shanks, maintains that the scrolls were not written at Qumran, and Professor Golb believes Qumran was a military fortress.
- Yitzhak Magen and Yuval Peleg, Israel Antiquities Authority, think Qumran was a pottery factory – there is limited support for this idea, mainly from people at the Hebrew University, Jerusalem.
- Alain Chambon and Jean-Baptist Humbert (authors of a volume on Roland de Vaux's archaeological work) believe the Qumran complex was a residential villa.
- Alan Crown and Lena Cansdale (University of Sydney, Australia) think Qumran was a trading post.

- Professors Robert and Pauline Donceel-Voûte, Louvain Catholic Seminary, Belgium, at first believed Qumran was a perfume factory, but then gravitated towards the theory that it was the home of a well-to-do Judaean. (They were initially entrusted with preparing a report on Roland de Vaux's original archaeological notes on the Qumran excavations, but were then denied publication facilities; their findings were heavily criticized by the Ecole Biblique team.)
- Professor Rachel Elior, Hebrew University, Jerusalem, posits that the Essenes never existed − she has some support from Lawrence Schiffman on the role of the Sadduceans, but has been heavily attacked for her central theory.

Appendix A lists the positions held by various scholars, academics and commentators on what was going on at Qumran during the period of the Essenic presence. This clearly shows the disparate nature of the minority theorists. To claim, as some like Norman Golb and the sensationalist media do, that these small groups, often only comprising one person, constitute a growing front of unified opinion challenging the consensus view is quite absurd.

It is rather like saying that theory:

$A \neq J$ and $B \neq J$

Therefore, as A and B lead to the same conclusion, they constitute a unified theory;

But $A \neq B$

A and B are completely at odds with each other, so one of them must be defective.

There is a basic error in the logic that needs to be knocked on the head and buried in some quiet corner of Qumran.

Certainly, the challengers have caused Dead Sea scholars to reassess their conclusions, and modify them somewhat. The resultant adjustments are described rather well by Edna Ullmann-Margalit. Whilst maintaining that alternative theories have dented the mainstream model she concludes, 'none of the alternative theories comes close to the theory of the consensus in comprehensiveness and its ability to account for the majority of the findings, and hence none succeed in posing a serious threat to it'.[3]

Almost the entire core belief group has spent an inordinate amount of time and energy rebutting the challengers. In my view this has largely been a waste of valuable resources and has deflected discussion from the real issues. Unfortunately, the media latches on to the latest challenge with glee, and a journalist, who usually writes the gardening or motoring column and knows almost nothing about Qumran or the Essenes, produces a story designed to catch the headlines. In fact many of the challengers express a view consistent with their own specialism and knowledge, ignoring the wider picture. This is what I call the 'George Brooke Syndrome'. Professor Brooke sees many of these divergent theories as reflecting the nature of the espousers. The very feminine, cultured Pauline Donceel-Voûte sees Qumran occupied by a wealthy upper class interested in making perfume and possessing fine ceramics and glassware; the aggressive Norman Golb sees a military fortress; ceramic experts like Yitzhak Magen and Yuvel Peleg see pottery manufacture; students of mysticism and philosophy, like Rachel Elior and Edna Ullmann-Margalit, see problems of imaginative semantics and philosophical ideology.

We can look at some of the 'origin theories', championed by individuals, which evince limited support from the rest of the Dead Sea Scrolls fraternity. Often their validity can be questioned in similar ways, yet opponents of the standard model claim that the sheer number of these alternative theories in itself constitutes proof that the consensus view is wrong.

A good example is Yizhar Hirschfeld's farm theory. The late Professor Hanan Eshel sums up Hirschfeld's position, that the main function of Qumran was as a farming establishment, in his review of *Qumran in Context*, written in 2004:

> In my opinion, Hirschfeld's book teaches more about the limitations of archaeology than about Qumran of the Second Temple period. If we were to adopt Hirschfeld's claims, then any archaeologist who would attempt to understand the nature of Qumran without consulting the scrolls would reach the conclusion that this is a fort situated in a completely illogical location, or a private agricultural estate built in an area completely deficient in water. We are fortunate that hundreds of texts were in fact discovered at Qumran. These texts bear

16

witness that a religious sect resided at this site at the end of the Second Temple period. The claims of an archaeologist, who believes that only he has the answers to the history of the settlement at Qumran and that consequently those scholars who research texts must accept his interpretations, are arrogant. There is no reason at all to decouple Khirbet Qumran from the scrolls. On the contrary, the ruins at Qumran should be understood in the same way as any other archaeological site, on the basis of all the finds discovered there.[4]

Professor Eshel cites the certain identification of a large number of *mikva'ot* (ritual immersion pools) within the site of Qumran as further proof that it was a religious site, and finds support amongst most scholars for this view. Whilst not disagreeing with this view, Hirschfeld still maintained that Qumran was initially a fortified settlement, and then became a farm, but seems to have backtracked on the claim it was a fortress *per se*, with comments like: 'We use the term fortress of the Judaean desert as almost a nickname . . . It is not logical to suggest that Qumran was built as a military fortress.'

The other theories will be dealt with as we encounter them through the book, with considerable attention devoted to Professor Golb's fortress theory and Magen and Peleg's pottery theory.

It is important to emphasize that, among the more than 100 scholars and academics, who have taken part in the extensive publication of the scrolls, not one has doubted the theory that a faction of the Essene religious sect worked at Qumran and lived nearby.

There are also fundamental disagreements on the attitude of the Qumran community to the Temple at Jerusalem. Most scholars say they looked on the Temple authorities in Jerusalem with disdain.[5] Others say they were favourably disposed to the authorities in Jerusalem.[6]

Because minority theorists deny that Qumran was a religious centre and insist that there was no connection between the site of Qumran and the caves where the scrolls were found, most of them claim the scrolls came from Jerusalem or elsewhere. The theories they put forward to explain the presence of the scrolls near Qumran, and how they got there, are varied, very imaginative, and generally quite implausible. They fail to take account of the mass of data that ties the site to the caves and the texts to the site. The following factors militate strongly against most of the scrolls originating in Jerusalem:

1 Caves 4 and 5 are within a stone's throw of the site, and from the pattern of pathways between the two, it is clear they were being regularly visited by the occupants of Qumran.
2 Cave 4 contained the remains of wooden shelves, almost certainly built to hold scrolls.
3 Fragments of storage jars, unique to Qumran, were found within the site and in the caves.
4 Linen wrappers on some of the scroll jars found in Cave 1 replicated a temple plan mentioned in some of the scrolls.
5 An *ostracon* found in 1996 catalogues property being donated to the *Yahad* (or community) by a certain Honi of Jericho. This correlates with the community's requirements set out in some of their sectarian documents, which also refer to the community as a *Yahad*.[7]
6 A pottery fragment found within the site of Qumran carries Hebrew letters in handwriting recognizable as that used by a scribe who also wrote some of the scrolls.[8]
7 More inkwells were found at the site than at any other site in Israel, indicating scribal activity.
8 An upper room, referred to as a scriptorium by most scholars, was almost certainly used for the preparation and/or writing of scroll texts.

When what I call the Röhrhirsch/Zias test[9] is applied to the circumstances of Qumran, its results — together with the other dominating factors of evidence from contemporary historians Josephus, Pliny, and Philo, the archaeology of the site, and the scrolls themselves — make it patently clear that the main activity at Qumran was religious.

The Röhrhirsch/Zias test challenges the various occupation theories against the indisputable evidence we have of a unique form of burial in the cemetery at Qumran:

• If it were a conventional villa, there would be no connection between the villa and the grave site. Pottery found at the settlement, for example, would be different from that associated with the graves. It is not; therefore the villa theory is false.

- If it were a military fortress, the graves would indicate normative Jewish burial rites. The graves and form of burial are unique to the location, and there are no signs of battle trauma; therefore the theory is false.
- If the graves were associated with a religious settlement, they would reflect the distinctive beliefs of its incumbents. They do; therefore this theory is true.

Joseph Zias sums up the reasoning as follows:

> The site [Qumran], however, on the basis of the cemetery, is unique and all attempts (being argued again by those individuals who have never studied Palestine) to argue that it was a military cemetery etc., are simply wrong. The cemetery defines the site and the clues to the correct assessment lie there, not at Ein Gedi or elsewhere.

The majority of scholars from the earliest times to today's leading figures recognize Qumran as a site where a devout, ascetic, male-dominated priestly community wrote, copied and curated the Dead Sea Scrolls. Nevertheless, the dissenters are numerous, nor are they lightweight academics, and continue to justify their views in learned journals, books and lectures. Even within the caucus of so-called orthodox views, there are major disputes – for example, on the date of the founding of Qumran, or their allegiance to the Jerusalem Temple.

The overall picture on the usage and origins of Qumran is one of disharmony and disarray, bordering on crisis.

Some scholars try and accommodate the fringe theories into a kind of quasi-Qumran. In my view, this is simply sweeping the problems under the carpet. Yes, there was farming, balsam- and perfume-making, pottery-making. indigo manufacture, leather production, but all of these activities were incidental to the main religious activity. In the same way as in modern monasteries the monks may possess valuable items and produce honey, wine, woven products and ceramics, these are for their own sustenance or to generate income, and are incidental to their main religious activities.

Qumran Site Features

A number of archaeological features found within the site of Qumran give a clue to the separate, unique nature of the community working there. Whilst archaeologists and Dead Sea Scrolls academics will endlessly discuss the detail of archaeological findings, they rarely ask themselves the reasons for these unique features in the geography and nature of Qumran.

The following are only some of the questions, to which, once again, there are no satisfactory or consensus answers. There are many other questions no one seems concerned even to ask. For objective scholars the response to many of these questions is often 'we simply do not know the answer'.

Questions relating to the site of Khirbet Qumran:

1 Why were there 10 *mikva'ot* (ritual baths) within the area of the buildings?
2 Why was one divided into four sections, unlike anything found elsewhere in Israel?
3 Why was some of the pottery unique to the site?
4 Why were the Qumran-Essenes carrying mattocks around when they left the confines of Qumran?
5 Why was their burial practice unique to the cemetery?
6 Why were virtually all the bodies buried N–S, with the head turned to the south?
7 Why were the main structural walls of the prayer hall in exact align-ment with the main structural walls of the Great Temple at Amarna?

The next dramatic statement may seem too radical for many sceptics. However, as there are no other proposals which lead to a cohesive interlinking set of explanations or that answer most of the problematic questions, it ought to be considered seriously – at least until a better proposal is forthcoming. The statement is:

> Almost all the unresolved problematic questions relating to Qumran and the Dead Sea Scrolls (and to the Bible) can be resolved in terms of known archaeological features found at the ruined site of Akhetaton and the beliefs that emanated from that critical period when monotheism held sway there.

Many other unique features that find their explanation in the Amarna period could also be considered, space permitting. Here are just a few:

1 There were ten ritual fonts in the inner court of the Great Temple at Akhetaton.

2 One of the fonts in the Great Temple was divided into four sections.[10]

3 Some of the pottery shapes appear to be copies of designs used at Akhetaton, as seen in the Petrie Museum in London.

4 During the reign of Amenhotep III, the father of Akhenaton, mattocks come into prominence for the first time in Egyptian history, and can be seen on the end of the rays extending from the Aton, for example in a relief in the tomb of Ramose, Amenhotep III's vizier. They also start to appear on small effigies of courtiers in the same period. What the spiritual significance of the mattocks might be is not clear, but they may be a reminder that the Aton, as the only God, provides humanity with tools which they must use to improve their lot on earth. The mattocks on the ends of the Aton rays certainly carry divine significance as the other emblems on the ends of the rays are usually the 'ankh' sign for life and 'hands' or 'yods' offering beneficence to the people. The Hebrew 'yod' is still a holy symbol representing the 'hand' of God.

5 The cemetery at Qumran contains about 1,300 burial mounds, and the 55 graves that have been excavated show that the burial procedure was completely different from the normal type of burial being practised by the Jewish community elsewhere. Whereas it was not unusual to find personal items interred with the body in burials outside Qumran, the inclusion of goods in the graves at Qumran was rare. Bodies were usually buried naked and unadorned, wrapped in a simple burial cloth. Prior to the period of monotheism, introduced into Egypt by Akhenaton, burial tombs of royalty and the upper classes were generally ornately decorated, and large amounts of worldly goods were interred with the bodies. For royalty and high officials the tomb would usually be furnished with all the accoutrements needed for the afterlife, including food, drink, jewellery and statues of servants for the deceased in his

or her journey to eternity. King Akhenaton swept away all these trappings and gifts for the afterlife and instigated burials in simple, unadorned tombs with no worldly goods included. It appears that the community at Qumran was following a similar style and philosophy of burial, eschewing adornments and gifts for the afterlife.

6 The heads of the corpses at Qumran were probably turned to the south, as an approximation to the direction of the River Nile at Akhetaton.

7 Because the community at Qumran had a memory of the layout of the Great Temple at Akhetaton and the alignment of the sanctuary in that temple, the geographical alignments of the main walls of the Amarna temple are within 1° of the alignment of the main walls of the large prayer hall at Qumran.[11]

Later on we will see many more examples of constructional similarities that indisputably prove that the Qumran-Essenes knew a great deal about the layout and practices of Akhenaton's holy city.

Chapter 3

The Black Holes

The huge disagreements or ignorance over what was going on at Qumran and the significance of the archaeology of the ruins and associated caves are only part of the story. When we come to look at the numerous central issues of the meaning of passages in the Dead Sea Scrolls themselves, there is virtually no agreement amongst scholars on what they are saying or why they are saying it – let alone the nuances of the actual translations. Black holes on a galactic scale abound, for which there are no plausible rationalizations.

Much of the effort of international scholarship on the scrolls has concerned itself with establishing *editio princeps* (primary translations) of the texts. When it comes to understanding the meaning of the texts there are a vast number of questions for which there are no consensus answers, or simply 'sticking plaster' answers. These are invariably based on assumptions which are unprovable and which do not consider the underlying or external factors.

Huge amounts of energy have been, and are still being, expended in chewing over an issue that most scholars accept as fact. Namely that Qumran was a religious centre. Side issues, such as the correct classification of texts, which might now need to be reclassified in the light of new evidence, preoccupy large numbers of students of the subject,[1] whilst excessive use of ambiguous words clouds relatively simple topics. All disciplines protect themselves from the uninitiated outsider by inventing a smoke screen of jargon, but in Dead Sea Scrolls scholarship the habit reaches extremes. Here is an example from an abstract of a paper by Alexander Andrason entitled 'Biblical Hebrew Wayyiqtol: A Dynamic Definition'. If you didn't know it was about biblical interpretation you might think it must have come out of a study on quantum physics!

23

This article provides a concise, non-reductionist and non-taxonomist synchronically valid definition of the Biblical Hebrew verbal construction labeled wayyiqtol. Basing his proposal on findings of evolutionary linguistics (to which belong grammaticalization, path and chaos theories as well as cognitive linguistics) and employing the panchronic methodology, the author demonstrates the following: all semantic and functional properties (such as taxis, aspectual, temporal, modal and discourse-pragmatic values) of the wayyiqtol – as distinct and superficially incongruent they appear – may be unified and rationalized as a single dynamic category: advanced portions of the anterior and simultaneous trajectories (which constitute two sub-clines of the resultative path), developed within the three temporal spheres and, additionally, contextualized by the incorporation of an originally independent lexeme with a coordinative-consecutive force ... and, finally, indicating certain weakness of his own explanation, sketches a plan of future research.[2]

Someone needs to look at Sir Ernest Gowers's *Plain English*!

Because there is a mind-set that almost everything in the Dead Sea Scrolls (and biblical material) is considered to be related to Israel/ Palestine, explanations for problematic passages are sought in the Hebrew Bible or in the influences of the post-exodus dominating powers – the Assyrians, Babylonians, Persians, Greeks and Romans. There is almost no recognition of Egypt and its persistent influences. A good example of this mind-set is the naming of one of the major Dead Sea Scrolls as the New Jerusalem Scroll, whereas the text never mentions Jerusalem and is obviously talking about a temple setting in a city that is far too large to be Jerusalem.[3] Similarly, the Temple Scroll of the Dead Sea Scrolls and the Hebrew Bible's descriptions of the Temple in Ezekiel and Deuteronomy never mention Jerusalem.

When the New Jerusalem Scroll, or New Akhetaton Scroll, as I believe it should be renamed, mentions the Temple, it does so in nuanced or direct terms that relate to Egypt at the time of Akhenaton. Recently published Aramaic fragments from Cave 4, some of the oldest sectarian commentaries, including 4Q554, speak of an apocalyptic vision given to a 'seer'. Who that seer was is debatable, but one eminent Qumran scholar, Eibert Tigchelaar, gets near to the truth when he suggests Jacob as a possibility.[4]

Any doubt that biblical Ezekiel could have known about the strategic geography and dimensions of Akhetaton, albeit blurred in memory by the passage of time, will be dispelled by analysis of his descriptions. For this memory to have survived eyewitnesses must have been present near to the time of 1350 BC, because the entire city of Akhetaton was destroyed and levelled within 30 to 40 years of Pharaoh Akhenaton's death in 1332 BC. In *The Secret Initiation of Jesus at Qumran*, I spell out evidence that pretty conclusively proves Israelites were present at Akhetaton. Their descendants must have brought out the information, which in turn was transmitted through Moses and preserved by the chosen priestly strain that attended the Tabernacle, but were estranged from the First Temple by King Solomon. This claim will be substantiated in later chapters.

The conventional way of dealing with these difficulties is to try and squeeze them into a preconceived mind-set and, when it becomes impossible to achieve that, to conclude that the texts are imaginary, visionary and not related to the real world. A typical excuse for this blinkered attitude, which also highlights the serious problems, comes from the website of the University of St Andrews in Scotland, mentored by Dr David Davila, in discussion of a Dead Sea Scroll called 'Songs of the Sabbath Sacrifice'. It highlights a common problem:

> There is the widespread assumption that the SOSS were composed (or at least used) by the sectarians to give themselves a 'virtual experience' of the Jerusalem Temple by bypassing the earthly Temple and projecting themselves into the macrocosmic Temple with the angels . . . This virtual-Temple theory is another plausible master narrative, and, like it, is in no small part a product of imagination to fill in *the enormous blanks in our knowledge* [emphasis added].[5]

These 'blanks' are huge black holes that appear throughout Dead Sea Scrolls and biblical scholarship. If this sounds like a provocative statement, try challenging any Dead Sea Scrolls experts you come across with any of the questions listed on the next pages. Questions, to which you will find there are no satisfactory, or consensus answers, and other questions no one seems concerned, or brave enough, even to ask. For responsible objective scholars, like Professor Vermes, the response to many of these questions is often 'we simply do not know the answer'. The rest will come up with a wide variety of unconvincing explanations with little hard back-up for their suggestions.

The Community of Qumran and their Texts

Who was the Plant of Righteousness?

Who was the Teacher of Righteousness?

Who was the Wicked Priest?

Who was Melchizedek to them?

Who was Seth?

Who was Metatron?

Who was the Youth?

What was their idea of the heavenly chariot modelled on?

Why were they awaiting two (and possibly three) messiahs – one kingly and one priestly?

Where did they get their ideas for these messiahs?

Why, when the messiahs arrived, was their first task to deal with evil in Egypt?

Why was the community following a different form of Judaism to the normal population?

Why did they follow a solar calendar, whereas the rest of the population, led by the Temple priests, followed a lunar-solar calendar?

Why do the Dead Sea Scrolls frequently refer to the appointment of priests at the time of Jacob and Joseph, in a temple context, long before there was a tabernacle in Sinai or a temple in Jerusalem?

Why did they celebrate festivals at different times to the rest of the population?

Why did they not celebrate Purim?

Why did they apparently celebrate festivals unknown outside their community?

Why did they denigrate the Temple in Jerusalem?

Why did their texts – the Temple Scroll, the so-called New Jerusalem Scroll – speak of a temple that was quite different from that at Jerusalem?

Why does Ezekiel in the Dead Sea Scrolls (and in the Hebrew Bible), whom the Essenes revered, also speak of a temple quite different to the one at Jerusalem?

Why has Akhetaton, Akhenaton's capital city, been identified as the most likely city the Qumran-Essenes are describing in their scrolls?

Why is the name of the high priest at Akhetaton mentioned in the War Scroll as a leader of the forces of light in the war against the sons of darkness?[6]

Was Jesus a member of the community at any period in his life?

Was John the Baptist a member of the community at any period in his life?

Were the Essenes mentioned in the New Testament?

The Copper Scroll (3Q15)

What is the explanation for the translated phrases in the Copper Scroll, agreed by most scholars, but whose meanings are not understood, and which do not make sense in a Judaic environment?[7]

Why were the Qumran-Essenes engraving on copper when no one else in Judaea before or since used such a material for engraving?[8]

Why were the Qumran-Essenes using 99.9% pure copper, which was by then not available in Judaea or elsewhere?

Where did they get the pure copper from?

What do the 14 Greek letters interspersed in the text mean?

Why does the name Akhenaton appear to be included in Greek letters in the text?[9]

Why does the Copper Scroll include Egyptian numbering?

Why are people now agreeing, largely as a result of my work, that the weight term (K or KK) that has been accepted since the 1960s as a biblical talent, approximating to 35kg and published as such in current versions of the translations, is wrong and should be a value closer to my suggestion of an Egyptian *kite*?

How can the term '*Nahal Hagadol*' in the text (Column 10), which virtually all translators agree means 'Great River' refer to anywhere near Jerusalem when there is no great river there or anywhere in Judaea?

How does anyone explain that by using the Egyptian *kite* value, the weight of light gold bars listed in the Copper Scroll tallies almost exactly with the weight of the light gold bars found at Akhetaton?

What does the word '*Kochlit*', generally translated as 'seventh year produce store' mean?

Where are the tombs said to be north of the 'seventh year produce store'?

Where are the colonnaded tombs referred to in the scroll?

Which queen is being referred to with the mention of the 'queen's jewellery' and 'queen's tomb'?

Where is the 'Hall of Foreign Tribute'?

Where is the 'House of Refuge'?

Where is the 'House of Rejoicing'?

Why are 'dovecotes' mentioned?

Why is only an eastern gate mentioned?

Where is the 'narrow pass of the potter'?

Amarna

How are the direct connections between Akhenaton and the standard Hebrew religion – spelled out by scholars expert in Egyptology, like Freud, Meyer, Krauss, Assmann, the Sabbahs, Groll, Davidovits, etc. – explained, if not by a contemporary presence of people who passed on the information?

How is Psalm 104's similarity to the Great Hymn of Akhenaton explained, if not by a contemporary presence?

How is it that so many features mentioned in the Copper Scroll are evidenced at Amarna?

Why were very early followers of Jesus apparently worshipping in front of a relief of Akhenaton on his chariot and venerating Nefertiti, his wife?

Elephantine Island

What is the explanation for the existence of a pseudo-Hebrew colony at Elephantine, in Upper Egypt, when most experts admit there is no current explanation for their presence?

Why does the layout of the pseudo-Hebrew settlement at Elephantine follow the city pattern at Akhetaton?

Why did the community on the island know nothing about the exodus and follow an aberrant form of Judaism quite different from that in the land of Canaan and Israel?

Vast tracts are simply avoided in discussion – because they are inexplicable and dangerous to consider, or perhaps because no one has a clue as to what lies behind the events of the texts. So they are avoided and ignored.

The first generation of scroll scholars, in the 1940s and 1950s, were anxious to try and identify the various people named in the scrolls by the use of sobriquets: the Teacher of Righteousness, the Wicked Priest, the Wrathful Lion, the Seekers-after-smooth-things. A tentative consensus thought the Wrathful Lion was to be identified with Alexander Jannaeus, who lived from 103 to 76 BC, but for others no generally accepted identifications were reached.

When any of these questions are put to experts in the field of Dead Sea Scrolls studies, very few clear answers will be forthcoming, and often no answer at all will be offered. Those that are forthcoming will invariably be opinion and lack any substance of evidence. Most scholars equivocate, and sit on the fence, although there are just a few, like the late Hartmut Stegemann, who are prepared to name names.[10] However, even he has no idea who the Teacher of Righteousness was, nor many other key characters described in the Dead Sea Scrolls.

One high-profile prolific academic author, Robert Eisenman, sticks his neck out and maintains that James the brother of Jesus was the Teacher of Righteousness. He happily dismisses what he calls 'external evidence', like archaeology, palaeography and carbon-14 dating, as unreliable. For him, the 'internal evidence' of the texts is sufficient, even though he finds it necessary, on occasion, to ignore the translations of other scholars and rely on his own versions. He ignores the fact that the 'internal' texts, on which he almost entirely relies, were written by people who were rarely objective, invariably had an agenda, and that their testimony has nearly always come down to us through transmissions which can, and often do, vary from the original work.

Professor Eisenman's conclusion in relation to the Teacher of Righteousness is in fact contradicted by the 'internal evidence' and the findings of many other scholars, which indicate that the Teacher of Righteousness came on the scene around 170 BC, led his followers to Qumran around 140–130 BC and died around 110 BC, long before the life of James the Just.

Talking about the dating of the Dead Sea Scrolls material, Professor Eisenman has said:

> If the results of these test and other external measurements such as archaeology and palaeography – some really not exact sciences in the true sense of the term at all – conflict with *the internal data*, then regardless of one's confidence in them, they must be jettisoned . . .
>
> This is the situation in Dead Sea Scrolls research today, the conclusions concerning which have been rendered inchoate and vacuous by the uncritical and superficial reliance on external data or parameters such as these.[11]

Professor Eisenman's views on technology appear to be quite archaic. For him, archaeology is dubious, and paleography, patina analysis, and carbon dating are 'pseudo-sciences'. Partly because of what he sees as science's weaknesses in testing the scrolls, and the gullibility of the scholarly community, he says: 'because they contradict the "internal evidence" of what the Scrolls themselves actually say – they made the Scrolls impossible to interpret, in effect, rendered them mute'.

The fact that there are so many unresolved questions on what are basic issues implies that something is seriously wrong with the façade being presented by scholars in their understanding of the scrolls. Some key factors are being missed that might give an explanation. It suffices to say that answers to all these questions come from one place and one source – Akhetaton, Akhenaton's holy city, and from his era.

The relevance for outside observers is that, when they cite Dead Sea Scrolls texts, they should be aware that the versions they consult and answers they obtain may be extremely subjective, and depend on who they consult and invariably take no account of the Egyptian dimensions. They should be aware of the 'crisis of understanding' that lies behind the façade. This is particularly true for makers of television documentaries and the popular press, who often inadvertently feed the public with a distorted version of the truth.

Chapter 4

A General Theory of Amarna–Qumran Relativity

Answers have been offered by disparate scholars to some of the questions that have just been posed, but they are invariably 'one-off' suggestions that lack plausibility, have little or no coherence and do not achieve consensus. Perhaps even more disconcerting is the lack of concern of Qumran scholars that most of the key personalities mentioned in the Dead Sea Scrolls remain unidentified – unidentified more than 60 years after the translation of some of the earliest scrolls and 100 years after the translation of Dead Sea Scroll material found amongst the Genizah collection.[1] For there to be so many difficulties in textual and site identifications, it has to be concluded that something fundamental is being missed – *some crucial factors are not being recognized.*

I now present a new set of circumstances in relation to Qumran and the Dead Seas Scrolls that offers deep plausibility and solutions to many of the unanswered and difficult questions that have dogged the scene from 1947 onwards. This will not be an easy worldview to take on board, but these answers have coherence and form part of an overall logical pattern of explanations. It will frighten many scholars, particularly academics, and those who have not been to Egypt or studied Egyptology, but it has a lineage of authority: the authority of the Hebrew Bible and the New Testament. Indeed, there is a growing corpus of scholars, most of whom we will meet in the pages of this book, who support the general theory, stretching from Sigmund Freud in the 1950s to Sarah Israelit Groll, the Sabbahs, Joseph Davidovits, the Lonnqvists, Professor Kris Thijs and Professor Harold Ellens in contemporary times.

The essential elements of a connection for the Hebrews to the Amarna period of Egypt were first proposed by Sigmund Freud back

31

in the 1930s in a work entitled *Moses and Monotheism*. More recently, a formidable amount of evidence has begun to emerge through the work of Erik Hornung, Jan Assmann, Joseph Davidovits, Roger and Messod Sabbah, Ahmed Osman, Minna and Kenneth Lonnqvist, Hugo Kennes, Kris Thijs and Michael Joyce. My own books, *The Mystery of the Copper Scroll of Qumran* and *The Secret Initiation of Jesus at Qumran*, carry forewords by George Brooke and Harold Ellens.[2] That does not necessarily imply their endorsement of the main theories, but it does imply that the ideas warrant serious consideration.

Many of the problematic texts cited (and many not cited through lack of space) make reference to Egypt and it is self-evident from sections of the Hebrew Bible, and the close relationship between the Essenes and another sect, the Theraputae of Egypt, that the Israelites had an ongoing and intense love–hate relationship with ancient Egypt.

When an Egyptian perspective is adopted, almost all of the difficult texts in the Dead Sea Scrolls can be explained and understood to relate to real historical people and circumstances. Why ignore the influences of a dominant power, adjacent to Canaan and Israel, which the Bible continually refers back to? Almost every important character in the Bible, from the earliest biblical period (c1550 BC) up to the birth of Christ (c4 BC) is said either to seek refuge in or flee from Egypt (examples appear in the table opposite). It would, therefore, be quite extraordinary if Egypt had not left its mark on the entire Bible.

As will be seen in later chapters, the central point is that the Hebrews were in Egypt during a period of prosperity which was followed by a period of famine when the pharaoh's vizier was Joseph and that Jacob and his family also interacted with the royal family.

The pharaoh in question was Akhenaton – a revolutionary figure, who turned Egypt away from pagan idolatry, instructing the smashing of all the carved images and removal of all the temple inscriptions relating to the previous gods, across the whole of Egypt. He abandoned the traditional pagan temples and structures of the capital city at Thebes and established a new capital and virgin city in central Egypt in a remote area now know as El-Amarna.

It seems likely that his father, Amenhotep III, was of the same mind, and that they governed Egypt as co-rulers for a limited period. As Amenhotep IV's commitment to one invisible God hardened, he

The Influence of Egypt on the Bible

Egyptians confirmed in the OT and NT	Drawn to or Flee from Egypt
Earliest Biblical Period	
Sarai's dalliance with unnamed Pharaoh.	Abram, Sarai.
Amarna Period	
Joseph's wife, children Ephraim & Manasseh.	Joseph (Manasseh, Ephraim), Jacob, Reuben, Simeon, Levi, Benjamin, Judah, Dan, Naphtali, Gad, Asher, Issachar, Zebulon.
Exodus Period	
Moses – a Prince of Egypt, Peleth of On, Korah, Dathan, Abiram. The Egyptian woman who is shunned. Son of an Egyptian father who is stoned.	Aaron, Miriam, Joshua, Caleb.
In Canaan	
Solomon marries a daughter of an Egyptian Pharaoh.	
Exilic Period	Jeremiah, Baruch, etc.
House of Judah	
Mered marries Bithia, a daughter of Pharaoh.	
Second Temple Period	
An Egyptian priest from Alexandria, Simon, son of Boethus, father-in-law of Herod the Great. Simon buried at Leontopolis in cemetery of Hebrews near Onias IV's temple.	Onias IV.
Early Christian Period	Jesus and his family, St Mark.

changed his name to Akhenaton and took the entire court, military and civil personnel, and a population of about 50,000 followers, to the newly constructed city on the east bank of the Nile, at the place he called Akhetaton, 'Place of the horizon'. Together with his queen, Nefertiti, and perhaps also with the inspiration of the biblical Jacob and Joseph, he ushered in a form of pure monotheism where only one supreme, invisible, all-powerful God was to be worshipped. He knew that God as Aton or Aten. Because the 't' and 'd' sounds are interchangeable in Egyptian hieroglyphs, it can also be read as 'Adon' – a term used in the Hebrew Bible for the name of God.

Chapter 5

Tout ce que j'avais rêvé[1]

Eurostar is, for me, one of the greatest advances in travel. I am not too fond of air travel and since its inception have travelled to France at least twice every year by train, often to play chess. On one chess trip I took the opportunity of seeking out Józef Milik, to discuss the draft of my book on the Copper Scroll. He was kind enough to see me in his Paris flat, and over a period of eight years, from October 1998, we had many long conversations on biblical subjects and the Dead Sea Scrolls. As a lapsed Catholic priest, he was party to the earliest excavations at Qumran and became the acknowledged doyen of Dead Sea Scrolls translation. As a man who was fluent in some 17 languages and gifted with a photographic mind for most of his life, one can only describe him as a genius – with a smile. Together with Zdzislaw J. Kapera, editor of the *Qumran Chronicle*, I co-authored a biography of Józef Milik, *Doyen of the Dead Sea Scrolls*, which has just been published.[2]

Leafing through dusty second-hand books in the shops in the Marais or Latin Quarter, or in the stalls along the Seine, I invariably find something I desire. More prosaically, Fnac, a chain of mammoth media shops, thronged with thousands of new books, always proves worth a few hours' meandering. As a result I keep abreast of French research in the areas of biblical study and especially in relation to Qumran. As far as understanding the influences of Egypt on these disciplines is concerned, the French are far ahead of their English-speaking counterparts. Inspired perhaps by adventurers like Napoleon Bonaparte and Jean-François Champollion, modern authors have done much to recognize the influence of Akhenaton and Egypt.[3] Messod and Roger Sabbah and Joseph Davidovits in particular have presented strong complementary evidence for my theories on Akhenaton.

Les Secrets de l'Exode, by the Sabbahs, looks at the Amarna and Tutankhamun periods and makes a powerful case for Psalm 104 in the

Bible to be a direct copying from the Great Hymn to the Aton, found in the tomb of Ay at Akhenaton's capital city. Others, like Jan Assmann and Eric Hornung, have also made the connection, but the Sabbahs go though the hieroglyphics letter by letter, comparing them with the Hebrew equivalents. Their findings are quite remarkable as they demonstrate that the Hebrew words mirror the Egyptian version and letters often take the shape of the Egyptian hieroglyphs and therefore confirm with absolute certainty the dependence of Psalm 104 on this 3,300-year-old inscription.

Explanations by conventional scholarship to account for the close relationship between the two texts, via some vague transmission process of popular memory, fall apart with the Sabbahs' submissions. Akhetaton was abandoned within tens of years of Akhenaton's death, and the city left desolated and isolated for about 1,300 years. Hieroglyphics would have been unintelligible to the Hebrews much after the time of Isaiah, when the Psalm came to be written down, so the transmission can only have been through a readable version of the Great Hymn or an incredible feat of memory. Psalm 104 is considered to be one of the oldest psalms, and in my submission *is* the oldest.

To buttress this assertion, Joseph Davidovits has rediscovered an inscription of great significance dating to the time of Akhenaton.[4] In 1935 two French Egyptologists, Claude Robichon and Alexandre Varille, unearthed a fresco at the Karnak funereal temple of Amenophis dating to the time of Pharaoh Amenhotep III, Akhenaton's father. It was not until 2005 that Professor Davidovits came across a book published by the two explorers and put two and two together. Having previously written a book, *La Bible avait raison – l'archéologie révèle l'existence des Hébreux en Egypte* ('The Bible was right – archaeology reveals the existence of the Hebrews in Egypt'), he was excited to find what he considered was further support for his ideas that placed the biblical Joseph as a contemporary of Amenhotep III. Translating the fresco, Professor Davidovits concluded that Amenophis son of Hapu (or Hapou), identified on the inscription, was none other than Joseph. The pharaonic names of the Amenhotep kings are also referred to in Greek as Amenophis, and to distinguish between Amenophis III and this contemporary, the contemporary was identified as Amenophis son of Hapu.

Professor Davidovits suggests that the priests who attended Hapu were Semites, which is a reasonable assumption, but in his 2005 book he has Joseph, aged 8–10, recruited by Pharaoh Tutmoses III, so he would be about 110 when he became vizier to Akhenaton. For this and other reasons, I do not go along with the assumption that Hapu, as vizier to Amenhotep III, equates to Joseph. I believe the vizier at the time of Akhenaton was the true Joseph.

Nevertheless, the professor's research adds yet another confirmation of a Hebrew presence at Amarna. The scenario could be that Joseph, as a prophetic, highly intelligent Semite in the priestly coterie of Hapu, came to the attention of Akhenaton, who appointed him as vizier, effectively second-in-command of all Egypt, and rewarded him richly. In recognition of the previous revered vizier he named him Amenophis Hapu.

A further detail shows where the genius of Professor Davidovits comes into play. Knowing that hieroglyphics can be read vertically, from top to bottom or bottom to top, and also horizontally from left to right or right to left, he noted that the name Amenophis son of Hapu in the fresco is out of phase and written back to front. He then looked at the name given to Joseph in the Bible. This is a name designated by pharaoh, but it comprises two unknown words that make little sense in Hebrew. Hebrew is invariably read only from right to left, so the name, in Genesis 41:45, reads: Zaphenath-paneah (or צפנת פענח). Reversing the Hebrew letters gives two words, and bearing in mind that there are no vowels at this stage in the development of Hebrew, they can be read as: H'NAPU SENOPHIS. So Joseph's given name could well be Hapu Amenophis

It is, of course, difficult to be categorical about this reading, but it does appear plausible, especially in the light of the inscription's similarity to the passage in Genesis (echoed in the Koran) which talks about Joseph and an Egyptian pharaoh. Some of the translations of the fresco reveal a quite remarkable and convincing connection for the Bible to the Amarna period, which Professor Davidovits refers to as 'the oldest text written word for word in the Bible'. The comparison is summarized in the table overleaf.

Joseph in Scripture and the Amenophis Fresco

Amenophis Fresco	Hebrew Bible Genesis 41:42–6	Koran Sura xii, Verse 54
He received ornaments of gold and all varieties of precious metals. He dressed him in linen of the finest quality. A collar of pure gold and all sorts of material was placed around his neck. At the age of 30 the great royal scribe bowed before his majesty	And removing his signet ring from his hand, Pharaoh put it on Joseph's hand . . . and he had him dressed in robes of fine linen and put a gold collar around his neck . . . thus Joseph was 30 years old when he entered the service of Pharaoh king of Egypt.	And the King said: 'Bring him unto me that I may attach him to my person.' And when he had talked with him he said: 'Lo! Thou art today in our presence established and trusted.'

Chapter 6

The Amarna Connection to the Dead Sea Scrolls

The area of Akhenaton's newly built holy city in Middle Egypt, with its vast Great Temple, is replete with locations that to this day philologically echo related biblical names – Bahr Jusef (Joseph's River), Amram, Sheikh 'Ibad (Amram and Jochebed were respectively the father and mother of Moses).

When Akhenaton died, almost certainly betrayed and killed by Ay, his chancellor, Egypt reverted to idol worship and Joseph and his family were *persona non grata* to the new ruler. The Hebrews, I maintain, were then ostracized and eventually taken into servitude and monotheism driven underground.

The sequence of how this suppressed religion and memories of Akhenaton's city re-emerged through Moses and was carried out of Egypt by a mixed company of Hebrews and armed wealthy Egyptians, with a priestly class from both groupings (Peleth of On, Dathan, and Kohath – all names with Egyptian origins) can be traced through the ongoing priestly struggles chronicled in the Old Testament from their very first emergence into Sinai. The mode of this transmission, from c1350 BC right down to the time of the priestly line that eventually settled at Qumran, is spelled out in detail in my previous books and documentaries, and has been supported by eminent authorities.[1]

There is not enough space to give examples of how all the practices, beliefs, architecture and other manifestations of monotheistic Amarna have impinged on both books of the Bible, the Koran and, more specifically, the Qumran-Essenes. A few examples, amongst hundreds, from the sectarian texts of Qumran, biblical sources, the Koran and modern archaeology in Israel follow.

Sectarian Texts and Qumran

The Temple Scroll

From the Temple Scroll (Col. 40) we read: 'to their daughters and to foreigners, who were bo[rn . . .] the width around the central courtyard will be six [hundred cubits(?)] by a length of about one thousand [six hundred] cubits from one corner to the other . . .'[2]

From excavations at Amarna we know the precise size of the Great Temple was 800 x 300m – a very close approximation to the 600 x 1,600 cubits specified in the Temple Scroll and a temple size far too large to fit on the Temple Mount at Jerusalem (the cubit is taken as 51cm). Whilst some people conclude that the description in the Temple Scroll is that of a visionary Temple, Yigael Yadin, in his classic book on the Temple Scroll,[3] has little doubt that the portrayal refers to 'an earthly temple'. (Some commentators take the design of the temple, set out in the Temple Scroll, as being in the form of concentric squares. This may have been for the inner areas, but I know of almost no square temples in the ancient Near East and the largest outside and key dimensions given in the Temple Scroll are clearly a width by a length, and cannot possibly give rise to a square outer wall shape.)

The mention of a 'Court for Foreigners' in the Temple Scroll is repeated in the Copper Scroll as a 'Hall of Foreign Tribute' and an area of 'Sunshade' (Cols. 2 and 7). This can hardly be a reference to a Temple in Jerusalem, whereas both a 'Hall of Foreign Tribute' and an area of 'Sunshade' are specifically named as being part of the Great Temple at Akhetaton.

Col. 56: 'But he is not to increase the cavalry or make the people go back to Egypt on account of war in order to increase the cavalry, or the silver and gold . . . He is not to have many wives . . .'

This clearly speaks from the perspective of a new king who is not to repeat the experience of the king in Egypt. It reflects Akhenaton's demonstrated monogamistic attitude to marriage (unlike the normal practice of kings in Israel), staying loyal to Nefertiti all her life despite the fact that she could only provide him with daughters.

Col. 60 makes it clear that the perspective of the Temple Scroll is pre-exodus: 'When you enter the land which I am going to give you, you shall not learn to emulate the depravities of those people.'

We will unroll more of the Temple Scroll later in the book, particularly the geometry it refers to, as this scroll was considered of great importance by the Qumran-Essenes. It was almost their 'Second Torah'.

Testament of Levi (4Q213)

These fragments from Cave 4 at Qumran, found in seven copies, include the passage: 'your priesthood from all flesh . . . When my father Jacob was separating the tithes'.

Tithes are specifically related to temple contributions, and the term was in use in ancient Egypt, and yet at the time of Jacob there was no Hebrew Temple, no Tabernacle, no associated priests. We know from examples of wine dockets and other descriptions at Amarna that tithes were being collected for donation to the Temple.

In her studies of the Testament of Levi, Dr Esther Eshel notes that there are continual references to the appointment of priests at the time of Jacob. Other commentators assert that the Ten Commandments were fully formed before the time of Moses.[4] These phenomena can readily be accounted for by their similarity to the tenets specified by the Pharaoh Akhenaton and confirm that the text of the fragment was formulated long before the Hebrews arrived in the Promised Land.

The conclusion has to be that the descriptions of Jacob's actions are based on an essentially true memory of real events. Later additional evidence on the Essenes' knowledge of the geometry of the layout of the city of Akhetaton proves they had a detailed awareness of the site, which can only have come from someone who was a contemporary of Akhenaton.

An Angelic Viewpoint

These areas of conclusion are ones no other scholars seem prepared even to consider, and yet the markers are all there, for all to see. One of the few scholars, apart from Józef Milik, who has delved deeply into the roots of priestly messianism and the Aramaic fragment of Levi, is Joseph L. Angel, of the Yeshiva University, New York. His interpretations are more plausible than most and shed a great deal of light on the real truth behind the fragments.

Joseph Angel notes that, unlike the book of Ben Sira (written c190–175 BC) which reflects the historical circumstances of Second Temple early 2nd century BC, the Aramaic Levi document removes the ideal priest from contemporary times 'placing him even before the time of any of the great priestly figures of the Bible' and elevating him to the role of high priest.[5] Apart from clear references to the 'priest of God Most High', and to Melchizedek, Levi's second son, Qahat is endowed with Jacob's blessing to be high priest for all Israel. An associated non-sectarian Aramaic composition, 4QApocryphon of Levi (4Q541), gives a tantalizing portrait of a grand unnamed priestly messiah figure whose teaching will be 'like the will of God' and 'his eternal sun will shine'. In the setting of the text this can only be referring to Pharaoh Akhenaton.

Jonas Greenfield, Michael Stone and Esther Eshel trace the wisdom instruction to Levi to Deuteronomy 33 and Malachi 2,[6] but Joseph Angel, in my view quite correctly, finds this attribution unconvincing. Apart from the fact that the priests are here teaching all Israel, in the Aramaic Levi document the teaching is directed to the Levites alone, and the subject of the instruction 'never comes close to identifying wisdom with the Torah'. Angel sees the 'recipe wisdom' as nearer to the Book of Proverbs. This makes the origins of the ideas, as set in the time of Jacob, Joseph and Levi, rather more obvious.

Proverbs and wisdom texts in the Bible have been clearly shown to relate to Babylonian and Egyptian sources, particularly Egyptian. In the case of the references in the Levi documents they are almost certainly more specifically related to the wisdom of Akhenaton, and he is therefore the tantalizing mystery figure so often referred to in Qumranic scrolls. This prince who became king/pharaoh took into his writings the 'Instructions of Amenhotep'[7] and other Egyptian wisdom texts. We know from records of his interests that he was continually teaching and instructing his followers, and the depth of his prowess in this area is self-evident from the dramatic changes in architectural, artistic, humanitarian, religious and philosophical practices he introduced during his reign. In the words of Jean-Claude Brinette, founder of the 'Historel' website:

> What characterizes Akhenaton (Amenophis IV) is his amazing simplicity of mind, so full of vitality; his will for peace, his constant concern to alleviate the daily life of the people and his wish to communicate his faith, his ideas of justice to them.[8]

The War Scroll

This relatively well-preserved scroll, found in part in Caves 1, 4 and 5 (1QM, 4QM, 5Q11), describes preparations for the final battle of the Sons of Light against the Sons of Darkness.

In Column 4, we find: 'On the standard of Merari they shall write the votive offering of God ... And the Prince of Light Thou hast appointed from ancient times.'

We know from Amarna texts and inscriptions that the high priest at Akhetaton was Meryre and that he was an hereditary prince in his own right, just as the priestly messiah awaited by the Qumran-Essenes is required to be. The kingly messiah to combine with the priestly messiah was most surely King Akhenaton and his high priest, Meryre.

In 1QM Column 15, we find: 'Those prepared for war shall set up camp opposite the king of the Kittim and the whole army of Belial that has gathered to him . . .'

The general assumption by the majority of scholars, that the 'Kittim' are the Romans, simply because they were the dominant power during the period of Qumran, and that the war can be set in Roman times, is quite unsustainable. The Romans did not refer to their leader as a king and Belial was a usual term for evil forces in ancient Egypt. Even a cursory reading of the references to 'Kittim' shows that they are anything but the Romans, but are the traditional enemies of Egypt – Moab, Asshur, Edom, the Philistines, Assyria. Even Column 1 refers to 'the Kittim in Egypt'.

Whilst the term 'Kittim' might be referring to Romans in the Dead Sea Scroll commentary on the book of Habakkuk, where the 'Kittim' are said to 'sacrifice to their standards and worship their weapons of war' (1QpHab 6:3-5), as this was a know practice of the Romans, it does not follow that the term always meant the same power. The Book of Daniel also seems to be talking about the Romans, but in 1 Maccabees the term is definitely applied to the Greeks. The origins of the term go back at least to the time of the Phoenicians where it was used to describe the Phoenician colony in what is now the island of Cyprus. In the War Scroll, which I suggest has a much earlier basic provenance, 'Kittim' are the final opponents in the eschatological battle of Israel against a foe led by a king (*melech* in Hebrew). It is quite clear that the term 'Kittim' was applied progressively to occupying powers, starting with the Assyrians and proceeding on to the Babylonians, Persians, Greeks and finally Romans. The application of the term in the War Scroll, in my view, is to the 'End Days' forces of chaos, that are equated with the original 'Kittim' enemy at the time of Pharaoh Akhenaton, in other words the Assyrians.

The question of who were the 'Kittim' and where was the 'Asshur' mentioned in Column 11 of the War Scroll was posed by me to the presenter of a paper on the War Scroll at the 2011 Society of Biblical Literature Conference held at King's College London.[9] The speaker, Hanna Vanonen, was reluctant or unable to give an answer to either part of my question, as was everyone else present at the session.

In fact Asshur almost certainly refers to what was the capital of Assyria,[10] as referred to in Genesis 2:14, and as such testifies to the antiquity of the setting of the War Scroll and excludes any possibility that the term 'Kittim' was referring to the Romans.

The Copper Scroll

The answers to most of the questions raised relating to the Copper Scroll were given in my previous book *The Mystery of the Copper Scroll of Qumran*, and other answers appear during the course of later chapters.

Chapter 7

The Amarna Connection
to the Bible

Science works on the principle that any theory has to be repeatable under the same experimental conditions and that a theory which has this characteristic will predict related findings when these are tested.

Not only are the Dead Sea Scrolls full of obvious memories of the Amarna period, as one might expect, but there are entire sections of the Bible itself that reflect life at the time of Akhenaton and the geometry of his holy city. If what I claim is correct, it would be surprising if they did not.

The Book of Ezekiel gives numerous clues that he is not talking about the land of Israel or the Temple at Jerusalem, when he talks about the Holy City and a huge temple:

> The House of Israel and their kings must not again defile my holy name by their apostasy and by the corpses of their kings at their death. When they placed their threshold next to my threshold and their doorposts next to My doorpost with only a wall between me and them they were defiling my holy name. *(Ezekiel 43:7–8)*

The kind of practice described has nothing to with Israelite burial custom. It is clearly a warning to Israel in their new land not to follow the Egyptian pagan practice of building a mortuary temple and housing the dead king in close proximity to the gods of the temple. This was the custom in the burial of kings and officials in ancient Egypt when a mortuary temple was built in front of the person's tomb to accommodate the funeral arrangements and mummification. None of the burials at Amarna included an associated traditional mortuary temple.

Ezekiel – The First Essene?

A careful examination of the geometry of the temple and city described in Ezekiel 40–48 demonstrates without any doubt that we are looking at the Great Temple of Akhetaton and the huge virgin city built for Pharaoh Akhenaton, as his holy city dedicated to Aton. I cite a few examples. Any explanation that tries to place this description in the land of Israel and relate it to the Temple at Jerusalem is quite absurd. Claims that the description is purely imaginary also fall, because they fail to answer where the knowledge of the landscape and setting for the building described came from, or why the accounts match so closely the layout and scenery at Amarna.

According to Ezekiel 40:44: 'There were chambers for singers in the inner forecourt'. There is no mention in the Bible of singers in the temples at Jerusalem, but depictions of singers can be seen in the side chamber of the Great Temple at Akhetaton.

Various measurements are given in Ezekiel 45:1–7. The total area designated for the Lord is 12,500 x 10,000m (taking cubits as 50cm); the area designated for the Levites is 12,500 x 5,000m; and the area designated for the city is 12,500 x 2,500m. This gives a total area of approximately 12.5 x 17.5km.

Ezekiel 46 also confirms the prophet's knowledge of Akhetaton, through the high priest of the Temple he is describing. In verse 12 we find: 'The gate that faces east shall also be opened for the Prince whenever he offers a freewill offering – be it burnt offering or offering of wellbeing . . .'

Detailed excavations at Amarna, under the supervision of Barry Kemp, and the work of N. de G. Davies, Geoffrey Martin and others, support both these points. They show that the area of the city of Akhetaton was defined by 15 boundary stelae and measured approximately 12.5 x 20km, very close to the city area recorded in the Book of Ezekiel. They also support the belief that the gate to the east would have been used by the high priest at Akhetaton.

Ezekiel 46:16 makes it clear that the high priest was a hereditary prince, which is inconsistent with the name of the high priests designated in the Bible. No high priest in the Bible is referred to as having previously been a prince. 'Thus said the Lord God: If the Prince makes a gift to any of his sons, it shall become the latter's inheritance, it shall pass on to his sons'. The high priest officiating at the Great Temple at Akhetaton was called Meryre, and he was a hereditary prince.

Also significant is the description in Ezekiel 47:

> He led me back to the entrance of the Temple, and I found that water was issuing from below the platform of the Temple – eastward, since the Temple faced east . . .
>
> As the man went on eastward with a measuring line in his hand, he measured off a thousand cubits and led me across the water; the water was ankle deep. Then he measured off another thousand and led me across the water; the water was knee deep. He measured off a further thousand and led me across the water; the water was up to the waist. When he measured yet another thousand, it was a river I could not cross; for the stream had swollen into a stream that could not be crossed except by swimming. 'Do you see, O mortal?' he said to me: and led me back to the bank of the stream. As I came back, I saw trees in great profusion on both banks of the stream.

Unequivocally, from this extended description, water in large quantities is flowing into the temple, which means the temple cannot be in Jerusalem near the Temple Mount. (Strangely enough Masonic rituals include tracing boards laid on the floor during ceremonies, which show a large temple, assumed to be that in Jerusalem, with water from a river running through it.)

The description is consistent with Ezekiel being led around to the outer gate of the Temple facing east and then made to walk eastward, as his guide starts to measure, using a typical Egyptian measuring device. They walk away from the Temple towards a very wide river. Taking a cubit as 50cm, the distance from the Temple to the edge of the river is 500m as specified by Ezekiel. This is almost exactly the distance from the edge of the Great Temple at Amarna to ankle depth in the River Nile. A suggestion that the Nile may have altered its course over the years and the distances mentioned might not be applicable today is contradicted by geo-archaeological studies. Fieldwork funded by the Amarna Research Foundation, looking at the course of the river concluded: 'the river was, in Akhenaten's day, more or less where it is today'.[1]

Go to Amarna and see for yourself. To this day the site of the Great Temple can be seen to have been 500m from the Nile and there are many trees on both sides of the river. The entire land is a flowering garden irrigated by a spring which has its source in the temple. The imagery is clear. There is no other source of water in candidate countries that would meet this description, except the Nile, and the temple has to be near that source.

A defining characteristic of the Nile is that, apart from a limited amount of rain, it is the only source of water for the whole of Egypt, and its annual flooding is essential for the irrigation of the land from the furthest south to the extreme north. In the New Jerusalem Scroll version of Ezekiel 47:8–12, we have one of the clearest confirmations that the river in question near the temple being described is the Nile. Water is said to emerge from under the threshold of the temple on the eastern side and descend from south of the altar to the outer court to irrigate the entire country!

> 'This water,' he told me, 'runs out to the eastern region, and flows into the Arabah; and when it comes into the sea, the sea of foul waters, the waters will become wholesome. Every living creature that swarms will be able to live wherever this stream goes; the fish will be very abundant once these waters have reached there . . . Fishermen will stand beside it all the way from En-Gedi to En-Eglaim . . . All kinds of trees for food will grow up upon both banks of the stream . . . because the water for them flows from the Temple.'[2]

The last verses here are of especial interest. The comparison above clearly shows that Ezekiel is talking about the temple at Akhetaton, but now he transplants the beneficial waters of the Nile that have flowed from the temple to the Arabah region of Canaan. The 'foul sea' must be the Dead Sea, and we are very near to Qumran with the mention of En-Gedi which is only a few kilometres away.

No one has yet put forward a reasonable explanation as to why the sectarians were led to Qumran by their Teacher of Righteousness. This passage in Ezekiel not only confirms a link from Akhetaton, it explains why the Essenes settled at Qumran to await the golden age associated with the true temple of God.

Strangely enough, one of the arch advocates of minimalist Bible reality, Niels Peter Lemche gets something right when he says Ezekiel's description (Chapters 40–8) of what people assume is a future temple 'in all probability really describes the original temple'.[3]

Knowing the thread of Ezekiel's connection to the Qumran-Essenes, as enunciated by Professor Wacholder,[4] and their connection to Amarna, there can be little doubt that his descriptions reflect a transmitted memory of the Great Temple at Akhetaton.

So when was Ezekiel writing about what I claim is the temple of Akhetaton? Ezekiel tells us himself. At the very beginning of his work (1:1), he says that: 'In the thirtieth year, on the fifth day of the fourth month, when I came to the community of exiles by the Chebar canal . . . it was the fifth year of the exile of King Jehoiachin'. This information puts the date at the fifth day of the month of Tamuz in the year 593 BC – seven years before the destruction of the First Temple in Jerusalem! It is generally accepted that the Book of Ezekiel was edited later than this period, but then one has to ask the question: why is Ezekiel continually talking about oracles concerning Egypt (Chapters 29–30) and especially about a heavenly throne chariot. So concerned were the rabbis of the Tannaitic period and later, over the sensitivity of this material, that the Mishnah requires that it must only be expounded by a 'sage that understands his own knowledge' (*Hagigah* 2:1). M. *Megillah* 4.10 states categorically that Ezekiel's writings on chariots should not be read at all!

One has to conclude, in the light of no other convincing explanations, that the original reason for these stringent stipulations was a knowledge that studying chariot, or 'Merkabah' stories, as they are referred to in Kabbalah, inevitably led back to Egypt and possible pagan indoctrination – or true knowledge of the origins of monotheism.

After dealing with his vision of the destruction of a temple, Ezekiel turns to descriptions of its rebuilding and the plan on which it should be based. Any doubt that this description is that of a memory of the Great Temple at Akhetaton has to be dispelled by the numerous identifying details which cannot possibly relate to Jerusalem.

Psalm 104

This psalm has been mentioned previously, but we can now look inside the cavernous tomb at Amarna where its *editio princeps* was originally engraved. The Great Hymn to the Aton can still be seen carved on the walls of the tomb of Ay at Amarna. It is paraphrased in consistent order of ideas and words in Psalm 104. Or, more precisely, Psalm 104 copies from the Great Hymn to the Aton.

When I first gazed in wonder at the huge floor-to-ceiling vertical lines of hieroglyphs, still readable after nearly 4,300 years, I listened as my guide, Dr Jocelyn Gohary, translated the text. Although there has been some deterioration since it was first discovered, the Hymn was fortunately copied in the 19th century when it was more legible.[5] The huge tomb is some 18m deep, originally with 15 tall support columns, and some of the colouring on the many reliefs still remains intact.

The proposition that the Great Hymn was somehow absorbed into the Bible through its general availability in ancient times is refuted by the fact that its central themes were only relevant during the short reign of Pharaoh Akhenaton (17 years) and after his death were expunged from Egyptian lore and memory. Virtually all inscriptions and images relating to him that could be found in the temples and monuments he had built were destroyed and 'cleansed' of his influence. These actions were a concerted attempt across Egypt to eradicate his name.

Carved in hieroglyphs, Akhenaton's name would not have been decipherable by later generations. Work by Erik Hornung and Jan Assmann demonstrates that the idea of a supreme invisible God who ruled both day and night was unique to the Amarna period and represented a key change in Egyptian religion. The detailed study by the French scholars Roger and Messod Sabbah already mentioned demonstrates that not only are the ideas in Psalm 104 and the Great Hymn identical, but the order of words and Hebrew letters follow the Egyptian hieroglyph shapes in exactly the same positions in the psalm. (The Hebrew *shin*, for example, as the 'racine' root letter in the word for vegetation DESHE, copies the Egyptian shape for vegetation – a wavy W.)

The description of ships 'going up and down the river' as given in the best translations of Psalm 104, and also written about in the Great

Hymn to the Aton, makes no sense in an Israel setting. The Nile, however, carried a constant stream of vessels carrying people, animals and goods. The Jordan River dwindles to a small stream by the time it gets near to the Dead Sea, and it carried only a few small boats, generally crossing from side to side rather than up and down.

Another indication of Qumranite knowledge of the Great Hymn comes from the order of festivals listed in the Temple Scroll from Cave 11. This is considered to be one of the most important scrolls for the Qumran-Essenes, and it was also unique to them. Although there are references to novel festivals in other sources, the Dead Sea Scrolls versions are the only ones where we get detailed descriptions. The Temple Scroll describes the celebration of a number of previously unknown festivals, and the order of listing follows exactly the order set out in the Great Hymn and Psalm 104.

When confronted with the kind of suggestion that links Akhenaton to the Qumran-Essenes, scholars like Professor Schiffman, one of the more receptive academics who has at least looked superficially at my work, cannot accept the premise and find the intervening distances and time too great to allow it to be credible, although Professor Schiffman cannot refute the actual linkages. He comments:

> Parts of the Bible may even be based on older traditions, so could come from Akhenaton. These types of parallels are even clearer in the Wisdom texts. However, the influences that come to the Qumran people come mediated by the Hebrew Bible, and there is not one stitch of evidence of a direct influence.[6]

In my submission there is not just one stitch of evidence but an entire wardrobe of proof. Professor Schiffman takes little account of the fact that many of the 'influences' he acknowledges existed cannot come via the Hebrew Bible as they are unknown in the Bible or from any other texts we know about, other than from Qumran.

Chapter 8

Confirmation from the Koran?

If the Bible, both Hebrew and New Testament, and the Dead Sea Scrolls contain large elements that I claim confirm a relationship for Judaism and Christianity back to Akhetaton, it would be likely that the Koran, which incorporates details of many biblical stories and events, might also show evidence of some similar connections or even new information. Clearly, as we progress through history, awareness of any connection would be strongest in the earliest parts of the Hebrew Bible and the Dead Sea Scrolls, less strong in the Tannaitic and rabbinic periods, New Testament and apocrypha, and even weaker in the Koran and the Hadith (comments on the Koran attributed to the Prophet Muhammad). If there was a progression through these various sources to Islam and a knowledge of their understanding of Akhenaton within them, then it would seem likely that Islam would know something – even if only a glimmer of the Amarna period.

It is certainly true that many of the ideas of Akhenaton and his morality are present in the teachings of the Koran, but is there anything more concrete in the texts to illustrate a comprehension of the pharaoh himself?

Qumran-Essene Philosophies, Akhenaton and the Koran

	Akhetaton	Normative Judaism	Qumran-Essenes	Christianity	Islam
Apocalyptic outlook	√√√	√	√√√	√√	√√
Reverence for Light	√√√	√	√√√	√√	√√
Predestination	√√√	x	√√√	√√	√√
Jesus as an Essene	–	x	√√√	√√√	√√
Resurrection	√	x	√√√	√√√	√√√
Qumran-Essenes mentioned in holy writings	–	√	√√√	√√√	√√√
Allusions to Akhenaton	√√√	√	√√√	√	√

There are several indications that Muhammad and the writing down of his revelations were influenced by a sectarian group of Jews. It was his custom to retreat to a cave in the mountains near Mecca for episodes of contemplation. It is said that some of his earliest followers were Jews. Could these possibly be descendants of Qumran-Essenes whose predecessors might have fled to the region after the destruction of Qumran in 68 AD? They were also 'cave dwellers' in their original site at Qumran.

Apocalyptic outlook

The idea of the End Days and apocalypticism seems to have first developed in the Books of Enoch and Daniel, in the late 3rd and 2nd centuries BC. For the Qumran-Essenes the apocalypse was a constant imperative and they expected its imminent arrival. A similar outlook is seen in Christianity and for both there was a much stronger expectation than in the rest of the surrounding religious communities.

The Koran picks up this theme with a belief in Day of Judgment when the life of every human being will be assessed by Allah to decide whether they go to heaven or hell.[1] There is also Sura 3, 'The Family of Imrân', 30:

> On the day when every soul will find itself confronted with all that it hath done of good and all that it hath done of evil (every soul) will long that there might be a mighty space of distance between it and that (evil). Allah biddith you beware of Him. And Allah is full of pity for (His) bondmen.

Reverence for Light

Light was an over-arching motif for the Qumran community, which I have suggested is a reflection of the same preoccupation apparent at Akhetaton. It is a theme powerfully picked up in Christianity and very evident in the Koran (Sura 24, 'Light', 35, 36):

> Allah is the Light of the heavens and the earth. The likeness of His light is a niche wherein is a lamp. The lamp is in a glass. The glass is as it were a shining star. (This lamp is) kindled from a blessed tree, an olive neither of the East nor of the West, whose oil would almost glow forth (of itself) though no fire

touched it. Light upon Light, Allah guideth unto His light whom he will. And Allah speaketh to mankind in allegories, for Allah is knower of all things. (This lamp is found) in houses which Allah hath allowed to be exalted and that His name shall be remembered therein. Therein do offer praise to him at morn and evening.

And a similar reference is found in Sura 39, 'The Troops', 69: 'And the earth shineth with the light of her Lord.'

Both these extracts express reverence for light, and Sura 24 is particularly interesting, with its explanation, as we are told throughout the Koran, that Allah speaks in allegories. The theme of reverence for light, from the time of Akhenaton through to the time of the *Yahad* at Qumran, is picked up in the Koran, and the description of the use of a lamp appears to be an allegorical description of its use in a synagogal context. After the destruction of the Second Temple in Jerusalem prayers were conducted in houses or buildings that were sanctified, and the main symbols of the rituals were the ark, where Torah scrolls were kept, and an oil lamp that was placed in front of the ark and was continually lit. Just as described in the Koran and as is still the custom in synagogues of today, prayers are said morning (*shacharit* – *shachar* means morning light in Hebrew) and evening (*ma'ariv*), and a perpetual lamp (*ne'er tamid*) lit with pure olive oil is positioned above the ark. The custom of prayers in the morning and evening may also be traced back to the ritual practiced at Qumran and other Essene centres.

Predestination

This is probably one of the strongest indications of an Essenic awareness in the Koran, as predestination was not the accepted understanding within conventional Judaism, but was a belief of Pharaoh Akhenaton's religion. For Muslims, Allah has knowledge of all that will happen, but that does not prevent humans from making individual free choices.

Jesus as an Essene

The Koran supports the contention that Jesus was 'out of circulation' for a long period of his life, commenced his ministry at the age of 30 and preached for a period for three years. This description, also set out in the New Testament, seems to indicate that Jesus was a member of the Qumran community, as a member could not become fully qualified as a 'master' within the movement before the age of 30.

Resurrection

The Koran (Sura 39, 'The Troops', 15, and Sura 75, 'The Rising of the Dead', 6) emphasizes the inevitability of resurrection, with a Day of Judgment separating the good from the evil:

> Then worship what you will beside Him, Say: The losers will be those who lose themselves and their housefolk on the Day of Resurrection. Ah, that will be the manifest loss.

> He asketh: When will be this Day of Resurrection?

Qumran-Essenes mentioned in Holy Writings

Whilst it is generally stated in the literature that the Qumran-Essenes are not mentioned in the New Testament, they are actually referred to many times in the New Testament under other names which they called themselves by – the *Yahad*, sons of light, scribes, eunuchs (in the sense of being celibate), the meek, Herodians and healers. A similar kind of procedure seems to have occurred in the Koran.

In Sura 2, 'The Cow', in the Koran we read:

> Jewish rabbis had often told their neighbours that a Prophet was about to come . . . So plainly did they describe the coming Prophet that pilgrims from Yathrib recognized the Prophet, when he addressed them in Mecca, as the same whom the Jewish doctors had described to them.

The term 'Jewish doctors' is unusual and has an inference of a Jewish group who were healers. This is the same terminology used by Roman and Greek historians to describe one aspect of the Essenes' abilities, as 'healers'.

Another term for a distinctive group, which appears several times in the Koran, is 'Sabeans'. There is no scholarly consensus as to who they were, but the Prophet Muhammad was obviously familiar with them. It has been suggested that they were the predecessors of the Mandeans, who are still extant in parts of Iraq and in the Iranian province of Huzistan. Today's Muslims refer to these people as 'Sabbas', and they have a distinguishing characteristic of being strongly Gnostic and espousing astrological ideas. These two characteristics are consistent with those of the Qumran-Essenes. The term 'Sabean' most likely means their later adherents.

The fact that the Koran was familiar with a group that can only have been followers of the original Jewish-style Qumran-Essene doctrines indicates their presence in Arabia, specifically at Yathrib. It is also possible that a group of non-Arabs that Muhammad came into contact with were what are sometimes referred to as Judaeo-Christians (I prefer to call them Yahad-Christians). These might have been descendants of some of the first followers of John the Baptist and Jesus who originated from Qumran. This might also help to explain why some scholars associate the Sabeans with the Mandeans (followers of formative Christianity rooted in John the Baptist).[2]

Allusions to Akhenaton

As discussed above, any naming of someone in the Koran or Hadith who could be identified as Akhenaton would be quite a surprise, with over 2,000 years separating him and the early days of Islam, but there are good indications that this is exactly the case as there are clear allusions to him.

In a previous book I postulated that Akhenaton and Jacob's form of monotheism went underground after the destruction of Akhetaton and came down to Moses through followers who probably originated at the pharaoh's court. It is worth quoting verbatim what I concluded more than ten years ago:

> We know Moses was brought up in the Court of the reigning Pharaoh, generally assumed to be Ramses II. His strong personality and outspoken manner won him few friends at Court and his enemies intrigued behind his back to get rid

of him. His name itself is perhaps a clue to his radicalism. There is linkage to the Tutmoses' family of pharaohs, and we know that this family almost certainly inter-married with, and was familiar with, the Amenhotep family philosophies that culminated in the thinking of Akhenaton.

We also know that after the death of Akhenaton, although there was a return to polytheism there was, nevertheless, a key change in the style of worship and approach to the reinstated old gods. Knowledge of the so-called 'heretic Pharaoh' of whom Moses, as a Royal Prince, might have been a direct descendant, would have been available to him – particularly as there is evidence from Manetho (a high priest of Heliopolis during the 3rd century BC) that Moses received much of his early education from priests at Heliopolis. If Moses was sympathetic to these ideas he would have been viewed as a radical at Court and made unwelcome.

This historical tradition fits in well with my theory that Moses learned, quite early on in his life, a philosophy of religion which flourished at Heliopolis during the time of religious revolution in Egypt, and which remained hidden there for centuries after.[3]

Sura 40, 'The Believer', 28, seems to confirm this hypothesis when it talks about a believer amongst the pharaoh's family:

> And a believer man of Pharaoh's family, who hid his faith, said: Would ye kill a man because he saith: my lord is Allah, and hath brought you clear proof from your Lord?

The sura is a recital of events around the time of Moses, so any previous 'believer' at the pharaoh's court must have been a monotheist in the line of Egyptian royalty. There is only one person who that could possibly be, and that is Pharaoh Akhenaton!

The question is, how could Muhammad have known about these hidden events? The answer for Muslims is simple. The information was given to him by divine revelation, and no one can deny that explanation. That the information might have been available at the time and place in history of Muhammad is nevertheless worth investigating. The suggestion that such oral traditions were available amongst groups in

Arabia is certainly indicated by parallels in the Koran, some of which came only from non-mainstream biblical writings. For example, Suras 2 and 7 talk about a mountain raised above the head of the people and it is clearly Mount Sinai that is being referred to. This idea is quite unlike anything that appears in the Hebrew Bible and one wonders where it can have derived from.

> And when We shook the Mount above them as it were a covering, and they supposed that it was going to fall upon them (and We said): Hold fast that which We have given you, and remember that which is therein, that ye may ward off (evil).
> *(Sura 7, 'The Heights', 171)*

There is a multiple sense in this episode: of the mountain from where Allah (God) gave the people the Ten Commandments being a protective cover for them; but that there was also a threat over their heads that it could drop and crush them if they disobeyed its entreaties. Michael Lodahl comments that there is nothing about this event in the Hebrew Bible, but there is a similar story in the Rabbinic tractates.[4] This demonstrates a Koranic awareness of rather obscure Talmudic knowledge which in turn implies a presence of especially learned Jewish people.

Chapter 9

Anomalous Artefacts in and around Israel

Symbols of the Aton and imagery at Amarna continue to be found across Israel and are a headache for religious historians.

Kuntillet Ajrud

An inscription found on a storage jar at Kuntillet Ajrud, in the Negev area, dated to the 8th century BC or somewhat earlier, has been interpreted as depicting God with His consort. Other inscriptions are read as: 'I bless you by Yahwe . . . and by His Asherah'. The idea of God having a consort is, of course, complete anathema in Judaism.

The scene on the Kuntillet Ajrud storage jar shows a small snake's head (Egyptian corn viper) in the top left-hand corner, near the nostrils of a male figure. In Egyptian legend this image is symbolic of life being breathed into an individual. In my reading of the scene the Bes-like figure (Egyptian image of entertainment) and the two other figures are representations of Akhenaton and his wife Nefertiti. They wear typical crowns of Egypt and are being entertained by a court musician. An identical small snake appears in a number of wall reliefs at Amarna where it is in exactly the same relative position to Akhenaton's nose as on the Negev inscription.

The Bes image was a particular favourite of Nefertiti. Nefertiti was seen as Akhenaton's personal co-ruler, and the inscription is better read as 'You and your consort are blessed by Yahwe'. (There is also an inscription at Khirbet-el-Kom, near Hebron, 'Blessed be Ariyahu and His Asherah, to Yahwe'.)

An Astarte/Asherah figuration does seem to surface in religious texts as being allied to God, prior to the 8th century BC, but in a different context to that seen at Kuntillet Ajrud. My tentative explanation for the persistence of this figure is that Astarte was a favourite god of Akhenaton's father, Amenhotep III, and the allegiance may have been mistakenly associated in defective transmitted memory with Akhenaton himself. Many Egyptologists believe, as I do, that father and son were co-rulers, sitting on the same throne for a period of years, so the confusion is not surprising.

Astarte/Asherah was also a powerful goddess in the ancient Middle East, as the promoter of fertility and beauty, and became firmly entrenched in most primitive cultures of the region. The influence of superstition ran deep and would have been difficult to eradicate in a general population where magic and folklore always remained strong.

Sun Discs, Ankh Signs, and Scarab Beetles

King Hezekiah of Israel, c720 BC, was particularly strong on mono-theism and practised a policy of purging the country of paganism, and yet he adopted an Egyptian winged sun disc and a beetle as his royal insignia. Related examples have been found on pottery jar handles and other artefacts across Israel.

More examples are seen from the rule of King Jehu in the 9th century BC and King Josiah (c625 BC). Again they are a headache for theologians who cannot explain the reason for their presence. A number of the seals show a two-winged scarab, and one shows a central sun disc with rays shooting out from above and below and an ankh sign of life on either side.[1] All three designs are Egyptian in origin and are especially associated with the Amarna period – the sun disc and ankh sign were the key elements of the Aton cartouche representing Akhenaton's name for God, and Pharaoh Akhenaton is often seen holding two ankh symbols. The form of the sun disc was dominant during Akhenaton's rule, and the scarab never more to the fore in Egypt's history. Clearly both Jehu and Josiah had an awareness of the symbology of Akhenaton's time and had an affinity with its deeper significance.

Within the limited space available, the evidence here presented is only the capstone on a huge pyramid of supporting information. Many other Qumran texts such as 4Q521 (Messianic Apocalypse), 11Q13 (Heavenly Prince Melchizedek), 4Q285 (Pierced Messiah), 4Q246 (Son of God), Songs of the Sabbath Sacrifice, Thanksgiving Hymns, etc., etc. can readily be accommodated within an Amarna setting. A detailed discussion is included in my previous books and these controversial texts will be looked at again in later chapters. Anyone involved in religious, archaeological or historical research who reassesses their own work in the light of an Egyptian perspective will no doubt come up with even more corroboratory material.

Identification of the Amarna period as the key to the origins of monotheism through an interaction between the patriarchs Jacob and Joseph and Pharaoh Akhenaton and his wife Nefertiti offers comprehensive answers to many of the problematic texts in the Dead Sea Scrolls and identification of many of the key personalities mentioned in the texts. It also clarifies many unexplained passages in the Old Testament, the Apocrypha, rabbinic writings and the New Testament. In addition the many apparently anomalous artefacts discovered across Israel and in areas traversed by the ancient Hebrews can now be seen as manifestations of this original heritage.

One final bonus is that the almost certain identification of pre-exodus patriarchs underlines the essential validity of the relevant passages in the Bible.

When confronted with the outline thesis, that the religion and nature of Amarna had a huge impact on the Dead Sea Scrolls and the Bible, many academic scholars simply shy away in bemusement. Those who do engage in a discussion, usually go on a 'fishing trip', trying to elicit information on areas they are familiar with in the hope of tripping me up! Others, who take the time to study the evidence in depth, are invariably convinced that the basic findings are correct. Typical of the type of sceptical response comes from someone I call 'Dr Decline':

> The theory that the treasures mentioned in the Copper Scroll could be Akhenaton's treasures and that they are somewhere in Amarna, Egypt, is absolutely ludicrous. There's no way that they could possibly be that, because the Copper Scroll is a thousand years after Akhenaton's time.

This comment comes from Dr Eric Cline, of George Washington University, and was made in a documentary by National Geographic called *Decoding the Dead Sea Scrolls*, first screened in 2008, in which we both appeared. Dr Cline was responding to the presenter in relation to my contribution to the programme. A more considered response might have been along the lines: 'On the face of it, the theory seems far fetched, but until I have had a chance to study the details, read Feather's work on the subject and study the evidence at Amarna, I am in no position to comment.'

So alarmed are many academics at the proliferation of what they call distorted information that a conference was convened in April 2009 at Duke University, on 'Archaeology and Media, Archaeology and Politics', attended by a sizeable contingent of mainly American scholars and academics.[2] People like Simcha Jacobovici (the 'Naked Archaeologist'), Vendyl Jones, and Jim Barfield were pilloried for their views.[3] As far as I am aware, my name did not get bracketed with these people.

Dr Cline attended this conference and presented himself as being in the forefront of defending the truth, in the face of inaccurate information and particularly TV documentaries that distort archaeology and history and harm the image of academic professionals. Despite a number of emails and letters sent to him concerning his comments in *Decoding the Dead Sea Scrolls*, he has so far not responded to me.

Professors are Dangerous

Like no other professional people academics are in a position to dominate and influence the thinking of those they impact upon, including the younger members of their colleges, who will later emerge as the teachers and opinion-formers of tomorrow. Their views, particularly in non-science subjects like history (described by Robert Birley, 1903–82, Headmaster of Charterhouse and Eton, as 'the most dangerous subject in the curriculum'), philosophy, art, psychoanalysis, economics or politics are especially dangerous. They are also likely to be more easily sustained in these subject areas where scientific analysis cannot easily be applied as a test of their validity.

By the time professors attain that lofty accolade, they are mature adults. Their minds, once flexible in ideas, tend to have become increasingly solidified by conclusions drawn on their early assessment of the available data, and they are already preaching their conclusions to an army of students. As time passes, repetition of these conclusions fixates them on the correctness of their analyses and their own positions, and they start to repeat their lectures, almost verbatim, year after year. From time to time, some of the more progressive and diligent exponents might modify their views in the light of latest research and findings, but few are prepared to change the basic patterns of their mind-sets. They have been trotting out the same material now, sometimes for decades. Why should they change their tune? Why embarrass themselves in front of their students or peers?

Other academics and professors in related fields are the only real potential threat to their reputation, but these they can avoid by not entering current debate, avoiding close scrutiny at peer conferences, or simply arguing their corner with self-righteousness.

The only time they come up against serious questioning of their views is in response to published material, in open conferences or in web peer groups. In every field there are those who try and keep up with events, but even then there are numerous examples where they find themselves in diametric opposition to fellow professors, sometimes even ridiculed and isolated. The end result is often that they are not invited to consensus-loving meetings or simply withdraw from the fray. There is little sanction against them from their own academic institutions – who also have a vested interest in preserving their employee's reputation – and more often than not do not even know about the criticism that a professor may be encountering.

As a supreme authority in his or her own environment, the professor is always able to retreat into the trenches of the lecture theatre, where they are the star. There they can continue disseminating their personal, sometimes flawed views to a captive audience of awed students, who in turn go out to the world to repeat the same biased analysis.

If you ask an academic or scholar who does not have a vested interest in a preconceived idea about a particular aspect of his or her discipline, you will generally get an objective answer. If you ask an opinion on a particular aspect of my work from such an expert, you will invariably receive a positive answer. But scholars and academics with a vested interest in a particular subject under discussion rarely agree with my proposals. Whereas scholars and academics with no vested interest in a particular subject under discussion invariably do agree with my proposals.

The next chapter discusses the theories and reprehensible behaviour of a high-profile American professor.

Chapter 10

The Ruined Fortress

The most destructive, obsessive and intractable of all the challengers to the validity of Qumran's religious credentials is Professor Norman Golb, of Chicago University. He started his campaign in the late 1970s, finally enunciating it to the American Philosophical Society in 1980,[1] and then intensifying it with articles and a book in 1995,[2] with claims that Qumran was not a religious centre but a military fortress, so we will look at his claims in some detail. The integrity of his views is somewhat undermined by the content of his doctoral dissertation at the University of Chicago where his conclusions conformed to the Essenic theory of Roland de Vaux.

One of his latest campaigns has been to dog the organizers of an exhibition that has been touring the United States displaying examples of Dead Sea Scrolls. The series began with an exhibition in Charlotte, NC, in spring 2006, and moved subsequently to Seattle, Kansas City, San Diego, New York and Toronto by summer 2009. At each venue he has written to the press and organizers and any other media that would publish his views, typically condemning the exhibitions in his words as 'a misleading and one-sided presentation of the Scrolls – in defiance of ordinary museum standards of scientific probity and fair play'. This quote comes from a long diatribe aimed at the organizers of the display at the San Diego National History Museum in 2007.[3]

Nit-picking his way through the Exhibition Catalogue, he refers to Khirbet Qumran as 'the desert fortress site claimed by various [unnamed] authors to have been eventually inhabited by a Jewish sect whose members supposedly wrote, copied and/or possessed Dead Sea Scrolls there'. Many of the arguments against his theory are similar to those set out in the following chapter, which rebuts Magen and Peleg's claim that Qumran was a pottery factory. Professor Golb cites their evidence as a direct confirmation of his fortress theory, whereas they never say that Qumran was a fortress, but at most a forward military surveying outpost. He obliquely refers to Magen and Peleg when he uses the phrase 'In 2004 a major team of archaeologists . . .', but refrains from naming them, in all probability because he knows they do not support his fortress theory. In the same way as it would be militarily naïve to position an early warning installation at the base of an overhanging cliff, when a far better location would have been at the top of the cliff, the siting of a fortress under a high cliff is unheard of. People will throw things down on your head!

Whilst Professor Golb is keen to point out the lack of any fragments of scrolls being found within the Qumran site, he avoids mentioning that the nearest main storage cave, Cave 4, where some 15,000 fragments were found, is no more than a 50m walk from the buildings at Qumran. Nor does he accept that signs of scribal activity, including some four inkwells and a long table-like structure, ideally suited to the laying out of long scrolls, were discovered within the Qumran buildings. Apart from other factors undermining his skepticism over what is referred to as the 'scriptorium' by most scholars, conclusive evidence tying the scrolls to the buildings is emerging from analysis of the ink in the inkwells and inks on the written scrolls.

Professor Golb, like Yizhar Hirschfeld,[4] believes that Qumran was not a religious site, and that soldiers were buried in the Qumran cemeteries. He never mentions that, throughout the series of excavations that have taken place over a period of more than 50 years from 1951 onwards, no weapons datable to the period of Essenic occupation have ever been found at or near the site, until the Roman occupation after 68 AD. Nor has any evidence of soldiers or weaponry been found in the burials in the cemetery. No examples of left-side injuries to skeletons, which would be expected for soldiers involved in fighting, have been seen. Nor have these characteristics been found in other cemeteries related to fortresses built in the Second Temple period.

Continuing his rampage through the catalogue, Golb categorically maintains that examples of Dead Sea Scroll material found at Masada were brought by fleeing refugees from Jerusalem. This, he claims, proves that the Scrolls originated in Jerusalem. There is nothing but circumstantial evidence to justify this claim, and it is much more likely that the material was taken to Masada by members of the Qumran community fleeing the onslaught of the Romans – the theory held by most scholars, including the excavator of Masada, Yigael Yadin.[5]

'However, what no scholar has ever been able to prove, for lack of evidence, is that the Yahad group lived at Kh. Qumran', is yet another inaccurate and loaded statement in the catalogue criticism. Few scholars actually claim that members of the *Yahad* lived at Qumran, but that they lived in nearby caves and tents.[6] The sectarian texts known as the Community Rule (Manual of Discipline) describe in detail the coming together of members to partake of a group meal every day, with strict rules of behaviour at the meal. The contemporary historians Josephus, Pliny the Elder and Philo, who indicate the location of the community settlement as being at Qumran, also describe elements of this communal meal which confirm many of the protocols described in the Dead Sea Scrolls. The idea that the group members came together to pray at the crack of dawn, conduct ritual bathing and eat together every day, but did not live very close by, is quite untenable.

When it comes to Golb's consideration of the Copper Scroll, found in Cave 3 in 1952, he attempts to use its contents to prove that the treasures described in it originated from the Second Temple in Jerusalem and therefore the scroll, like all the others, must have come from Jerusalem. Whilst he is correct in stating that most scholars believe that the treasure so described came from the Second Temple, many do not, and the fact is not one single item mentioned in the Copper Scroll has ever been found in Israel. My own study of this 'mysterious scroll' demonstrates a convincing case for the treasures to be located elsewhere than in Israel, and I have located some of them![7]

Jerusalem, O Jerusalem

A central theme of Golb's attack is that it is 'the view of a growing number of scholars, based on the present totality of actual evidence, that the Scrolls are of Jerusalem origin and have nothing to do with a claimed sect living at Kh. Qumran'. However, exactly the opposite is the case. Father Roland de Vaux's basic original theory has now been bolstered by a whole new raft of solid evidence. The internal and external evidence has mounted over the years, a few of the key facts being:

- the finding of an inscribed *ostracon* mentioning the *Yahad* and the description of a potential member offering to donate his worldly goods to the community;
- a sundial whose design is consistent with its use as a solar calendar, as described in their texts;
- neutron activation studies that confirm the scroll jars found in the nearby caves were made within the site of Qumran;
- identification of a large number of religious *mikva'ot* used for ritual washing;
- the clear connection between the scrolls and the way of life of the Qumranites;
- unique burial practices, indicating a unique society;
- recent studies showing that samples of ink from some of the scrolls contained high levels of bromine, consistent with the use of water from the Dead Sea; this evidence further undermines claims that none of the Scrolls were written at Qumran.[8]

Golb's 'growing number of scholars' represents about 1% of the corpus of Dead Sea Scrolls researchers and commentators, and even the 1% do not agree with each other's basic theories. To extrapolate from a subsidiary conclusion, that if the scrolls didn't come from Qumran, they must have come from Jerusalem, is to accept that all 15 or so differing theories on what was going on at Qumran are correct, and that is logical nonsense.

That the scrolls represent a cross-section of what must have been going on in greater Judaea and Jerusalem and do not represent a contradictory religious philosophy is not sustained by the contents of the scrolls – especially the sectarian versions. A cursory look at the different religious and belief structures exhibited within the scrolls shows that the stance of sectarian scrolls differs from the rest of the wider Jewish population in some one-third of the scrolls – confirming the separatist nature of the group. Are we really to believe the supposed fleeing refugees from Jerusalem comprised a group who brought with them distinctively non-conformist texts and other groups with normative biblical texts and they all hid their scrolls in the dead of night, in a series of 11 caves, mixing up the contents? It sounds like something out of a Marx Brothers film!

Some of the Scrolls found in the Qumran caves may well have come from Jerusalem, but most were copied, written or curated at the religious centre of Qumran. Consider the logic of Golb's theory, and that of Magen and Peleg, who take the same view in relation to the scrolls' origins in Jerusalem. The rebuttal which follows in the next chapter also applies to the other challenger theories, which require the scrolls mainly to have come from a source in Jerusalem.

Consider again the claim that refugees fleeing from an impending attack by the Romans brought scrolls with them and hid these scrolls in caves near Qumran. About 900 scrolls were recovered from the caves between 1947 and 1956, so assuming each refugee carried about ten scrolls, there would have been about 90 of them. Quite reasonably, not wanting to deposit precious material in the caves without some form of protection, they went to the buildings at Qumran and 'lo and behold' found several dozen large jars in good condition which were suitable for storing some of the larger scrolls. Not only that, some kind person gifted them stoppers and bitumen to seal the jars, and fine linen cloth with embroidery to help wrap them. Then, according to Magen and Peleg, and Professor Golb, who holds to a similar scenario, in the dead of night they scrambled around in the cliffs behind Qumran and hid their scrolls in one of 11 caves between 50m and 3km from Qumran. All this in a climate of urgency in anticipation of an imminent attack by the Roman army. No doubt they carried oil lamps and night-vision goggles!

One great problem with all this is that, if there was no religious community at Qumran, some of the 11 caves they are supposed to have hidden scrolls in would not have existed at the time of these new arrivals. The reason is that there is evidence that some of the caves were carved out for the very purpose of storing pottery scroll jars, and some of the pottery can be clearly related to a scribe who wrote some of the scrolls.

Although there are at least 30 natural caves in the vicinity of Qumran, which would have been suitable for hiding scrolls material in, our refugees decided to spend several weeks, perhaps months, cutting seven new caves into the marl terracing, notably Caves 4Qa–b, 5Q, 7Q, 8Q, 9Q, 10Q. And in two of these 'new' caves, 4a and 4b, they decided to install shelving to hold the scrolls!

Of course the caves did exist, and they were man-made; they were cut by members of the *Yahad*, Cave 4 being within a few minutes' walking distance of their settlement and the one they accessed most frequently. No wonder the organizers of the exhibitions that have toured America, and have been mounted elsewhere around the world, ignore, or give only a brief mention to, viewpoints propounded by a tiny minority of scholars. To do otherwise would be to confuse the lay public and distort the general consensus view.

Interviewed by the *National Post* of Canada, Dr Risa Levitt Kohn, curator of the Dead Sea Scrolls exhibition staged at the Royal Ontario Museum, Toronto, told Adrian Humphreys that she, and others like Dr Jodi Magness, Dr Robert Cargill and Dr David Noel Freedman, had been subjected to harassment that should be the subject of criminal sanction:

> Our hard work, our professional competence and, in my case, my integrity, intelligence and the exhibitions over which I have spent years of my life have been fodder for attacks. Our universities have been contacted, the media has received letters and published articles that defame us, the museums where I have been curator have been subjected to a stream of angry anonymous letters, and more.[9]

However, matters got a great deal more serious for the obsessional professor when his son, Raphael Haim Golb, was arrested for allegedly 'creating multiple aliases to engage in a campaign of impersonation and harassment relating to the Dead Sea Scrolls and scholars of opposing viewpoints'. The 50-year-old New York real-estate lawyer was accused of identity theft, criminal impersonation and aggravated harassment, and arrested on 5 March 2009, on the instruction of Manhattan District Attorney Robert M. Morgenthau. Using computers at New York University, the younger Golb is alleged to have created dozens of internet aliases to hide his own identity during the period July to December 2008.[10] One of the people he allegedly impersonated was respected New York Professor Lawrence Schiffman, and by using an email account 'larry.schiffman@gmail.com' he pretended to be Dr Schiffman and purported to admit to plagiarism, whilst in other emails he had the temerity of accusing Professor Schiffman of plagiarism.

Defending his son's arrest in the Israeli newspaper *Haaretz*, Professor Golb said: 'Raphael, my son, is very devoted to my research. He realized years ago that there was an effort to close the door on my opinions. And so he started debating bloggers who were against me, using aliases. That's the custom these days with blogs, as I understand it.'[11]

This statement was tantamount to admitting the alleged charges against his son, and one has to wonder if the father himself had not coached his son in some of his attacks on scholars his son had never met. In the same *Haaretz* article Magen Broshi is said to have spoken of Norman Golb's theory as 'foolishness and mean-spirited', and of the Professor himself as a 'mediocre scholar who went into an area not his own'.

Three of the identities Raphael Golb is alleged to have hidden behind, as well as the one he used to represent Professor Lawrence Schiffman, were Charles Gadda, Paul Kessler, Jeffrey B. Gibson and Steve Frankel. These 'entities' have been active on numerous blog sites, all peddling a pro-Norman Golb line. In fact the mastermind behind the aliases marshalled an army of officers and soldiers and sent them out to do battle with Professor Golb's enemies on scholarly websites, blogs, chat rooms, newspapers and magazines. Wikipedia articles on Qumran and the Dead Sea Scrolls were also targeted for adulteration until the administrators clamped down on the infiltrators and started deleting their inputs. A concerted attack focused on the museums exhibiting the Dead Sea Scrolls, including letters and emails to the organizers, local newspapers, and anyone who would listen.

One scholar who has made it his business to try and unearth the person allegedly behind the many masks is Dr Robert R. Cargill of UCLA. He has tracked down about 80 different names fronting the hidden source. A tactic he noted in the campaign was the coordination of an attack, with aliases cross-referencing each other and supporting each other's arguments by serializing their comments on targeted sites. Various of the offending missives are included in Appendix B, courtesy of Dr. Robert R. Cargill.[12] It is worth looking at these to see the tone of the provocative material, especially as one mentions my name.

The latest chapter in this sorry saga was played out in a Manhattan courtroom when proceedings against Raphael Golb began on 13 September 2010. Golb went on trial facing criminal charges of online impersonation, identity theft and harassment. He pleaded not guilty, though his lawyers conceded plagiarism had occurred, but argued that the writings amounted to typical biosphere banter, which they claimed is not a crime, and were made in the spirit of satire. The prosecution lawyers maintained Raphael Golb configured an elaborate camouflaged pastiche in order to support his father's stance on the origins and purpose of the site of Qumran and the writings of the occupants. Some of the blogs posted by Raphael Golb accused Professor Lawrence Schiffman of stealing from Norman Golb's work! Assistant District Attorney John Brandler called the whisper campaign 'a disturbing pattern of conduct', involving 70 phony email accounts and hundreds, if not thousands of hours of endeavour. Schiffman said he was forced to devote weeks of time responding to inquiries from colleagues, students and New York University officials to defend his good name.

The jury found Golb guilty on 30 counts of identity theft, forgery, criminal impersonation and aggravated harassment. On 18 November 2010 Golb was sentenced to six months in prison and five years' probation. At the time of writing he was free on bail of $25,000 and his lawyers were reportedly planning an appeal.

The outcome of the case has inevitably tarnished the reputation of Professor Norman Golb, and is yet another episode in a series of distracting side issues which have wasted the time of serious scholarship into the more important issues of the Dead Sea Scrolls.

Chapter 11

How Potty Can You Get?

In 2007 Yitzhak Magen and Yuval Peleg, accredited archaeologists with the Israel Antiquities Authority, put their name to a preliminary report on their excavations at Qumran between 1993 and 2003, which threw the world of Dead Sea Scrolls scholarship into yet another turmoil. Having been working intermittently in the area for over ten years, it suddenly dawned on them that the entire site was 'a large pottery manufacturing center'.[1] In their study Magen and Peleg rightly complain about the lack of any final report being published on the work of Roland de Vaux and disagree with some of his preliminary findings, but agree with much of his excavation work. For example, they agree with de Vaux that pottery production first began on the site during the first half of the 1st century BC.

Whilst rejecting the idea that Qumran was a fortress, or farmstead, or anything other than a pottery in its later usage, Magen and Peleg assume that Qumran was initially a forward observation post for the Hasmoneans, with stables for cavalry. These buildings, they claim, were later converted into a ceramics manufacturing area. As mentioned above, throughout the series of excavations that have taken place over a period of more than 50 years, from 1951 onwards, no weapons have ever been found at or near the site, until the Roman occupation after 68 AD. Nor has any evidence of soldiers, horses or weaponry been found at the site or in the burials in the cemetery.

Excavations were conducted at Qumran under the auspices of the Staff Officer for Archaeology in Judaea and Samaria beginning in 1993, renewed between 1996 and 1999, between 2001 and 2002, and again in 2004. It was only at the end of their 2004 season of work, whilst digging in locations 71 and 58 at Qumran, that Magen and Peleg 'found a layer of clay used for the manufacture of pottery'.

It is a measure of the illogicality of their treatise that they talk about amounts of clay found at the bottom of these two pools as being used to make pottery. If the clay is *in situ*, it has not been used for anything! This alluvial clay would have built up over tens or perhaps scores of years, and then only during periods of intense flash floods. Magen and Peleg estimate the presence of about 3 tons of high-quality clay, which they assume could be used to make 'thousands of pottery vessels' (later they revise the total amount of clay found to 6–7 tons.) This, they say, means that material for producing pottery was not brought in from outside, and that the potters were in fact exporting clay products all over Judaea. It also implies that the occupants of Qumran had no need to import clay pots.

This is completely contradicted by recent research into the origins of the clay vessels at Qumran. Neutron activation analysis by Marta Balla has shown that only about one-third of the pottery analyzed, from a cross-section of pottery found at Qumran, actually originated in Qumran.[2] The rest have a chemical fingerprint showing the sources as Jericho, Hebron and Edom/Nabatea. Incidentally the research also demonstrates a clear connection between the pottery used at the settlement and that from clay vessels found in the Dead Sea Scrolls caves. Why would there be any need to import pottery when thousands of vessels were being manufactured at Qumran, as Magen and Peleg claim? A final nail in their argument comes from the work of Frederick Zeuner whose analyses showed that sedimentary clay washed into the pools at Qumran and that the Lisan marls found nearby would have been unsuitable for the manufacture of pottery.[3]

This conclusion is borne out by an ingenious tangential analysis by Eyal Regev.[4] He looks at the ideology of the occupants of Qumran as indicated by their rituals and their resistance to conventional behaviour as a measure of their social boundaries. Concentrating on the archaeology of the site, rather than the content of the sectarian texts, he analyses the burials, ritual baths, eating habits and pottery assemblage and concludes that: 'the inhabitants of Kh. Qumran subscribed to a sectarian ideology or bore social characteristics typical of a sect'. Among the strongest findings are that, of the vessels listed in Roland de Vaux's notes, an astonishing 84% are tableware – more than double the findings at any other contemporary site – and that many of the vessels were not locally manufactured. This leads to a conclusion that: 'The pottery production center theory therefore cannot be sustained.' The abundance of tableware is also said to be related to a 'complex hierarchical structure of ritual meals in which participants emphasized their social solidarity and the exclusion of outsiders. This pattern of behaviour is characteristic of elite groups of outsiders.'

In talking about the large amounts of water needed in pottery manufacture Magen and Peleg continually refer to rivers bounding the site – an indication of their mind-set in trying to demonstrate the availability of large volumes of water. These routes are wadis, which remain dry for almost the whole year. To support their theory they challenge the work of Ronny Reich, an expert in *mikva'ot*, who has indentified ten of the cisterns as pools used for ritual immersion.[5] There are some 16 pools within the Qumran complex and a number of the large, very deep ones are undoubtedly cisterns for water storage. To 'convert' many of Ronny Reich's ritual immersion pools, Magen and Peleg maintain that steps and dividing structures within the pools were there for structural purposes to strengthen the side walls. This makes little sense in constructional terms as the small dividing walls run parallel to the side walls. They also question the halachic (religious law) requirement for the construction of the immersion pools, citing Talmudic sources, which had not yet been written down at the time of the construction of the ritual baths. Nor do they seem to be aware that the *Yahad* at Qumran had their own version of Halacha, quite different from the normative Jewish practices.

The extreme scarcity of water in the region seems not to deter Magen and Peleg from their claims of massive floods of water being available and stored for use in pottery making. The real reason for the large water storage cisterns was almost certainly to sustain the community during the long periods of drought. Annual rainfall is normally 100–200mm per year!

Little mention is made by the pottery advocates of where the large amounts of combustible supplies for the clay firing kilns would have come from. Wood was a scarce commodity in the region and they fail to suggest a possible source of fuel.

Apart from all the other internal and external factors that confirm Qumran as a communal religious centre, the nature of burials and the cemeteries, adjacent to the site, are a defining characteristic. The arguments put forward by Magen and Peleg, that the burials in the cemeteries were not unique, and that 'this burial method was typical of the Second Temple period in general', are simply invalid. They cite other examples of field burials in dug graves, such as at Ain-El-Ghuweir, but fail to acknowledge that it is the 'form of the burials' that is quite unique, not the fact that there are other examples of dug graves. Most of the graves at Qumran are marked by a small pile of stones, with a dark marker stone invariably positioned in a north–south direction. The bodies were buried naked, placed in shallow trenches, with no adornments, and the heads carefully turned towards the south. Perhaps with one exception, all the bodies in the main cemetery were males. No other cemeteries in Israel exist with these kinds of defining characteristics. Descriptions by Pliny the Elder of a 'celibate community living near the Dead Sea close to Ein Gedi' also resonate with the finding that virtually all the skeletal remains found in the main cemetery at Qumran were male.

Despite quoting Joe Zias in support of some of their arguments, they fail to mention his profound views on the Qumran cemetery. He describes it as 'the defining characteristic of the site, which defines the nature of the Community'.[6] Other authorities, including F. Röhrhirsch and O. Röhrer-Ertl, who have made an extensive study of burials at Qumran, including examining many of the skeletons excavated from the cemetery, come to the same conclusion as Zias.[7]

In Magen and Peleg's imagined scenario, Qumran was at first inhabited by soldiers and then became an industrial pottery factory. The stables, according to their postulation, were converted to pools to facilitate pottery production, which commenced in the first half of the 1st century BC. Nevertheless, these quite different groups, they maintain, followed the same burial practices.

Having been editor of *Ceramic Industries Journal* for a number of years in the early 1980s and visited Staffordshire, home of the pottery industry in the UK, many times, I am familiar with the factors and geographical prerequisites needed for establishing a ceramics industry. The essential ingredients are a plentiful supply of fuel, clay deposits, and a reliable and abundant supply of water. That is exactly why the pottery industry was first established around Stoke, on the River Trent and near large coalfields. None of these ingredients is present at Qumran. There is certainly evidence of a few small kilns and small-scale ceramic materials production at Qumran, but to describe Qumran as a dedicated pottery factory, exporting its products all over Judaea, is simply unsustainable.

The Dead Sea Scrolls

When Magen and Peleg come to consider how the scrolls got into the caves and whether they had any connection to Qumran, we are told: 'Such a connection was assumed before excavations began', as if there was no prior evidence. Eleazar Sukenik,[8] who acquired the first three of the major scrolls from Cave 1 in 1948, was one of the first to make the connection, on the basis of the texts he was translating, the testimony of Josephus, Pliny and Philo, who collectively described a location for Qumran and its occupants in some detail, and on the letter by Timotheus.[9] As more archaeological and textual information has come to light over the years, the evidence has increased dramatically in support of the main conclusions of de Vaux. Magen and Peleg's claim that there is no evidence that members of the sect lived in caves on the fault scarp or in tents near the scarp is contradicted by the archaeological findings published by Hanan Eshel and Magen Broshi.[10]

According to the pottery factory theorists, 'the scrolls were hidden in the Qumran caves, since these were located on the route of the fleeing refugees', when the Romans were attacking the Jerusalem area, prior to destruction of the Second Temple in 70 AD. Evidence of occupation of the caves, reported by Eshel and Broshi, is now ascribed to these fleeing refugees by Magen and Peleg, based on their reading of a 1999 report by Eshel and Broshi. Magen and Peleg believe no one would stay in these caves for long, but that the refugees found 'scroll jars' at the site of Qumran and used some of them to store scrolls they had brought with them. They allegedly hid the scrolls in a random manner, at distances of anything up to 3km from the main site and worked at night! I do not recommend anyone to try and climb to Cave 1 at night without climbing gear and lights.

This, of course, is all conjecture, and Magen and Peleg fail to understand the 1999 report or take account of additional work carried out by Eshel and Broshi in 2000 which reconfirmed their earlier findings, that the caves were occupied for lengthy periods over a considerable amount of time. En passant Magen and Peleg also dispute the work of Hirschfeld, who found an Essene dwelling at nearby Ein Gedi dated from the second half of the 1st century to the early 2nd century AD.[11]

Magen and Peleg's assumptive theory also fails to explain how the scrolls were deposited in various caves in related subject groups, with a mother lode in Cave 4, within 50m of the Qumran buildings, and why the refugees decided to seal some of the jars with bitumen and wrap some of them in cloth with complex woven patterns, and build a set of shelves in one of the caves to store them in an orderly fashion.

Magen and Peleg's treatment pointedly ignores all the other external evidence from independent contemporary historians, who describe the Qumran community and its locations in great detail, details which tie up with the content of the sectarian texts found in the Qumran caves. They also ignore other archeological finds from Qumran that do not suit their case – the sundial evidencing the anomalous solar calendar which some of the Dead Sea Scrolls describe in detail; the *ostracon* describing a deed of gift to the Community; etc.

The Magen and Peleg theory is yet another crackpot claim that needs to be knocked on the head and buried in some quiet corner of Qumran.

Chapter 12

Sadducean Mysticism

No doubt more peculiar theories will emerge out of the woodwork, but at the time of writing the latest challenge to the standard model has come from a Professor of Jewish Mysticism at Hebrew University, Jerusalem, Rachel Elior. She has come out with the incredible statement, followed up in a book, that the Essenes never existed and that the scrolls were authored by the Sadducees in Jerusalem and carried to Qumran in advance of the Roman threat to the Second Temple.[1] There are certainly some Sadducean influences in the scrolls, but there are also many other influences. Even Lawrence Schiffman, who advocated this idea long ago, has modified his views in the light of later scholarship and talks about the Qumranites originally being Sadducees, but that they broke away and therefore could no longer be classified as such by the time they reached Qumran.[2] This claim is severely challenged by Dwight D. Swanson, amongst others, who comments that in identifying the sectarian origins with what becomes the party known, via Josephus and the New Testament, as the priestly opponents of the Pharisees, 'The problem is that, in both sources, the Sadducees post-date the supposed withdrawal of the sectaries, and are part of the Temple establishment. How do documents of the hyper-establishment Sadducees end up in the library of the hyper-anti-establishment Zadokites?'[3]

Another big problem, amongst others, for those claiming the Qumranites were Sadducees, is the fact that the scrolls quite clearly and repeatedly describe the community's belief in divine predestination, whereas the Sadducees denied this possibility. This attribute is confirmed by the writings of Josephus, who also confirms the Sadducees denied any interference of God in human affairs (*Antiquities*, xiii). Professor Schiffman's claims are convincingly refuted by a number of scholars, including Moshe David Herr, Hebrew University Jerusalem.[4]

Impure Semantics

Professor Elior studies mysticism, and I am inclined to comment she should stick to what she knows! The idea that the scrolls were brought to Qumran just before the Temple was threatened and then destroyed is quite unsustainable. She fails to take account of Josephus, Philo, Pliny and the archaeological connections between the scrolls and Qumran and its date of occupation. The cemetery is one of the defining proofs, as mentioned earlier, and she completely ignores its significance. Whilst quoting extensively from the work of Joseph Zias, she ignores his statements that confirm Qumran as a religious centre where the scrolls were authored, copied or stored. In an attempted defence of her case, Elior refers to 'non-historical legendary Essenes of the first century AD', and there being no reason to dismiss the priestly concerns of the scrolls prior to that date. Her arguments are impure semantics, and no one who maintains the existence of the scrolls community, otherwise referred to as the Essenes, suggests that they did not have an earlier ancestry.

Elior claims that descriptions of Essenes by Philo, Pliny, Josephus and others were all made up and, in the case of Josephus, designed to cater to Roman admiration of asceticism and a Spartan way of life! It is rather like saying we should not call the religious Temple officials 'priests', because they did not speak English and called themselves Cohanim, Zedekim, etc., so 'priests' never existed. All three of the main contemporary historians who refer to the Essenes are obviously talking about the same group, as their descriptions overlap and are complementary. The fact that the group never referred to themselves as 'Essenes' does not alter the validity of the descriptions.

Unhappily, Professor Elior is way off beam, and her thesis has been rejected by virtually all senior Dead Sea Scrolls/Qumran scholars. Hanan Eshel commented that Elior has never published anything on the scrolls in a scholarly journal and ignores 60 years of research on the subject. Dr Adolfo Roitman, curator of the Shrine of the Book in the Israel Museum, Jerusalem, where a number of the scrolls are kept, says that the fact that the Essenes are not mentioned in the scrolls or elsewhere 'is irrelevant': 'No one should expect the Dead Sea Scrolls to mention the Essenes, a Greek word. The Scrolls composed at Qumran are in Hebrew and Aramaic: the Qumranites never composed in Greek.' (They did, of course, include Greek terms in some of their scrolls – for example, in the Copper Scroll – and Cave 7 contains a number of scroll fragments in Greek). Professor James Charlesworth has little doubt that Josephus was describing a real religious sect when he referred to the Essenes, and that some of sect members were located at Qumran, and that they were not Sadducean.

To give Professor Elior some credit, she has bravely responded to her critics, in various media. One of her contentions in these responses is the assertion that there is no connection between the caves and the settlement occupants at Qumran. Of course she is quite wrong. Here is a brief listing of some of the connections:

1 Josephus, Pliny and Philo describe a community with behavioural and belief systems that are reflected in the Dead Sea Scrolls. The descriptions of these three historians cannot be about anything but the *Yahad* community at Qumran and their colleagues scattered across Judaea, even if they use their own term to describe these communities.

2 Pliny the Elder describes a location by the Dead Sea where 'the Essenes' lived, near Ein Gedi, which is a few kilometres from Qumran.

3 Pliny refers to the community as leading an ascetic lifestyle – refraining from sex – and Josephus gives similar information on the celibacy of 'the Essenes'. These descriptions conform to the lack of any legislation on marriage and procreation in the Dead Sea Scroll Community Rule (compared to the Rule of the Community, Damascus Documents, War Scroll and Temple Scroll which do deal with marriage and procreation). The main cemetery, in close proximity to the Qumran buildings, has approximately 1,180 burials, and of the 55 so far excavated all were found to be male, except possibly for one example of a female, and there are no infant burials in the main cemetery.

4 Pliny refers to the community as denouncing the accumulation of personal wealth. Josephus gives similar information on the Essenes' resentment of wealth. The Damascus Documents also describe the giving up of personal property and possessions to the community.

The *ostracon* already mentioned appears to be a deed of gift of a new member giving over all his belongings to the community. This procedure is supported by evidence from fragments of Dead Sea Scrolls that refer to deeds of land (4Q342–358).

5 No scrolls were discovered within the Qumran site, but archaeological evidence shows that the same pottery types were found at the site as in some of the scroll caves. These tall, cylindrical 'scroll pots' are virtually unique to Qumran.

6 An inscription on a shard of pottery found in the cemetery is in the same handwriting as in one of the Dead Sea Scrolls.

The evidence is overwhelming for the standard model of Qumran as a religious centre where many of the Dead Sea Scrolls were composed, copied and curated.

Chapter 13

Akhetaton and the Great Aton Temple

Many current Dead Sea Scrolls scholars remain closeted in their universities, like the philosopher Immanuel Kant once was. Living in isolation, Kant knew about ideas, but knew little about the world from which they sprang and wrote down his thoughts in the most obscure academic language, dragging philosophy back into hermeneutics. Whereas other thinkers had striven to free philosophy from the restraints of scholasticism, Kant sought to separate reality from intellect and systemize reason.

One of the biggest black holes in the Dead Sea Scrolls, and biblical and koranic study relates to the almost complete lack of comprehension and understanding of the role Pharaoh Akhenaton played in the formulation of the so-called 'religions of the Book'. Most scholars and laypeople are living in the Dark Ages of biblical/historical awareness. There is a desperate need to enter a new Age of Biblical Enlightenment ('ABE') illuminated by the Sun of the Aton, inaugurated by Sigmund Freud, characterized by Ben Zion Wacholder and Sarah Israelit Groll, and discussed in this and my previous books.

If we take a look at the absurdity of what present-day scholars make of the numerous references to 'the Temple' in the Dead Sea Scrolls and in the Hebrew Bible, we get a flavour of their static Kantian mind-set on these and many other historical texts. There are four main sources that talk about the Temple:

1 The Dead Sea Scrolls – The Temple Scroll, the so-called New Jerusalem Scroll.
2 The Bible – 2 Samuel, Isaiah, 1, 2 Chronicles, 1, 2 Kings, Ezekiel, Ezra, the Gospels, Revelations, Acts.[1]

3 Rabbinic writings – Talmud, Midrash, etc.

4 Historical sources – Josephus, Pliny, Philo, etc.

In talking about these four sources of information on the Temple most scholars automatically assume that the Temple in question has to be the one at Jerusalem, either the First Temple, which was destroyed in 586 BC by the Babylonians, or the Second Temple, destroyed by the Romans in 70 AD. Their intolerance to new ideas leaves them nowhere else to go! However, none of the most informative texts of these sources – the Temple Scroll, the New Jerusalem Scroll, and 1 and 2 Chronicles, 1 and 2 Kings, or Ezekiel – ever mentions Jerusalem as the place where the Temple was located. Even Deuteronomy is reluctant to mention Jerusalem and the name of the land that is to be distributed to the tribes in the Promised Land. In fact biblical texts often deliberately avoid mentioning the city in which the Temple was located.

One would have thought these clues would be sufficient in themselves to alert translators to a problem, but no. They plough on, filling in the word Jerusalem whenever there is a lacuna or any doubt about an unnamed place. They even title one of the scrolls the 'New Jerusalem Scroll', whereas once again, in a very lengthy and detailed description of a vast city and huge temple, the word Jerusalem never appears and there are no geographical markers to identify it as Jerusalem.

I will now examine in more detail the Temple Scroll and the so-called New Jerusalem Scroll. In this process I draw heavily on the work of five key scholars, who I believe have read the material far more acutely than most others, but nevertheless fail to join up the dots: namely Yigael Yadin, Florentino García Martínez, Michael Chyutin, Shlomo Margalit, Ben Zion Wacholder and Sarah Israelit Groll.

The Temple Scroll

This scroll, recovered by Yigael Yadin in 1967 from Bethlehem where it had been concealed by an Arab dealer named Kando, is considered one of the most significant of all the Dead Sea Scrolls. It was undoubtedly held in high esteem by members of the *Yahad* at Qumran and has even been described as a second Torah. However, for students of the Temple Scroll there are intractable problems that have not been resolved, and as yet there are numerous puzzling questions:

Why does the scroll conflict with so many teachings of the Pentateuch?
When was it composed?
Where does the author draw his information on previously unknown
festivals?
Why, when the author gives the name of God, are the Hebrew letters
in a script dating back to the 10th century BC?
Why was it regarded as holy scripture by the *Yahad*?
Why does the Scroll never mention Jerusalem in its detailed
descriptions of a temple?

The least understood section of the Temple Scroll relates to its long
dissertation on the measurements of the Temple. As Yigael Yadin
points out in his seminal book on the Temple Scroll:

> . . . although one of the principal obligations of the children
> of Israel was to build a Temple once they were established
> in the Holy Land, there is no Torah, no divine law recorded
> in the Bible, governing the plan of its construction. Already
> in ancient times Jews were perplexed by the absence of such
> biblical directions. True, there are descriptions of the Temple
> of Solomon [as we see in Kings and Chronicles discussed next]
> but there is no divine law presented by God to Moses as to how
> the Temple was to be built, as there is on how the Tabernacle
> was to be fashioned.[2]

In fact there is something radically wrong with the dimensions of
the Temple given in 1 Kings 6. These would create a small building
only 60 x 20 x 30 cubits about 30 x 10 x 15m (100 x 33 x 50ft), and
the cherubim would hardly fit inside the walls! These two figures
were to adorn the golden shrine of the Ark, but with each having an
outstretched wing of 10 cubits there would have been no room for the
bodies of the creatures in a room measuring 20 cubits in width.

In addition to the cherubim and Temple furniture, some 4,000
congregants are said to have been accommodated in the prayer hall,
which with the partition for the Holy of Holies left a space only
about 20 x 10m (65 x 33ft). An average shoulder to shoulder space
of 60cm/2ft could allow for a reasonable 16 people per row but the
depth of each row would be no more than 15cm/6in! And building

Solomon's modestly sized Temple involved more than 150,000 people working over a period of seven years! Something appears wrong with the given dimensions and the task force.

In 1 Chronicles 28, King David is forbidden to build the Temple, but announces that his son Solomon has been chosen to succeed him on the throne and to build the Temple. Then we have the astonishing news:

> Then David gave Solomon his son the plan of the vestibule of the temple, and of its houses, its treasuries, its upper rooms, and its inner chambers, and of the rooms for the mercy seat; and the plan of all of that he had in mind for the courts of the house of the Lord, all the surrounding chambers, the treasuries of the house of God, and the treasuries of the dedicated gifts; for the division of the priests and the Levites, and all the works of the service in the house of the Lord; for all the vessels for the service in the house of the Lord the weight of gold for all golden vessels for each service, the weight of silver vessels for each service, the weight of the golden lamp stands and their lamps . . . [and] the golden chariot of the cherubim . . . All this he made clear by the writing from the hand of the Lord concerning it, all the work to be done according to the plan.

So there had been a plan! But it was not evident from the Torah. So where was it? What was it? Why is there a reference to a golden chariot?

I think we now know the answers to some of these questions. The plan was in the Temple Scroll, idealized by the strain of priests – Ezekiel's 'Benei Zadok 1' (this is Professor Ben Zion Wacholder's designation for what he sees as a separate strand of priests) – who stood outside the Temple hierarchy from the time of Solomon down to Seleucid times, and handed on by them through the Teacher of Righteousness into the hands of the Qumran-Essenes.

Confirmation that there was a plan, and that it was in the Temple Scroll, comes from two sources of rabbinic writing:

> The Temple Scroll which the Holy One, Blessed be he, committed to Moses while standing . . . Moses stood and

transmitted it to Joshua while standing . . . Joshua to the Elders, and the Elders to the Prophets, and the Prophets to David, and David to Solomon . . . *(Midrash Samuel)*

And David said before him: Master of the Universe, make me arise for the sake of the Temple Scroll that Samuel the Prophet transmitted to me; I pray you: Make it possible for me . . . That I may rise from this bed and transmit to them the Scroll for building the Temple. *(Agadat Bersit – Legends of Genesis)*

Now, not only do we have good evidence, from three different sources, that the Temple Scroll was a real plan, but its documented ancestry, back to the time of Moses, takes knowledge of the plan right back to within a hundred years of the time of Pharaoh Akhenaton and his Great Temple at Akhetaton.

Yadin is reluctant to claim that the Temple Scroll he recovered in Bethlehem was a copy of the one the Prophet Samuel gave to King David. He is, nevertheless, convinced that it was the passage in 1 Chronicles 28 that prompted the author to write the Temple Scroll. Yadin's modesty begs the question. Would the author dare write such a text, unusually, in the first person, as if dictated directly by God? Where did he get his detailed descriptions from? Why are the Levites accorded special rights not given to them in the canonical Torah? If the writer was inspired by the Torah writings, why did he make up so many new prescriptions and festivals, and contradict the Torah in so many critical areas? How did he get the dimensions and physical descriptions so close to known equivalents of the Great Temple at Amarna?

To answer some of these questions we need to unroll the 8.5m of the precious Temple Scroll and read what is says. Analyzing the Temple Scroll in depth would take another book, so we will confine our attention to some key elements, some 'black holes' that remain a mystery to modern scholarship. The Temple Scroll is divided into subject sections as follows: Geometry of the Temple Buildings; Courts and Holy Areas; Festival Calendar; Purity Laws; Laws of Polity; Law of the King.

Geometry of the Temple Buildings

In order to see how the Temple Scroll descriptions of the Temple and its city diverge from a location in Jerusalem we need to look at the respective sizes, numbers of courts, holy areas, etc.

We have seen that the Temple Scroll gives a very precise measurement of the size of the Temple it is describing. The dimensions are almost exactly those of the Great Temple at Akhetaton. The Temple Scroll gives 1,600 x 600 cubits (800 x 300m) and the ground measurements of the Great Temple at Amarna are very close to this. In addition, many other dimensions and details of the courts, gates, towers and so on are enumerated. It is also true that the alignment of the main prayer hall at Qumran is almost exactly the same as the orientation of the main wall of the Great Temple at Amarna. To deny knowledge of the layout of the Great Temple to the authors of the Temple Scroll and that that knowledge was known to the community at Qumran who possessed the Temple Scroll – unique texts not known from any other source – is tantamount to saying black is white.

Many significant features of the Great Temple at Akhetaton are described in the Temple Scroll. Among these is this passage:

> . . . you shall make a spiral staircase to the north of the Sanctuary: a square building of 20 cubits from corner to corner, its four corners matching, located 7 cubits away from the wall of the sanctuary, north-east of it . . . in the loft of this building you shall make a door opening to the roof of the Sanctuary and a passageway made in this door to the opening [of the roof of the] Sanctuary, by which one can enter the loft of the Sanctuary. You shall cover all this building of the spiral staircase with gold.[3]

From the ground plan of the Great Temple, recovered by modern excavations, and extant illustrations on the tomb walls at Amarna, we know many of the architectural details of the Great Temple. Much of this information is taken from a major campaign of excavations conducted under the auspices of the Egypt Exploration Society between 1926 and 1936. This work shows that to the north-east of the sanctuary there was a building, about 20 cubits square, about 7 cubits from the temple wall. Work by N. de G. Davis has shown the existence of a spiral staircase, almost certainly allowing access via the roof of the temple and direct access to the sanctuary.

There is no mention of a spiral staircase in the Bible or of access to the sanctuary via one, and yet here we have a description in the Temple Scroll of one.

Integral with the northern wall of the Great Temple, excavations have revealed a structure referred to as the Hall of Foreign Tribute. This location is mentioned in the Copper Scroll, and in the Temple Scroll we find: 'You shall make a third courtyard . . . to their daughters and to foreigners.'[4]

The presence of foreigners, almost certainly including Hebrews, would be quite feasible at Pharaoh Akhenaton's court, as it was for his immediate predecessors. This tolerance conforms to Akhenaton's policy of opening up his new religion to all the population, but completely contradicts biblical custom, as non-Jews or foreigners were not permitted to enter the Temple at Jerusalem. The only logical conclusion, once again, is that the Temple being described in the Temple Scroll is not at, nor meant to be at, Jerusalem.

Yet some scholars will try and pick holes in individual congruences, ignoring or trying to moderate the fact that the hundreds of what they term coincidences are unique correspondences. In doing this, they conveniently ignore the myriad of clear protocols from the Amarna period that are described throughout the Bible, the Dead Sea Scrolls and other sources, protocols and practices that are often reported in detail in these sources, for a place that was destroyed within 30 years of Akhenaton's death and the existence of its society expunged from the records in Egypt.

Whilst it appears that the central courts of the Aton temple were configured in concentric square formation, some casual students of the dimensions given in the Temple Scroll read the entire temple to be shaped as a square. This interpretation falls on a number of grounds.

The Temple Scroll clearly gives the outer dimensions as 1,600 cubits by 600 cubits. Florentino García Martínez in his major study and translation of the Temple Scroll is unambiguous in his reading. For some reason, some interpreters 'lose' the 1,600 cubit figure and ignore it in their reconstructions. The main outer dimension clearly establishes a vast rectangle, encompassing the inner square courts.

All the legitimate temples described in the Hebrew Bible are rectangular. Why would the author of the Temple Scroll suddenly invent a square temple? Square temples are extremely rare in the ancient Near East. The only one I am aware of is the Temple of Bel in Palmyra. Indeed, Josephus cites an old prophecy in his comments on Herod's Temple that 'if the Jews ever squared the Temple, it would be destroyed'.[5]

In the same column of the Temple Scroll (Column 40), we find further confirmation, as pointed out by Dwight D. Swanson, that the temple being described cannot possibly be the Jerusalem Temple, past, present, future or imaginary.[6]

Whilst a number of gates are mentioned for the various tribes of Israel, it is obvious that these names were added to the original description as they are for 12 sons of Jacob and not the 12 tribes of Israel. Manasseh and Ephraim are not mentioned.

The altar before the Holy of Holies is the most important feature of the Temple, and one would therefore expect handed-down memories, or even written records of its structures, to be fairly accurate – if there are any in the Dead Sea Scroll material and the mainstream Bible. In fact we find very convincing evidence from a Dead Sea Scroll, the so-called New Jerusalem Scroll, Ezekiel and other Biblical texts. Here are a few more revealing examples.

Leviticus 1:11, when referring to burnt offerings, is usually assumed to be talking about procedures in the Jerusalem Temple when it says 'it shall be slaughtered before the Lord on the north side of the altar'. Is it just a coincidence that the slaughtering area seen in reconstructed plans of the Great Temple at Amarna shows it to be on the north side of the altar? Again, in Leviticus 1:14: 'If his offering to the Lord is a burnt offering of birds, he shall choose his offering from turtledoves or pigeons.' Is it just a coincidence that the detailed relief on a wall of the tomb of Huya at Amarna shows turtledoves or pigeons being stored within the Temple?

There are just too many congruences for chance to have played a role in the descriptions we find in the Dead Sea Scrolls, Apocrypha, pseudepigrapha, rabbinic writings and the Bible itself, of a Holy Temple and the Great Temple at Amarna.

Joseph's Signature Work – The Storehouses

Now I posit another set of facts that, in their own right, regardless of all the other confirmatory factors, should be sufficient to convince any court of law in the land that the Temple Scroll records knowledge of the layout and geometry of the Great Temple at Akhetaton. They also prove beyond reasonable doubt the existence of the biblical vizier Joseph.

A block plan of the central city of Akhetaton can be established from the extensive excavations carried out under the direction of J. D. S. Pendlebury in the seasons 1926–7 and 1931–6.

In the Bible, we are told that Joseph was set in overall control of the gathering and control of the crops that were to sustain the country through a seven-year period of famine. If this is true, he would have been responsible for the building of storehouses for the grain. Pendlebury's excavations uncovered the remains of a series of storehouses. The main ones are nearest the Great Temple, abutting the Royal Road, in an area designated by Pendlebury as 'Temple Magazines'. The Temple Scroll (Column 40) specifies the location of the largest store-rooms nearest to the Great Temple as 'fifty-two store-rooms, their rooms and their huts'.

Why does the Temple Scroll describe 52 separate store-rooms for provisions in these storehouses? Where does this figure come from? There is no mention of store-rooms of this type in the Bible, but in the ground plan of the city of Akhenaton it is seen that there were exactly 52 silos in each of the main storehouses nearest the Great Temple!

If there is one building skill the Hebrews developed, we learn, from evidence at Ramses in the Delta region and Medinet Habu near Thebes, as well as from the Bible, it was building storehouses for the pharaoh. The Bible confirms this as a task set for them, and it is not surprising that this skill would have been developed by Joseph under the purview of Akhenaton, if my contention about their relationship is correct. This skill might have been specifically handed down to his Hebrew followers and been something they became known and respected for in Egypt.

The contention that the biblical Joseph was vizier to Pharaoh Akhenaton, as shown by a weight of direct and indirect evidence in my previous books, is now reinforced. Egyptologists like Alan

R. Schulman have long recognized the Egyptian elements in the Joseph story,[7] and when we look at the flavour of the Joseph story as handed down through the Bible, we find it quite in harmony with the environment of the 14th century BC. For example, Genesis 37:28 records the sale of Joseph into slavery for 20 shekels, a figure consistent with the average price of a slave for the second half of the millennium, derived from external documentary sources. By the time of the first millennium, from around 1000 BC, the average price had increased to 50 or 60 shekels.[8]

What's in a Name?

Quite often, when you are introduced to someone, you can get a good idea of their age from their first name, and even the place of their birth. Parents tend to choose names that are popular at the time of their offspring's birth, and certain names that were fashionable, say, in the 1920s, are simply no longer in vogue. The etymology of personal names used in the Joseph story is extremely instructive when viewed from this perspective, and gives us a chronological horizon that fits neatly into the likelihood that those he interacted with were contemporary with the Egyptian 18th Dynasty. We find: Potiphar – Joseph's master (Genesis 39:1); Asenath – Joseph's wife (Genesis 41:45); Potipherah – Joseph's father-in-law (Genesis 41:45); Zaphenath-Paneah – the Egyptian name given to Joseph by Pharaoh (Genesis 41:45).

This last name does not obviously conform to the pattern of Egyptian names of the period but, as analyzed in Chapter 5, it is almost certainly the Hebrew version of an Egyptian hieroglyph relating to Amenophis son of Hapu. The others are clearly Egyptian.

After Joseph's betrayal by Potiphar's wife, he was incarcerated in prison and we have another series of dream interpretations which are said to turn out to be accurate. Is there any possible external confirmation of this story and the date of the dream? The answer is a qualified 'yes'.

The suffix 'rah' is seen as connecting Potipherah's name to the ancient temple city of On (modern Heliopolis), the traditional location of the Sun god Re. Potipherah is said to have been a priest at this religious centre (Genesis 45: 41). By the time of Amenhotep III and Akhenaton, On had been converted into a temple for the new pharaoh's religion and the pagan imagery destroyed. It is not surprising that the name of On is revered in Judaean tradition and the Hebrew name for On is a vocalization for the Egyptian '*iwnw*', often pronounced as Zion. On, as Zion, is remembered in Hebrew prayers. Even today the name of Jerusalem is coupled with the name of Zion in Jewish prayers, but it is clear that they are two separate places.[9]

The name Asenath has long been thought of as deriving from the Egyptian name '*ns-nt*' ('She who belongs to the goddess Neith'), but Professor Kenneth Kitchen has rejected this interpretation. He says: 'In a forthcoming book I will provide evidence that suggests a definite connection to the goddess Neith and that the name is tied firmly to the role of the High Priest at Akhenaton's Temple, so that the original link may well be correct.'[10]

Joseph's given name of Zaphenath-Paneah has been the subject of much debate as to its meaning. Kenneth Kitchen, I believe, comes up with a likely explanation, in view of its link to Akhenaton's reign, although that of Joseph Davidovits (see Chapter 5) is more compelling.[11] Kitchen postulates the name as '*dd (w) n.f Ip-cnh*, which means 'Joseph who is called Ip-Ankh' or 'He who recognizes Life'. The significance of this interpretation is that the *ankh* reached its peak of employment as a religious motif, and can be seen as a key element, in the Amarna period, with the *ankh* sign attached to the end of the life-enhancing rays in the symbology of the Aton.

Some Egyptologists, like Donald Redford[12] and Alan Schulman,[13] date these names to the 21st to 22nd Dynasties, but Kenneth Kitchen places them at an earlier time and concludes that the transition to the forms seen in the Bible began at the start of the 18th Dynasty. Thus, the names recorded by the Bible for the Joseph narrative are entirely consistent with the probable dates and location of Joseph and his family that I have suggested – the 14th century BC and the holy city of Akhetaton in Middle Egypt.

A study of the Elephantine papyri, written by members of an Aramaic-speaking pseudo-Jewish group that lived on the island of Yeb, in southern Egypt, shows that similar name patterns to those used in the 18th Dynasty occur in the recording of Semitic birth names and given Egyptian names. This is not too surprising. My contention is that the settlers on Yeb Island, who were there for hundreds of years before 400 BC, were originally refugees from Akhetaton, with all that implies.

Later this style of names was also applied to Semitic slaves attached to Egyptian estates.

Was Panehesy the Biblical Joseph?

Panehesy's titles as 'Superintendent of the Oxen of the Aton, and Superintendent of the Granary of the Aton', certainly accord with the role of Joseph in the Hebrew Bible. As vizier, the Bible says he was second only to the pharaoh, and put in charge of coping with the impending seven-year famine he had predicted. He does not appear to have had the formal title of vizier, but the name of Panehesy is attested as vizier under the Pharaoh Merneptah.[14] One has to wonder if Panehesy was not in fact the Biblical Joseph! Inscriptions in his sepulchre also confirm that he was gifted gold necklaces and abundant valuable rewards by Pharaoh Akhenaton and left the presence of the king in his own special chariot to the acclaim of the populace. All these factors fit well with descriptions of Joseph's treatment by the pharaoh. Perhaps even more significant, the Egyptian name given to Joseph by the pharaoh (Genesis 41:45) was Zaphenath-Paneah, and the name Paneah could well have derived from the hieroglyphic form of Panehesy. This possibility might also help explain why the early Christians chose Panehesy's tomb, rather than any of the many others they could have selected, to establish a place of worship, knowing through the Qumran-Essenes, and through Jesus' intimate knowledge of many of their innermost secrets, that Panehesy was a Hebrew ancestor.

Ezekiel's Views

It is worth spending some time, once again, with Ezekiel to try to resolve some of these issues, as he was a key figure for the Qumran-Essenes and one of the pivotal transmitters of information gleaned about Akhetaton.

Living at the time of the Babylonian conquest and destruction of the First Temple in Jerusalem by Nebuchadnezzar, Ezekiel ben Buzi was probably exiled to Babylon shortly after 597 BC. Most of the Judaeans were deported to areas along the River Cheber, near the flourishing city of Nippur. They were able to continue their religious practices and became well integrated into parts of Babylonian society, adopting Aramaic as their language and entering commerce.

Little hard evidence exists, in addition to Ezekiel's testimony, of this period in Babylon, but we do know from Babylonian records dating from 595 to 570 BC that:

> The King of Akkad [Babylon] . . . laid siege to the city of Judah [iahuda] and the king took the city on the second day of the month of Addaru. He appointed in it a new king of his liking, took heavy booty from it, and brought it to Babylon.[15]

This Babylonian chronicle helps explain a fragmentary record on ceramic tablets, found near the Ishtar Gate in Babylon, listing rations of oil and barley provided for the exiled king of Judah, Jehoiachin, and his entourage, who were being held as privileged prisoners. It also confirms Ezekiel's recording of events. During the siege of Jerusalem King Jehoiakim was assassinated and his son Jehoiachin took command, but almost immediately surrendered the city to Nebuchadnezzar, hence the favouritism shown towards him whilst in captivity. We also know from the 5th century BC Marashu collection of some 700 tablets,[16] that the Hebrew population in Babylon became well integrated into banking and business activities, laying the foundations for a well-educated, thriving Jewish presence in the following centuries.

Ezekiel's key descriptions of the temple and the city of the temple come in Chapters 33-48 where he lays down guidelines for a restored temple and covenant society. In the myopic eyes of most scholars, his statements in these sections are to be regarded as divorced from reality and Ezekiel is relegated to the position of a visionary priest with an over-active imagination. They are quite happy to take much of his testimony as valid, but when it comes to his descriptions related to the temple he is simply 'making it all up'.

Ezekiel saw the temple as the ultimate symbol and guarantee of God's eternal contract with His people, and as we have seen, he did not invent a building and a city on behalf of God. He would not have been so presumptive, and in fact he had a very good source for his descriptions. Whilst Ezekiel's descriptions differ markedly from those in 1 Kings 6–8 and 2 Chronicles 2–4, and scholars cannot explain these

Seal of The Living God

This special prayer is a Gift from
God the Father given to prophet
Maria Divine Mercy for the
protection of all God's Children.

All who accept this Seal will be offered
protection for each and every one of you
and your families during the period in
the lead up to the Second Coming of Christ.

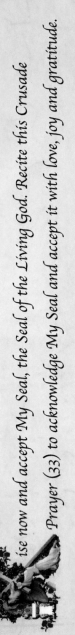

...ise now and accept My Seal, the Seal of the Living God. Recite this Crusade
Prayer (33) to acknowledge My Seal and accept it with love, joy and gratitude.

O My God, My Loving Father, I accept with love and gratitude Your Divine Seal of Protection

loved ones with this special Seal and I pledge my life to Your service forever and ever.

I love You Dear Father. I console You in these times Dear Father. I offer You the Body, Blood, Soul and Divinity of Your dearly beloved Son In atonement for the sins of the world and for the salvation of all Your children.

Amen.

Go, My children and do not fear. Trust in Me, Your beloved Father, who lovingly created each of you. I know every single soul, every part of you is known to Me. Not one of you is loved less than the other. Because of this I do not want to lose one soul. Not one.

Please continue to pray My Divine Mercy Chaplet every day. One day, you will understand why this purification is needed.

Your Loving Father in Heaven

God the Most High

differences, Ezekiel lived at the time of the First Temple in Jerusalem and, as a priest, must have known what it looked like.

The simple answer is that whilst the authors of Kings and Chronicles were describing the Temple in Jerusalem, Ezekiel was describing a temple in another place. Many of the scrolls from Qumran reflect a view that the sanctuary built by Zerubbabel during the rebuilding of the Temple after the return from Babylonian exile was quite wrongly designed. This sentiment is reflected in Qumran texts such as the Aramaic Testament of Levi, the Cairo-Damascus Documents, the Book of Jubilees, the New Jerusalem Scroll, and the Temple Scroll. All these texts refuse to recognize the legitimacy of the Second Temple. All those who served in this Temple were seen as utterly idolatrous. They did not carry the legitimate badges of office, the *urim* and the *thummim* (divination devices), or wear the correct *ephod* (high priestly garb). These items of legitimacy are seen in the *shabti* figure of Meryre in the Metropolitan Museum in New York. According to Ezekiel, the only true Benei Zadok were those descended from Levi, and, as Esti Eshel pointed out to me, the Dead Sea Scrolls continually insist that the Levite priests were appointed at the time of Jacob, long before there was a temple in Jerusalem, and have to be related to another place.

How do the Dead Sea Scrolls relate to Ezekiel? Ben Zion Wacholder was a partially sighted Professor of Hebrew Studies at Cincinnati University, but he saw more clearly than most of his contemporaries. He regarded the bulk of the non-biblical Qumran texts, even though not written at Qumran, as sectarian, either early or late *Yahad* sectarianism, and posed the questions: Who inspired this movement of thought? When did it begin? He differentiated between Ezekiel's early sectarianism of what he calls the Benei Zadok-1 and the Qumran Cairo-Damascus version which he calls Benei Zadok-2.[17]

Professor Wacholder notes that, ever since the 19th century, the views of scholars like Abraham Geiger and Julius Wellhausen have dominated, with the theory that the Benei Zadok-1 were to be identified with the theocratic state founded by Jeshua ben Jozadaq and Zerubbabel, and that they ruled from around 520 BC to the rise of the Seleucids. Professor Wacholder profoundly disagreed with this understanding, insisting Ezekiel's Benei Zadok-1 reflected, 'a movement that stood in opposition to the sacerdotal authorities who controlled the First Temple from the time of Solomon, and whose descendants ruled Judaea until the Seleucid persecution'. In other words the Book of Ezekiel should be read as an indictment of the pre-exilic high priests, as it was by the Essenes of Qumran and the rabbinic sages. Ezekiel was in effect a 'textbook' for sectarian Judaism in the Second Temple period.

According to Professor Wacholder, Ezekiel contradicts the Deuteronomist teaching in the rest of the Hebrew Bible, that Israel prospered when it obeyed God's commandments but lost its protection when it turned to apostasy. He notes that Chapter 20, for example, recounts Israel's history 'as one of unbroken idolatry and lawlessness . . . Israel had been an apostate nation ever since their sojourn in the wilderness.' He continues: 'if one prophet can be designated the "father of apocalypticism", that prophet would be Ezekiel, and his vocabulary in its most characteristic form survives almost exclusively in the Qumran sectarian writings.' What Professor Wacholder is effectively saying is that there was a link of sectarianism right the way back from Qumran via Ezekiel to the time of the exodus.

Ezekiel's visions in Chapters 1 and 10 describe a scene we are familiar with from Panehesy's tomb – intertwined winged creatures, chariots and a heavenly throne glowing with light. The Qumran-Essenes' texts have a much clearer view of the scene and describe it in words that demonstrate the memory of an eyewitness account – words one might well use today for the incredible pictorial representations of Akhenaton's chariot and the Great Temple structure and chambers that can still be seen in the tombs of Amarna. A series of Qumran texts, including the Songs for the Sabbath Sacrifice, specifically describe and praise 'wall images and movements of a chariot throne', and this is but one of many examples of references to these scenes recalled in the Qumran scrolls. One would be hard pressed to find an Israelite setting for these notions:

> The Cherubim praise the vision of the Throne-Chariot above the celestial sphere, and they extol the [radiance] of the fiery firmament beneath the throne of His glory. And the holy Angels come and go between the whirling wheels, like a fiery vision of

most holy spirits; and around them stream rivulets of molten fire, like incandescent bronze, a radiance of many brilliant colours, of exquisite hues gloriously mingled. The Spirits of the living God move in constant accord with the glory of the Wonderful Chariot. The whispered voice of blessing accompanies the roar of their advance, and they praise the Holy One on their way of return . . . The vestibules by which they enter, the spirits of the most holy inner Temple . . . engraved on the vestibules by which the King enters, luminous spiritual figures . . . Among the spirits of splendour there are works of [art of] marvellous colours . . . glorious innermost Temple chambers, the structure of [the most ho]ly [sanctuary] in the innermost chambers of the King.[18]

The question has to be asked: how can this reference to engraved images possibly be reconciled with descriptions of the inner sanctum of the temple in Jerusalem?' The simple answer is it cannot be. There can be little doubt it recalls a scene in the temple at Akhetaton, reproduced in the tomb of Panehesy, if for no other reason than that images would have been forbidden in the Jerusalem temple.

We are therefore left with limited choice. There can be no doubt that the king being referred to in this passage is not an Israelite king. There are no biblical descriptions that match these temple chambers. Nor can there be any doubt that the description of the heavenly chariot matches the reality of a pharaonic state chariot of the period of Akhenaton:

The decorative panels are made of heavy gold foil worked in a repoussé linen, with scenes of the chastising of foreign foes by the king as a sphinx. The gold is enhanced with bosses and borders inlaid with coloured glass, faience and similar ornamentation, to produce a gorgeous and dazzling appearance.[19]

Pharaoh Akhenaton made the chariot his preferred mode of transport, as opposed to the traditional state palanquin, and the wide, straight roads in his new city were designed for use by state chariot processions. These vehicles seem to have had some profound ritualistic meaning, and the wealthy aristocratic charioteers formed a *corps d'élite* around the divine king.

Mosaics

One of the most striking features of excavations across Israel has been the finding of large mosaic floor decorations, dating to around 400–500 AD, in ancient synagogues at Sepphoris, Hammat-Tiberias, Beit Alpha, Na'aran and Ussifeyeh amongst others. Even though the appearance of a human being and astrological signs within mosaics in a synagogue is thought to be unacceptable and in contravention of the Second Commandment these show a zodiac with a figure, assumed to be the Greek god Helios, riding a chariot at the centre.

The director of the excavations at Sepphoris (in the Galilee region) of a building presumed to be a synagogue, Professor Zeev Weiss, wrote: 'As surprising as it may seem to find a zodiac sign in a synagogue, it is even more shocking to find a depiction of the sun god, Helios, riding in his chariot drawn by four horses (the quadriga).'[20] Weiss tried to find a reason for the extraordinary sight. He assumed that the figure of Helios was meant to be a reminder of God's omnipotence, but why a Greek god should be used for this purpose was beyond him.

I maintain that it is wrong to take the image as being Helios, and that the clues are all there to indicate the truth behind this series of mosaics. The building at Sepphoris is aligned east–west with the result that the worshippers would not face Jerusalem, as was normal in a synagogue. It is also noteworthy that the chariot that the figure rides is not of the 5th century AD period. The chariot construction shows a thin rim and 6-spoke wheels, characteristic of the Amarna period. Chariots subsequent to this period used more spokes and 12 or 18 were typical of later periods. This observation confirms we are not looking at an Israelite, Greek or Roman chariot design. The radiating rays of the sun around the head of the rider and the figurative style of the horses also mean only one thing. These images are all of a distant memory of Pharaoh Akhenaton riding his dazzling chariot, portrayed by people who knew a deeper secret meaning behind representing him, apparently, as the Greek god Helios.

This is not unique. The Book of Secrets (*Sefer ha-Razim*), a text of the late third century AD, written in Hebrew, fragments of which were found amongst the Cairo-Genizah collection, refers to Helios, but the wording, sense and style are again those of the Great Hymn to the

Aton. 'Holy Helios, who rises in the east, good mariner, trustworthy leader of the sun's rays . . . Who of old did establish the mighty wheel of the heavens . . .'[21] There are also connections to the mystery works of the Qumran-Essenes and their interest in astrological/zodiacal studies.

One has to assume that the use of the name and apparent figure of Helios is a euphemism for Akhenaton as the representative of the Aton, just as the horses of the sun at the entrance to the temple in Jerusalem are thought to be pagan monuments.

More Names from the Scrolls and the Bible

One element that has disappointed historians is the failure in the books of Genesis and Exodus to name the pharaoh for many of the important episodes in Egypt. The Hebrew rendition of the title 'pharaoh' is derived from the Egyptian 'pr c3' meaning 'Great House'. As a reference to the pharaoh's palace, this goes back to the Middle Kingdom, but shortly before the reign of the 18th Dynasty Pharaoh Thutmoses III (c1479–1425 BC), the epithet was applied to the monarch rather than his palace. In Egyptian records, from their inception up to the 10th century BC, it is a stand-alone description, with no additional detail. After this period the name of the pharaoh is given. This pattern is followed precisely in the Bible, where the pharaohs related to the Abraham, Joseph and Jacob, and Moses episodes are not named, but for events after the 10th century BC the pharaoh is named – Pharaoh Shishak, Pharaoh Neco and Pharaoh Hophra. (Pharaoh Ramses is indirectly referred to in Exodus, but not specifically named.)

It has to be concluded that the biblical Hebrew writers were well acquainted with contemporary Egyptian practice, in relation of the naming of the Pharaoh at the time of Joseph, and refrained from giving his name for this very reason. There are many other examples of correlations between Egyptian records and the Hebrew Bible's version of events in the Joseph story, and I hope to return to these in a subsequent book.

Later on, we will learn that the detailed intimate data the forebears of the Qumran-Essenes had of the pre-10th century BC period gave them knowledge of the names of personalities right the way back to the times of Abraham and Sarah, and that they knew the name of the pharaoh who they interacted with. This is a revelation never before given in print, and will be forthcoming in its full context later in this book. In a sequel book, I also intend to reveal the hidden name of the Patriarch Joseph and the full secret name of Moses!

Two other names, which occur in Exodus 1:15, are Shiphra and Puah, midwives charged by the Egyptian king to kill Hebrew males immediately before they were born. Here again, they are familiar Egyptian names for the 12th and 11th centuries BC, and carry a ring of truth giving further credibility to the strength of oral memory.[22]

Courts and Holy Areas

According to Leviticus 16 and the Temple Scroll, the anointing of the High Priest takes place in an identical manner, which may seem to undermine my claim that the Temple Scroll is talking about a much earlier time than Moses. There can be little doubt that biblical accounts drew on previous knowledge as well as contemporary experience, but the variants in details are memory markers for the truth. The difference between the two accounts exemplifies these discrepancies. In the Temple Scroll, the ceremony is fulfilled by the elders of the people, a function reserved in Leviticus for Moses alone. The reason for omitting any mention of Moses in the Temple Scroll is highly significant as it cannot be a deliberate omission. The reason must be that he was not yet on the scene when the Temple Scroll text was originally composed.

The New Festivals

In his study of the Temple Scroll, Yigael Yadin concludes that the scroll's author seems to make use of injunctions in Leviticus (23:15–16) and Exodus (34:22) to describe three previously unknown festivals – of new barley, wine and oil – in addition to the biblical festivals of First Fruits, Shavuot and Pentecost. The truth may well be the other way around – that the biblical account drew some of its information from contemporary versions of the Temple Scroll. All sorts of reasons have been put forward to try and explain where the Scroll's author got his information from. There are no scriptural references which can help.

A pointer to this process is seen in the ceremony of the Waving of the Sheaf festival described in the Temple Scroll, which has been interpreted as referring to the First Fruits festival of barley, or Sukkot (or Succoth), an autumn festival celebrated by Jews to this day. Interestingly, in the Temple Scroll, the waving of the *lulav* (palm frond) sheaf is elevated to a major ritual. As this is not a requirement in the Pentateuch, what could the biblical source have been for this? Yigael Yadin is perplexed and comments: 'Since he [the scroll author] never introduced any new ritual arbitrarily, but always based himself on his own interpretation of the Pentateuchal text, what was the biblical source for his radical departure from normative Judaism?' What indeed!

I believe that these festivals, particularly the Waving of the Sheaf ceremony, had their origins in earlier Egyptian times. Sukkot, as one of the three pilgrim festivals, predated the festivals of Rosh Hashanah (Festival of the New Year) and Yom Kippur (Day of Atonement) and was almost certainly the main festival (or the 'Ha Hag', the foremost festival of the time) prior to the introduction of these two festivals. Yadin goes on to identify an additional Temple Scroll festival of six days' duration, which he concludes was yet another new festival – of wood.

So what were the festivals being observed at Akhetaton? As far as we can tell, the festivals celebrated by Pharaoh Akhenaton were related to the crop cycles, organized around the spring and autumn harvest products, and would have paralleled those described in the Temple Scroll. So is there any other evidence to tie in the four festivals mentioned in the Temple Scroll, three of which – wine, oil and wood – are completely new and previously unknown?

The answer, I believe, is spelled out precisely in Psalm 104 of the Hebrew scriptures and its relationship to the Great Hymn of Akhenaton. This long hieroglyph inscription refers to the fruits that come forth out of the earth, and the sequence of products mentioned exactly matches the sequence of festivals of wine, oil, wheat and wood in Psalm 104:14–16:

> That he may bring forth food out of the earth: and wine that
> maketh glad the heart of man, and oil to make his face to shine,
> and bread which strengtheneth man's heart. The trees of the
> Lord are full of sap.

Professor Witold Tyloch came to an interesting conclusion in relation to the Festival of New Oil. He notes that Josephus, in *War*

2.123, says that the Essenes refrained from anointing themselves with oil, an unusual inhibition, and as the Temple Scroll specifies using new oil once a year as a means of expiation and purification, Tyloch takes this as an explanation of Josephus' report. Oil was only to be used for a holy event. Together with the employment of a solar calendar by the Essenes, this is taken by Tyloch as 'decisive proof to support the identification of the members of the Qumran Community as Essenes'.[23] One of the rituals described in Mishnah Yoma (holy writings compiled in the Rabbinic period shortly after the destruction of the Second Temple) talks about the Days of Atonement ceremony in the Temple, with a choir and orchestra, cymbals and two silver trumpets being played. All these musical features are seen in wall reliefs of rituals in the Great Temple to the Aton at Akhetaton. Strangest of these mishnaic descriptions is the statement that the silver trumpets were blown with the notes *'Teki'ah'*, *'Teru'ah'* and *'Teki'ah'*. These same notes are today blown on a ram's horn (*shofar*) at the high holiday festivals.

It would appear that the original ceremony in the Jerusalem Temple, and possibly also in the Tabernacle, required the blowing of a silver trumpet. This custom of blowing trumpets seems to have been in vogue at Akhenaton's temple, but were the trumpets silver? The answer is almost certainly 'yes' and we know about trumpet tooting from Tutankhamun!

When Howard Carter entered the royal tomb in 1922 he discovered two long trumpets measuring 49.4cm and 58.2cm (19.5 and 23in) respectively – one copper and one silver. Tutankhamun was the immediate successor to Akhenaton (apart from a transitory pharaoh called Smenkhkare), so the trumpets in his tomb would almost certainly have been exactly the same as those sounded in the Great Temple to the Aton. Because drawing out and shaping the metal trumpets required sophisticated specialist skills, developed over centuries by the Egyptian metalworkers, it is also almost certain that the trumpets sounded in the Jerusalem Temple would have been identical to those found in Tutankhamun's tomb and would have been acquired from Egypt. The transmission of the information to the mishnaic rabbis implies a direct line of knowledge stretching over a time span of several hundred years. There seems little alternative explanation for a ceremony which was only curtailed with the destruction of the Second Temple and replaced in synagogues by the blowing of the *shofar*. The Arch of Titus in Rome shows a trumpet pillaged from the Second Temple being carried in triumph back to Italy, and the trumpet is visually identical to the trumpet seen in the tomb of Tutankhamun. Another example of the ancient trumpet can be seen on a relief in the temple of Medinet Habu dating to the 12th century BC, which shows a battle scene. These facts underline the certainty that the Israelite trumpet-blowing ritual in the First and Second Temple must have been enacted in the same manner, using identical musical instruments as those employed in important festivals at the temple of Pharaoh Akhenaton and Queen Nefertiti.

The truly astonishing fact is that we can actually listen to the sound of the Tutankhamun silver trumpet being played today! In 1939 the BBC persuaded the Egyptian custodians of the trumpet to allow it to be played and the sounds broadcast to the public, and this can be listened to on the BBC website.[24]

Perhaps just as extraordinarily intriguing is the indication that the ceremony of Waving the Lulav, the most important of the First Fruits Festivals for the Essenes, which is observed to this day during Sukkot by Jews around the world, is almost identical to a ceremony seen in the Great Temple of Akhetaton and must therefore have originated in Egypt of the 14th century BC, long before the existence of a temple at Jerusalem.

Five days after the Day of Atonement Festival, Jews around the world celebrate the Festival of Sukkot – and have done so for nearly 3,000 years. It is known as a Festival of Rejoicing over the bringing in of the fruits of the harvest. From the information available to us, we do not have to look too far for clues to see how the procedures in the festival have derived from memories of the Great Temple at Akhetaton. We can even get a good idea of where the ceremony must have commenced in the temple and the route of the celebratory procession. The altar, in the first of the three courtyards of the Great Temple, faced east, and to the north of it was 'The House of Rejoicing'.[25] Processing from here, a line of priests would have wound their way around the temple walls, entering the main precinct through the east gate and on into the protected courtyard leading to the altar.

The importance of the autumn festival, variously referred to as Sukkot, Tabernacles or Booths, is demonstrated by its referencing in Deuteronomy 16, Numbers 29 and, as quoted below, in Leviticus 23:39–40:

> Mark, on the fifteenth day of the seventh month, when you have gathered in the yield of your land, you shall observe the festival of Adonai seven days; a complete rest on the first day, and a complete rest on the eighth day. On the first day you shall take the product of hadar trees, branches of palm trees, boughs of leafy trees, and willows of the brook, and you shall rejoice before Adonai your God seven days.

All three biblical references include the instruction for the people 'to rejoice' and during the service of Sukkot in synagogues songs of joy in a section of the Psalms called 'Hallel' are sung and palm leaves shaken and paraded. Notably the songs contain pointed references to activities at Akhetaton and reverence to the sun and light:

> Praise God, Servants of the Eternal, praise the name of the Eternal! May the name of the Eternal be blessed now and evermore. From the rising of the sun to its setting praised be the name of the Eternal. *(Psalm 113)*

> 'The Lord is God; He has given us light; form a procession with the branches up to the horns of the altar.' *(Psalm 118)*

The Altar

What the altar in the Temple in Jerusalem might have looked like is fascinating to contemplate, and one of the strongest linkages demonstrating that the writers of the Bible, and more particularly the writers of the Dead Sea Scrolls records, knew the format of structures and ceremonies pertaining to Akhetaton.

The description in 2 Chronicles 4:1 of the altar in King Solomon's Temple, known as the First Temple, specifies: 'He made an altar of bronze 20 cubits long, 20 cubits wide and 10 cubits high'. The description (Exodus 27:1–2) of the altar in the earlier Tabernacle, in the desert of Sinai, is somewhat more modest: 'You shall make the altar of acacia wood, five cubits long, and five cubits wide – the altar is to be square – and three cubits high. Make its horns on the four corners, the horns to be of one piece with it; and overlay it with copper.' Ezekiel

43 also talks about the dimensions of an altar, which roughly conform to the dimensions above. He also talks about four horns projecting upward, an upper base and a surrounding rim of 1 cubit. For him, the stairs leading up to the altar are towards the east and are 14 cubits long.

So what did the altar look like in the Great Temple at Akhetaton? Did the altar in Solomon's Temple resemble the altar in Akhetaton's Great Temple? How do we know anything at all about its design?

There are three distinct sources of information for knowledge of Akhetaton: the evidence of archaeology at the site; drawings and inscriptions on the walls of the tombs of the nobles to the north and east of the vast plain of Amarna; images and inscriptions on reconstructed *talatat* building blocks that were taken away from Akhetaton during its destruction and recycled in other buildings around Egypt.

A scaled reconstruction of the sanctuary and the altar area can be made, based on archaeological studies. This shows that the altar in the Hebrew Tabernacle, described in the Bible, was almost exactly half the size of the altar in the Great Temple, whilst the dimensions of the altar in Solomon's Temple were almost exactly double those of the altar in the Great Temple. Both the Tabernacle and the First Temple in Jerusalem copied the square shape of the Amarna altar.

The height of the altar at Amarna is difficult to determine from archaeological work, but we have another firm clue, which helps in the analysis. A detailed drawing of the Amarna sanctuary can still be seen on the wall of the tombs of the high priest at Akhetaton, Meryre I. The Egyptians at this time were not able to show images in three dimensions and used overlays of two dimensional representations to illustrate a third dimension. It is therefore not easy to determine the dimensions of the altar from the wall relief, except in relative terms to other objects depicted. However, the proportions of the altar are clearly seen in the sideways drawing and the height of the altar can be calculated as 60% of the width – almost exactly the same as the ratio of height to width for the Tabernacle. In Solomon's Temple the height is 50% of the width of the altar. Since construction of the Tabernacle preceded that of the Jerusalem Temple by about 200 years, it is only to be expected that the central feature would be more accurately remembered.

Close examination of the illustration of the altar on the wall of the high priest's tomb at Akhetaton, in the left-hand bottom corner, and in the centre of the upper square section showing the altar laden down with offerings, show that the top surface of the altar edges appears to curve upwards to form what were referred to as 'horns' in later designs of sacrificial altars.

Interestingly, in the lower left-hand section of the relief can be seen accoutrements of the sanctuary, including a hide shape, which is the designation of a copper sheet and, to the right of it, what appear to be rolled-up scrolls. I will say more about these shortly.

Another illustration of the altar appears on the tomb wall of Huya at Amarna. An illustration which I have previously pointed out carries an unmistakable representation of the figure of the Patriarch Joseph (see *The Mystery of the Copper Scroll of Qumran*). Here the blocks leading up to the altar are clearly illustrated with 13 (possibly 15 to reach ground level) on the top surface, and 17 on the lower part, with what is apparently a border running up the side of the stairway. To represent a third dimension another view is shown in the two-dimensional drawing as underneath or on top of the two-dimensional picture. Here the length of the stairway is almost exactly 14 cubits, just as described in Ezekiel 43, and the ramp illustrated in the tomb of Huya, at Amarna, clearly shows that there was a border running alongside the steps of the ramp, just as described by Ezekiel.

To summarize: the details of the altar described in various parts of the Hebrew Bible match almost exactly, or are in simple ratio to, those known to have existed in the Great Temple at Amarna and are as follows:

1 Both altars were square.
2 The tops of both altars had four horns, one on each corner.
3 The altar described for the Tabernacle was almost exactly half, and the altar in Solomon's Temple almost exactly double, the size of the altar in the Great Temple.
4 The direction of the stairway leading up to both altars was eastwards.
5 The stairway for the Amarna Temple was almost exactly 14 cubits long, with a half cubit border, just as described in Ezekiel 43, and the ramp illustrated in the tomb of Huya, at Amarna, clearly shows that there was a border running alongside the steps of the ramp, just as described by Ezekiel.[26]

Fresco of King Akhenaton riding his royal chariot, in the tomb of Panehesy, Amarna.

Drawing of a relief on the wall of the tomb of Apy at Amarna, showing twelve loaves of bread on the table in front of the altar.

Images of Queen Nefertiti and King Akhenaton marked with the early Christian symbols of the alpha and omega, in the tomb of Panaehesy at Amarna. To the left is the baptismal font carved out by early followers of Jesus.

Examples of clay jars and containers found at Amarna and now in the Petrie Museum. Similar-shaped jars have been found at Qumran and at Ain Feshka.

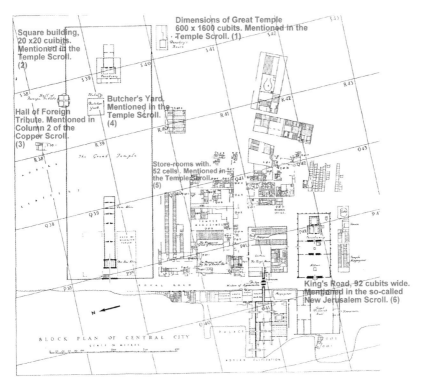

Square building, 20 x20 cubits. Mentioned in the Temple Scroll. (2)

Dimensions of Great Temple 600 x 1600 cubits. Mentioned in the Temple Scroll. (1)

Hall of Foreign Tribute. Mentioned in Column 2 of the Copper Scroll. (3)

Butcher's Yard. Mentioned in the Temple Scroll. (4)

Store-rooms with 52 cells. Mentioned in the Temple Scroll. (5)

King's Road, 92 cubits wide. Mentioned in the so-called New Jerusalem Scroll. (6)

Plan of the city of Akhetaton.

(Left to right) George Brooke, Hanan Eshel and Lutz Doering at the Brown University conference on the Dead Sea Scrolls in November 2002.

Excavations at Qumran by the Magen/Peleg team in 2002, during which they claimed to have found evidence that the site was a pottery factory.

Elephantine Island viewed from the direction of Aswan, showing huge boulders shaped like elephants that made the Greeks change its name from Yeb to Elephantine.

Geza Vermes, Emeritus
Professor of Jewish
Studies at Oxford
University.

John Franks, the man
who freed up publication
of the Scrolls.

Professor Emanuel Tov, the last editor-in-chief of the Dead Sea Scrolls
publication team, at a lecture in Manchester.

Examples of *shabtis* carrying mattocks, on display in the Metropolitan Museum, New York.

John Marco Allegro with a mattock he excavated at Khirbet Qumran.

Pottery fragment with lettering identical to that used by a scribe who wrote one of the Dead Sea Scrolls.

Scene from the window of appearances, showing mattocks on the end of the Aton rays.

Józef Milik (*left*) with Robert Feather in Paris, 2001.

Professor Harold Ellens (*right*) with Robert Feather.

The possibility that these details were included in the Hebrew Bible and, by chance, almost exactly mirrored the dimensions known to have existed in Akhenaton's Great Temple at Akhetaton, is the hardest possible evidence. It is beyond credibility that it is coincidental. It has to be concluded that knowledge of the size and layout of the altar at Akhetaton was brought out by eyewitnesses, or a copy of the temple's plan somehow became available to the biblical writers.

The lower image in plate 1 in the colour section of this book comes from a scene in the Great Temple at Akhetaton and shows priests in a ceremony waving a palm sheaf. The clinching evidence is the four binding rings wrapped around the long palm. These palm-leaf wrappings are not part of the palm, but were added to bind the fronds together. They appear in the same manner, position and number as on the palm fronds used today in synagogue services.

If there can be any lingering doubt that some of the festival ceremonies enacted in synagogues today are rooted in ceremonies that were introduced at the time of Jacob and Joseph in the Great Temple of Akhetaton, a visit to the first floor of the Museum of Luxor will dispel it. Engraved on a long wall, composed of reconstructed *talatat* showing scenes in and around the Great Temple of Akhetaton, is the figure of a priest parading a covered, decorated scroll. The Tree of Life (Hebrew *Etz Chayim*) central binding pole and disk ends are designed in precisely the same manner as the Torah scrolls that are carried around synagogues to this day. This is not a happening seen in any other temple in Egypt, or anywhere else for that matter. There are dozens of examples across Egypt, carved on temple and tomb walls, of papyrus scrolls being carried or *in situ*, but there are no other examples of a scroll matching that being paraded in the Great Temple at Akhetaton.

Close examination of the scroll cover shows that it might actually have been incised on copper, with decorations of pomegranates – Hebrew *rimonim*, a traditional Hebrew emblem for fertility – a decoration said to have been used on the robe of the high priest (Exodus 28:33). The two cartouches on the cover of the elevated scroll appear to carry emblems related to the Aton.

I believe this kind of revelation does not devalue the authenticity of modern Judaism or of the Hebrew scriptures. On the contrary, it verifies the ultimate antiquity of its traditions and the reality of its central characters like Jacob and Joseph. In effect, it confirms that many of the stories of the Hebrew scriptures are not, as some detracting minimalists claim, based on fiction and myth, but instead on hard, engraved fact.

How exactly the images of the festival processions of the Lulav and Torah scroll being paraded around the Great Temple at Akhetaton came to be repeated in the Jerusalem Temple, and are copied right down to this day, is a matter of conjecture. The fact that there is no certain record of the transmission mechanism in no way contradicts the assertion that it must have happened. One can speculate that a mental picture of the processions may have been carried out by Hebrews or diaspora priests when the Great Temple was destroyed. However, to recreate the elevated scroll so precisely would have been difficult. I prefer to conclude that a precursor of the Torah scroll was carried out of Egypt by Moses – perhaps as the 'Testament', which we are told in Exodus, was kept in the Ark of the Covenant.

In relation to the waving of the sheaves, it makes sense that Levi, Joseph's brother, and some of his attendants, may have held a priestly role in the Great Temple and that Joseph put some of these Levitical priests in charge of preparations for the binding of the sheaves, in his role as vizier and superintendent of crop storage. They would, therefore, have been in an ideal position to become acquainted with the binding procedures and pass them down *'d'or v'dor'*, generation by generation.

There is another possibility. Some time between the destruction of Akhetaton and its Great Temple and the construction of the First Temple in Jerusalem, some Hebrews might have made a nostalgic journey to Amarna – to the birthplace of their religion. They would have been confronted with a scene of utter devastation, but around the site of the destroyed city the tombs of Akhenaton and his officials would still have been intact, as they are to this day. They could also have seen some of the 15 boundary stelae in isolated places that encircled the site of the city, with visual records of Akhenaton and Nefertiti. Perhaps some of the drawings on the walls of some of the tombs would have awakened long-neglected memories of the splendours of the holy city. They would have seen examples of the layout of the Great Temple and scenes from inside its courtyards. However, the scenes I quote, of the carrying of the scrolls in the Great Temple of Amarna, would not have been available to them, as, when the city was destroyed within 30 or 40 years of Akhenaton's death, these particular images were broken up and carted off to Luxor for re-use.

All of these mechanisms of transmission might have been supplemented by material taken out from Akhetaton and eventually brought out in the exodus. All of these suggested mechanisms of transmission apply equally to the other similarities already discussed.

The King's Law

The dating and interpretation of the Temple Scroll is an ongoing contentious issue. According to Lawrence Schiffman the scroll's date hinges on the meaning of a section in it known in Hebrew as *Torah Ha-Melech* ('Law of the King'). Professor Schiffman says this section contains 'the clearest references to historical events'. He concludes that legal and historical material in the scroll point to the Hasmonean period, citing the reigns of Jonathan (160–143 BC) and John Hyrcanus (135–104 BC) for the dates of the composition.[27] Yet this assumption is fraught with difficulties, and Professors Hartmut Stegemann, Johann Maier and Hans Burgmann date its composition to several centuries earlier. Professor Stegemann is scathing about people who think the Temple Scroll relates to Hasmonean or Herodian times and places it in the early post-exilic period.[28] I agree with the three professors in that the scroll may have been copied in these periods, and indeed that it was not composed in Hasmonean or Herodian times. But I believe the composition of the scroll dates to a still earlier era for the following reasons.

Much of the sense of this section on the Law can be seen to come from sources in the Hebrew scriptures, but descriptions of regulations relating to the queen, provision of a round-the-clock royal bodyguard, the king's army council, conscription in the case of war and division of booty are not found in the Bible. The stipulation regarding the queen in fact goes against the Bible in requiring the king to stay with her all the days of her life; in the Bible it is entirely permissible for the wife to be 'sent away'.[29]

The question of where the author of the Temple Scroll got his information from has always been a conundrum. It may not now be a surprise to discover that the circumstances in the Temple Scroll are closely aligned to what we know about Pharaoh Akhenaton and Queen Nefertiti. If the king being referred to was Akhenaton, we know from inscriptional records that he remained, for a pharaoh, unusually faithful to his wife, and that he was constantly attended by bodyguards. Assuming a background of Akhetaton, and that the requirements of the Law of the King related to an idealized renewal in Israel, many of the anomalies of the Temple Scroll fall away and reasonable explanations are forthcoming. For example, the phrase 'He should not return the people to Egypt for war' which appears in the Temple Scroll, makes little sense for any candidate kings of Judaea or Israel unless there was some locus in Egypt. The king's army council is aptly described in Cyril Aldred's insightful *Akhenaten, King of Egypt*.[30] The army commanders 'formed a council of management around the king, like henchmen around their warlord' – in almost a paraphrase of the description in the Temple Scroll:

> All those selected, which he selects, shall be men of truth, venerating God, enemies of bribery, skilled men in war, and they shall always be with him day and night . . . He will have twelve princes of his people with him and twelve priests and twelve Levites who shall sit next to him for judgment and for the law. He shall not divert his heart from them or do anything in all his councils without relying on them. No decisions on going to war were made without their consultation.[31]

The author of the Temple Scroll, in fact asserts that the words of God in the Temple Scroll relate to a one-time revelation in Sinai, (c1200 BC) and the entire setting of the instruction in the Temple Scroll is for Israel *before* the people enter the land of Canaan. It is certainly feasible that the style of copying of the text might reflect its composition at a much later date (Perhaps around 700–600 BC), and the content might have been modified by knowledge of that period. For the original author or authors, however, to have included eyewitness accounts of contemporary events relating to kings of that period would have completely blown their cover and undermined claims for a setting in Sinai of hundreds of years earlier. No contemporary reader would believe what was being said.

Most commentators assert that the scroll draws on sections of scripture – Exodus and Leviticus, but particularly Deuteronomy – whose composition is generally dated to the reign of King Josiah in the 6th century BC, but this assumption does not make sense. As Professor Ben Zion Wacholder has shrewdly noted, Deuteronomy flies in the face of the beliefs of the teachings in Ezekiel and is not likely to have been acceptable as a source to the author of the Temple Scroll and the sectarians of Qumran, who placed such esteem in the Temple Scroll and Ezekiel. Deuteronomy 1:1–4, like the Temple Scroll, has its premise at the time of Moses, before entry into the Promised Land:

> These are the words that Moses addressed to all Israel on the other side of the Jordan . . . It was in the fortieth year, on the first day of the eleventh month, that Moses addressed the Israelites in accordance with the instructions that the Lord had given him for them . . .[32]

The Temple Scroll commences in the same time frame, but unlike Deuteronomy, it is not Moses who is speaking to the people, but God Himself:

> For it is something dreadful that I will do to you. I myself will expel from before you the Amorites, the Canaanites, the Hittites, the Girgashites, the Perizzites, the Hivites, and the Jebusites. Take care not to make a covenant with the inhabitants of the country *which you are to enter* so that they may not prove a snare for you. [*Beginning of the Temple Scroll 11QT 27; my emphasis*]

The Temple Scroll is unambiguous. It was composed before the Israelites entered the land of Canaan, that is c1200 BC.

This conclusion is reinforced by one of the more perplexing narratives in the Temple Scroll. The author asserts that the Lord revealed to Jacob at Bethel, as he did to Levi (confirmed in another Dead Sea Scroll, the Testament of Levi), that the Levites would be the priests in the temple of the Lord. There is no such mention in the Bible, where the Levites are not appointed as priests until the time of the Tabernacle and Moses. This identification of Levitical priests prior to their appointment by Moses implies a history for the Temple Scroll dating back to the time of the patriarchs Joseph and Jacob, and inevitably their contemporary Pharaoh Akhenaton.

Aramaic fragments of the Testament of Levi found at Qumran refer to the coming 'reign of the sword' and 'anointing of Levi', and making him 'greater than anyone'. He is then dressed in priestly clothing by Jacob and invested as the highest priest.[33] Another clear example of the understanding the Qumran-Essenes had of the earliest role of priests comes from 4Q 213–14. Here Levi is talking about his father, Jacob, as he goes about tithing (giving a tenth of all he earns or grows) to God, while Levi is for the first time at the head of a procession of priests and Joseph teaches Torah (from holy scrolls). The setting is a place with an altar, presumably a temple, which is being used to make offerings to God. All these functions are testified to by wall reliefs and archaeological finds at Amarna, and yet the period must be several hundred years before Moses appoints any priests and 400 years before there is a Temple in Jerusalem. Views of a line of Egyptian priests, unusually interspersed with a foreign-looking priest – whom I identify as a Hebrew from his headgear and garb – can still be seen at Amarna, as can the parading of what appears to be a Sefer Torah-style scroll as used in synagogues today. Offering jars, labelled as tithes, have also been found at Amarna.

The evidence is there for anyone to see in the Museum at Luxor, and in Cairo, London, New York, and in many other museums and sites in Egypt, as well as in my previous books.

Jacob fights with an Angel

There is another intriguing episode relating to Jacob that warrants consideration. In the middle of Genesis 32, from verse 25 onwards, a very intrusive, bizarre episode is dropped into the storyline:

> Jacob was resting [near the River Jabbok] alone. And a man [generally assumed to be an angel] wrestled with him until the break of dawn. When he saw that he had not prevailed against him, he wrenched Jacob's hip at its socket, so that the socket of his hip was strained as he wrestled with him. Then he said, 'Let me go, for dawn is breaking.' But he answered, 'I will not let you go, unless you bless me.' The other said, 'What is

your name?' [Odd that the angel/man should attack a person whose name he did not know.] He replied, 'Jacob.' Said he, 'Your name shall no longer be Jacob, but Israel, for you have striven with beings divine and human, and have prevailed.' Jacob said, 'Pray tell me your name.' But he said, 'You must not ask my name!' And he took leave of him there. So Jacob named the place Peniel, meaning, 'I have seen a divine being face to face, yet my life has been preserved.' The sun rose upon him as he passed Penuel [apparently an alternative spelling of Peniel], limping on his hip, since Jacob's hip socket was wrenched at the thigh muscle.

So what is going on here? I believe this is another example of the scribes or priests writing up the history of the Hebrews and drawing on distant handed-down memories of the period they believed relevant to the story, and filling in details with filtered memories. Commenting on this passage, Rashi, the great French rabbi of the Middle Ages, said that it relates to the articulation of the hips and that the Hebrew letter *kaf* signifies the spoon-shaped socket of the hip becoming deeply rounded and potentially causing a problem.[34]

One image, or recollection, that may have come down to the scribes was the unusual physical stature of Akhenaton and his prominent wide hips. The elongated limbs and wide hips exhibited by Akhenaton, seen in a number of statues and illustrations of him, have led some medical experts to suspect that he and some members of this family may have suffered from a disease called Marfan syndrome. A symptom of this disease is that the socket of the hip joint, or acetabulum, becomes deeper than normal during childhood growth, leading to a condition known as *protrusio acetabulae*, which, in adulthood, can result in the affected person developing a limp. Did the biblical authors insert this passage in recognition of a story they knew was significant, but did not understand why?

Naming the Pharaoh Sarai Encountered

An even clearer example of this kind of attempt to recreate the setting for the early biblical period of Abraham comes from Genesis 14:14 where we are told he maintained a household with 318 retainers. This must have equated to a very large mansion, comparable with a palace. Abraham would not have been a contemporary of Akhenaton, but the scribes may have used information they had about Akhenaton's father, Amenhotep III, who maintained a household of 317 retainers[35] to dignify Abraham at the level of an Egyptian king they knew something about.

How could the Hebrew scribes have learned any details about the inner workings of a pharaoh's household? A clue to the dates of Abraham comes in Genesis 12, early in his lifetime, before his name was changed to Abraham and his wife's name to Sarah. Abram and Sarai venture into Egypt to seek food, and the ruling pharaoh learns of Sarai's stunning beauty, through one of his courtiers. Neither the courtier nor the pharaoh is named in the Hebrew Bible, but the courtier is named in the Dead Sea Scrolls version of the story. Sarai is taken to his palace and would therefore have been able to relay details of the inner workings of his household when she is eventually returned to Abram. I quote from a version of the Genesis Apocryphon (a scroll found in cave 1 at Qumran) by Daniel A. Machiela:

> Now there was a famine in all of this land, and I heard that there wa[s] w[h]eat in Egypt. So I set out to go . . . [ ] to the land that is in Egypt . . . [ ] . . . and there was [ ] I [reached] the Carmon River, one of the heads of the River, [I] sai[d] '. . . [ ]. . . [until] now we have been within our land.' So I crossed over the seven heads of this river, which af[terwards en]ters [int]o the Great Sea [o]f Salt.[36]

The Genesis Apocryphon contains much more detail about this period of biblical history than any known Bible, and the above section includes quite an astonishing revelation. We are told Abram reaches the River Carmon or Qharmon (Hebrew לכרמונא) and crosses seven branches of the Nile.

The ancient Nile delta branches have been recognized in various historical maps. There were between three and 16 distributaries, though most of them have now silted up. In the 1960s, Manfred Bietak traced all the former branches of the Nile and dated them by the pottery found on their former banks. It was found that the Tanitic branch of the Nile did not exist during Ramses' reign, and that the

Pelusiac branch was at that time the easternmost one. It is now known that the Pelusiac branch began silting up c1060 BC, leaving the city without water when the river eventually re-established a new course to the west now called the Tanitic branch.[37] It would therefore seem impossible for anyone writing about the Nile after 1,000 BC to have been aware that prior to that date it had seven distributaries, which, as far as can be ascertained the river had at some period in the 19th to the mid-18th Dynasties, that is 1570–1350 BC. This indicates that the Genesis Apocryphon preserved the record of an eyewitness memory or knowledge of the geography of the delta region, perhaps dating back to the time of Abram himself.

The description of Abram and Sarai's venture into Egypt, as recorded in the Genesis Apocryphon, actually names the Pharaoh they encounter:

> and three men from nobles of Egypt. . . his [ ]. . . by Phara[oh] Zoan because of my words and my wisdom, and they were giving m[e many gifts They as]ked erudition and wisdom and truth for themselves, so I read before them the book of the words of Enoch.

Whereas the Hebrew Bible simply says Sarai was 'a beautiful woman', in the Dead Sea Scrolls version we have a full, rapturous description of her beauty:

> . . . how irresistible and beautiful is the image of her face; how lovely h[er] foreh[ead, and] soft the hair of her head! How graceful are her eyes, and how precious her nose; every feature of her face is radiating beauty! How lovely is her breast, and how beautiful her white complexion! As for her arms, how beautiful they are! And her hands, how perfect they are! Every view of her hands is stimulating! How graceful are her palms, and how long and thin all the fingers of her hands! Her feet are of such beauty, and her legs so perfectly apportioned! There is not a virgin or bride who enters the bridal chamber more beautiful than she. Her beauty surpasses that of all women, since the height of her beauty soars above them all! And alongside all this beauty she possesses great wisdom. Everything about her is just

right! Now when the king heard the words of Herqanos and his two companions – that the three of them spoke as one – he greatly desired her, and sent someone to be quick in acquiring her. When he saw her he was dumbfounded by all of her beauty, and took her for himself as a wife.

No wonder pharaoh became obsessed with taking her into his court and into his bed, but who was Pharaoh Zoan?

For those who have patiently waited to discover the name of the pharaoh alluded to earlier in this chapter, it may be disappointing to learn that Zoan was a place rather than a pharaoh, and probably a place where the pharaoh who desired Sarai resided at the time of his interest. Zoan was an ancient city of Lower Egypt, called Tanis by the Greeks, meaning 'place of departure', located on the eastern bank of the Tanitic branch of the Nile. It existed in its earlier course long before the time of Abraham, and Ramses II, in the period of the Exodus, and is mentioned in the Bible.[38] The clue to the pharaoh's name comes in Column 20:8 of the Apocryphon above where we learn the name of the courtier who brought Sarai to the pharaoh. He was 'Herqanos'. In another section of the Genesis Apocryphon the courtier's name is given as 'Hyrcanus'. They are almost certainly one and the same.

My attention was drawn to the name Herqanos in 2000 by Esther Hanan, who was working on the Genesis Apocryphon and asked me to try and identify the Hebrew name in Egyptian records. After a protracted investigation I found a close match for the courtier's name in an obscure hieroglyph record designating a court official by the name of 'HqAnkAS' dating to the mid–15th century BC, from which it is possible to infer the name of the pharaoh who sanctioned the kidnapping of Sarai as Thutmose III, who ruled 1457–1425 BC.[39] Apologies to Esther Eshel for taking so long to come back to her with an answer!

Back to the Temple Scroll

So where did the Temple Scroll originate from? Who composed it? Why does it advocate such different ideas from the conventional biblical prescriptions? I do not profess to have all the answers, but without doubt the confusion amongst scholars in comprehending its difficult passages suggests that something fundamental is being missed.

Some key elements in the original background to the Temple Scroll are not being understood.

The most likely scenario is that the Temple Scroll was assembled from previously existing texts, combining oral and/or written information, and that it was written down not too long after King Solomon banished the Benei Zadok-1 from the Temple in Jerusalem and exiled the High Priest Abiathar to Anathoth. There appear to be five separate sections of text, dealing with five different topics, and I quote Professor Stegemann, for part of this reasoning:

> The breakthrough to a more adequate valuation of the textual complexity of the Temple Scroll was provided by Andrew M. Wilson and Lawrence Wills, with many helpful suggestions from John Strugnell. Starting from the division of the Temple Scroll into five different sections on the basis of their contents, they conclude that at least the bodies, or main parts, of these sections were at the same time literary sources, independent documents, which the author utilized in the composition of his final book.[40]

One of the sections, the 'Law of the King', is an example of sustained original writing in the Temple Scroll. It does not rely to any significant extent on rewritten scripture. When the Temple Scroll speaks of laws and oaths, it has a totally different agenda, literary form, exegetical technique and end results. There is little agreement with the Book of Jubilees and other Dead Sea Scroll edicts which castigate the Temple authorities over questions of law and procedure. For conventional understanding, as Professor Schiffman maintains: 'It is impossible to show direct correspondence between the Temple Scroll and the other systems of Jewish law as known from the available sources.'

This last statement would not be a surprise if what I claim is true: that the Temple Scroll records conditions and rules for a much earlier time prevailing in the Amarna period in Egypt.

The New Jerusalem Scroll

If there is one other Dead Sea Scroll group of texts, not known from any previous source, which sets intractable problems for scholars, it is the so-called New Jerusalem Scroll. I say so-called, because that label is a complete misnomer. It never ever mentions the word Jerusalem, and it should be renamed the New Amarna Scroll, something that becomes patently transparent as we unravel the true sense of its contents.

Several examples of the scroll were found in Caves 1, 2, 4, 5 and 11, and the Herodian Aramaic orthography of the text has been dated to the late part of the 1st century BC and early part of the 1st century AD. Although the various recovered pieces of the scroll probably amount to only half of the original, there are meticulous descriptions of the planning of an enclosed temple city, its streets and houses, the temple and ceremonies conducted in the temple, the Holy of Holies, the High Priest, the priests' rotas, Sabbath and other ceremonies, and a scenario for the End Days.

It soon becomes clear that the New Jerusalem Scroll is talking about a location for the temple quite different from Jerusalem and that it has a tendency to detract from the sanctity of King Solomon's temple, the first temple to be built in Jerusalem, and favour the design of the Tabernacle. There are some similarities to the description in Ezekiel, with the author being conducted around by an angelic guide, whereas in the Temple Scroll the commentary comes directly from God. In the New Jerusalem Scroll and the Temple Scroll, the order of descriptions is opposite to that in Ezekiel, going from inside the temple to outside.

One common denominator of all three sources is that none of them mentions Jerusalem, or defines Israel as the setting for the temple being described. Most scholars express surprise at these omissions, but some take the view that these works had to be talking about Jerusalem and therefore there was no need for it to be mentioned. Detailed analysis of each of the sources soon elucidates that none of them can possibly be talking about Jerusalem. Instead, when the translated text of the New Jerusalem Scroll is considered in detail, it immediately becomes obvious to anyone with a modicum of familiarity with Egyptian phrasing and content that there are Egyptian cognates. I cite a few examples.

Column 3 refers to the placement of seven crowns on the head of the high priest. This procedure is not known from any other scriptural source. Nor would knowledge of the seven crowns be available to others outside the inner circles of the Egyptian court (it was unknown by Western historians until relatively recently). Traditionally, the pharaoh would wear several different crowns indicating his (or her) area of authority for a particular event. We now know that the seven crowns were the: Atef Crown; Double Pschent Crown; Red Crown; Blue Khepresh Crown; Hemhem Crown; White Crown; and the Nemes Crown. Awareness of the seven crowns implies an intimate knowledge of Egyptian ceremonial procedures, dating back to at least the 18th Dynasty.

Column 4 refers to a throne in the Great Hall, near to the holy of holies, on which the king or possibly high priest would have sat. Written in Aramaic as כורסיא – *kûrsiyā* – the word is repeated three times, and is taken as a version of the biblical word '*kisse*', the seat of judgment where the Israelite king would sit. The term *kûrsiyā* appears in other ancient languages of the 13th and 14th centuries BC and, significantly, is found in the El-Amarna letters received by Pharaoh Akhenaton and his father Amenhotep III, in correspondence between vassal states and Egypt. For these reasons it seems much more likely that the biblical word was derived from the much earlier Aramaic-Akkadian word, before the Bible was even written down in Hebrew.

Michael Chyutin, in a defining comprehensive reconstruction of the meaning of the New Jerusalem Scroll, comes to some remarkable conclusions, but does not follow through to deduce the full significance of his findings.

There is no mention in the Bible of a throne in the temples in Jerusalem, but we know there was a throne in the Great Temple at Akhetaton. In his monumental study, Chyutin has no reservation in stating that: 'In my opinion, the kûrsiyā which appears in the ceremony described in the New Jerusalem Scroll is a real throne that served as a seat for the High Priest during the ceremony.'[41] I agree with Chyutin on the reality of the proceedings and the throne, although as the high priest is not mentioned in Column 4, I am inclined to believe the throne refers to a seat for the king, Akhenaton, or one possibly used by both.

Whilst the Bible describes ceremonies that were held in the court of the temple, it says very little about the ceremonies held inside the temple building itself, with only the priests and king present. The New Jerusalem Scroll reveals ceremonies unknown in tradition, in which the high priest is crowned with seven crowns and reads from the Book of the Temple, receives gifts, presides over the ceremony of changing the priestly shifts, and finally enters the Holy of Holies. None of these actions can be reconciled with a Jerusalem temple setting and mean that the so-called New Jerusalem Scroll must be talking about a different temple.

Because of the undoubted knowledge the author has of Egyptian protocols, and because some of his (or her) original statements can be cross-checked with realities existing in Akhetaton, the conclusion can only be that the scroll is describing real scenes inside and around the Great Temple at Akhetaton.

Columns 6 and 7 refer to sapphire doors, the altar covered in copper, and walls made of pure gold and overlaid with gold. As a virgin city, we know from archaeological studies that Akhetaton was constructed with the prolific use of precious stones, including red marble and jasper (mentioned in Column 16), and gleaming white lime materials. Copper, in a temple context, was considered as a metal of the gods and of special intrinsic religious significance. When you visit the 'Amarna Room' on the ground floor of the Cairo Museum, you will see a large section of what must have been a temple wall coated in thin gold foil.

Column 7 also refers to a wall which surrounds 'living water'. Living water, in a biblical sense, always means a natural flowing stream or river. There is, of course, no 'living water' near the Temple of Jerusalem, but there was at Akhetaton – the Nile.

Column 10 reads as follows: '. . . into the Great Hall . . . and they baked twelve loaves . . . And they took the loaves and they set them in two rows, six loaves in each row upon the pure table.' Crucially, the table before the altar in the desert Tabernacle of the Israelites was also, according to biblical instruction (Leviticus 24:5–6), specifically required to contain 12 cakes of bread, *just as they are seen on the offering table in front of the altar of the Great Temple at Akhetaton*. Examples of this procedure, where the bread is placed foremost on top of jars of wine, can be seen in the tombs of Apy and Panehesy at Amarna.[42]

Column 20 says: '. . . and he showed me all the houses that are inside the boundaries of the city'. Whilst the ancient city of Jerusalem was almost certainly surrounded by a protective wall, explorations have shown that Akhetaton was demarcated by 15 boundary stelae, rather than walls.

The New Jerusalem Scroll descriptions of the courts, the colonnades and the gates are radically different from those given in Ezekiel, Josephus and the Mishnah tractate *Middot*, and when we come on to the overall conclusions of Michael Chyutin we will see why.[43]

As the guided tour moves outside the temple, we get detailed description of the surrounding houses and streets. It is here that I turn again to Michael Chyutin's analysis.

Starting near the walls of the temple, there is mention, in Column 14, of a 'House of Joy', the meaning of which is not understood by conventional translators. There is no biblical reference to such a building in the Jerusalem temple. The explanation comes from the images of the Temple seen in tombs at Amarna, which include an area designated as the 'House of Rejoicing'. We then move to a vast bounded area measuring 100 x 140 *ris* or 18.5 x 26km (where a *ris* is 350 cubits. The *ris* was based on the length of the side of the Great Pyramid of Cheops at Giza of 440 royal cubits = 1.25 *stadia*, and the perimeter of the base of the pyramid is 5 *stadia*, as reported in ancient Greek sources. The *stadia* are called *ris* in the Mishnah, and appear to be the same measurement as used in the New Jerusalem Scroll). The city plan is an orthogonal grid of streets of different widths, enclosing blocks of houses. The sides of these blocks are 51 rods = 357 cubits, surrounding alleys of 21 cubits and streets of 42 cubits. When you compare the city area and the total area encompassed by the boundary stelae, derived from archaeological surveys of Amarna, it is seen that they mirror the dimensions given in the Temple Scroll.

The scroll says that within the residential areas there are 'communal eating houses' with 22 couches for a large number of people to eat together. This practice would seem to be quite unusual, but makes a direct connection to the practice at Qumran. Both Josephus and Philo say that communal meals were one of the defining characteristics of the Essene sect. The practice is indicated in an apocryphal psalm from Qumran, which refers to eating and drinking in community together, whilst the Rule of the Community Scroll talks of assemblies of members of the sect. Chyutin notes the connection and comments: 'The description of these eating houses, halls for communal gathering, perhaps hints at a connection between the description of the city and the custom of the sect.'

Chyutin does not follow through to deduce the full significance of his findings. Having made the connection, he fails to follow up on the implications, even when he comes to the astounding conclusion in his assessment of the city plan, as set out in the New Jerusalem Scroll, that it patterns the layout of the city of Akhetaton. This conclusion was also reached by another Israeli architect, Shlomo Margalit.

Running along the east–west axis of the city there are three main streets, two are 70 cubits wide and the third, running from the temple, is 126 cubits wide. This is referred to by Michael Chyutin as the 'King's Way'. The north–south axis has three main streets, two of which are 67 cubits wide and the third is 92 cubits wide. These streets are exceptionally wide for an Egyptian city, or for any city of the ancient Middle East.

When you compare the layout, direction, widths and lengths of the street plan derived from archaeological surveys of the central area of Akhetaton, it is seen that they mirror the descriptions and dimensions given in the New Jerusalem Scroll.

Akhetaton, Sesebi and Elephantine

In analyzing the plans of the temple and city described in the New Jerusalem Scroll, Chyutin finds he cannot make sense of the dimensions unless he uses an Egyptian cubit unit. When he does this, he comes to a number of important conclusions. He firstly recognizes the grid pattern of the street plans, defined by closed enclosures as residences, temples, storehouses, army barracks and palaces, and concludes that Akhetaton is the closest fit of any cities known from history. The other places he singles out as fitting the layout described in the New Jerusalem Scroll is Sesebi, and, rather surprisingly, the Hebrew settlement on Yeb/Elephantine island in the far south of Egypt, near Aswan – and incidentally the similarity also applies to Medinet Habu, but that is another story. These remarkable conclusions seem to be completely ignored by conventional scholarship, as this has no explanation for the relationships.

Michael Chyutin is also at a total loss to explain why the author of the scroll should choose, or even know about the design of an ancient Egyptian city, and comments:

> Why did the author of the Scroll describe a city planned in
> an archaic Egyptian style, rather than describing a Greek city

or a Roman castrum? It is almost certain that at the time the Scroll was composed, Alexandria, a Greek hippodamic city, was a flourishing and familiar city. The Roman castrum too was well known in every place where a Roman legion was encamped. It is probable that the author of the Scroll wished to create an archaic model of description of the city, and to return to an ancient tradition of city building. The New Jerusalem appears like a city planned during the period of the First Temple, the times of King David and Solomon, when the Egyptian influence on the material culture in the land of Israel was strong.[44]

His instincts are, I believe, basically correct, but he has no rationale to explain why the author should want to recreate this early period in the first place. Even at the time of the first kings of Israel, Jerusalem bore no resemblance to the city described in the New Jerusalem Scroll.

As, I think, has now been firmly established, the Qumran-Essenes and their texts were well aware of Akhetaton. On the face of it, the towns at Sesebi and on Elephantine island might not be expected to be involved in the connections, but there are good reasons why. Sesebi, located near the 4th Cataract of the Nile was also built by Akhenaton, so it is not surprising he applied the same designs.[45] The reasons for the similarity of Elephantine's town layout are not quite so obvious.

Chyutin, and other independent assessors of the city layout, show that the ancient paleo-Hebrew settlement on Elephantine island follows the pattern described in the scroll. Not only is the overall town of similar design, but the houses are similar to those described in the scroll, typically being of two storeys surrounding a central courtyard.

So why were the town layout and the houses of the Hebrews who were living on the island until around 400 BC patterned on the same design as those at Akhetaton? The origins of this aberrational community are discussed in detail in my previous book *The Mystery of the Copper Scroll of Qumran*, and the bottom-line conclusion agrees with the conclusions of one of the most comprehensive analyses of the settlement's origins: '. . . that it was a form which could not have existed in a Hebrew group which had been exposed to the influences of Sinai and Canaan after the settlement'.[46] In other words, Maclaurin rules out any possibility, as I do, of the Israelite settlement at Elephantine island having derived from outside Egypt after the exodus. These conclusions are not just based on the design patterns of the town but also on a host of other factors that define the settlement's religious and social structures. Until recently, the position of the temple described in the Aramaic scrolls (known as the Elephantine Papyri) was unknown, but its location and size has now been discovered.

The reason why the town layout and the houses of the pseudo-Hebrews settled on the island were patterned on the same design as that at Akhetaton was that the people who established the original settlement were familiar with the city of Akhetaton. They, or their ancestors, must have fled from the area of Akhetaton in the wake of Pharaoh Akhenaton's death and the destruction of his holy city around 1350 BC.

Numerous unconvincing and conflicting explanations have been put forward to try and explain the anomalous community at Elephantine island, but there is just no other suggested scenario that makes sense. Even the eminent historian Sir Martin Gilbert fudges an explanation. In earlier editions of his *Atlas of Jewish History*, first published in 1969, he ascribes the colony at Elephantine to the dispersions of 722 and 586 BC – the periods of Assyrian and Babylonian conquests of the Northern and Southern Kingdoms of Israel. He arrows the dispersees as being taken from Jerusalem northwards, and also to Alexandria and Elephantine in Egypt.[47] However, neither of these invading powers conquered Egypt as far south as Elephantine and therefore could not have dispersed refugees to the area of Syene or to that island. The map in Gilbert's book also shows Elephantine and Syene in completely the wrong locations. Elephantine is mistakenly positioned 550km further north than it really was. I pointed out the anomaly to him several years ago, orally and in writing, and he agreed that the mistake should be corrected in the next edition of his book. Needless to say, the seventh edition of the book, published in 2008, repeated the errors.

One widely held view is that the community arrived in the time of King Manasseh, who sent soldiers to help the Egyptians under Pharaoh Psammeticus I guard their border with Nubia. This idea makes little sense as there is absolutely no archaeological evidence of any military presence in the colony, or mention of military activity in their writings.

Yeb was not the southern border of Egypt by many kilometres, nor was there much need for it to be guarded as Psammeticus II led an invasion into Nubia (Kush) in 592 BC inflicting a heavy defeat on the Nubians. Kushite power was crushed, and their threat was nullified thereafter, to such an extent that the Nubian rulers moved their capital much further south from Napata to Meroe.

Another similar conventional understanding is that the settlers were Jews who returned to Egypt after the destruction of the Temple in Jerusalem in 586 BC. This theory fails to explain many anomalies in the practices of the community, for example that they did not follow the Ten Commandments, intermarried with local Egyptians, and appeared to worship more than one god.

In addition to the wealth of evidence for a different understanding of Elephantine presented in my previous books, recent excavations at Dra Abu el-Naga, in the northern area of western Thebes, have unearthed an inscribed wooden board used for writing practice.[48] This is of some significance to the dating of activities at Elephantine. Images on the board indicate it dates from the 18th Dynasty between 1450 and 1320 BC, whilst the reverse side carries a text in hieratic known as the 'Book of Kemit'. It opens with a respectful epistolary formula for the commencement of a letter to a person of superior status. This formula goes back to around 2000 BC. Known as the 'Memphite formula', it fell out of general use after the 18th Dynasty, but astonishingly there is a letter in the Brooklyn Museum, New York, written by a member of the community at Elephantine, which follows the same formula.[49] The Brooklyn letter was written by a son to his father, and has been dated to the 5th century BC, and yet the son was familiar with a form of address long since abandoned in Egyptian writing. The implication is that the people at Elephantine had an awareness of the period of the Pharaoh Akhenaton and continued to use styles and writing their ancestors had learned at his court.

Another clue connecting Elephantine, Jacob, Akhenaton and the Qumran scrolls emerged from publication of the 37th volume of *Discoveries in the Judaean Desert*, in 2009. Preliminary versions of these Aramaic texts were published by Józef Milik many years earlier, but others have been kept back for over 40 years. Many of the Aramaic texts from Qumran indicate a very early provenance. For example,

4Q570 makes repeated use of a final '*mem*', which typifies a very early form of Aramaic lettering, as seen in the Book of Ezra and the Elephantine papyri. We know that these last texts date at least to the 5th century BC and derive from much earlier periods. These texts continually use anonyms and toponyms (oh dear, I've caught some of the jargon disease!) dating to distant antiquity – an unnamed prophet, elect one, a chosen/beloved one, and Egypt, Media, Persia, Assyria, Cush.

Ceremonies

Whilst dimensions and layout comparisons in the Temple Scroll and New Jerusalem Scroll show absolutely certain congruences with Akhetaton, descriptions of previously unknown temple ceremonies and priestly procedures are even more difficult to explain away, especially as these relate to sacrosanct procedures and holiness in the temple. How and why would the authors fabricate completely new religious practices, often in direct contradiction of those spelled out in Torah?

Ceremonies described in the Temple Scroll and New Jerusalem Scroll include:

The Seven Crowns ceremony
The Throne ceremony
The Reading from the Book ceremony
The Changing of the Shifts ceremony
Conclusion of the New Year Sacrifice ceremony
Beginning of the Days of Ordination ceremony
Ceremony of the Sacrifice of the Ram of Ordination
Ceremony of the Sacrifice of the Bull of the Congregation
Beginning of the ceremony of the Showbread
Conclusion of the ceremony of the Showbread
Ceremony of Eating from the Basket and the Ram of Ordination
Passover Sacrifice ceremony
Ceremony of Eating the Passover Sacrifice
Seven Cups and Glasses ceremony

There is not enough space to analyze all the different ceremonies in this book, but we have already seen that the Seven Crowns ceremony can only have originated in Egypt and that the Ceremony of the Showbread is directly dependent on the ceremony played out at Akhenaton's Great Temple. It will not be a surprise to find that most of the ceremonies fall into the same category.

The only ceremonies I could have difficulty with are those listed above referring to Passover. If, as I contend, the congruences are with the Amarna period of the 14th century BC, then the ceremonies cannot describe Passover, a celebration relating to an event which had not yet happened. Indeed, Michael Chyutin believes Columns 11–14 describe the traditional Passover or Feast of the Unleavened Bread ceremony. However, closer examination of the Hebrew text shows that leavened bread is involved, and the setting for the ceremony is in the temple and not in the family home, as specifically prescribed in Exodus 12:3–4. Clearly the ceremony described in the New Jerusalem Scroll is a different ceremony to that celebrating the exodus from Egypt and should not be labelled as a Passover ceremony.[50]

Chapter 14

Christians in the House of Akhenaton!

In the same way that a recent series on Channel 4 of British television, *The Bible As History*, hosted by historian Howard Jacobson, allowed the outlandish claim that Abraham was a Muslim to go unchallenged,[1] there cannot possibly have been Christians at Pharaoh Akhenaton's capital city. However, there is every likelihood that very early adherents of Jesus went there, and perhaps Jesus himself was taken to Akhetaton by his family. Much of the evidence supporting this claim was documented in my book *The Secret Initiation of Jesus at Qumran*,[2] and more work at the site of El-Amarna, conducted by resident archaeologist Barry Kemp in 2006–7, has provided additional information.[3]

There is clear proof that the hillsides were the abode of pilgrims numbering several hundreds, clinging like birds to the summit of the cliffs, in spite of the great inconvenience and dangers in such primitive anchorite dwellings an hour's walk from the River Nile. There is no indication that the first arrivals were Copts, although inscriptions inside the tomb of Panehesy testify that the presence of pilgrims continued on into the Coptic period.[4]

During the period of Pharaoh Akhenaton's reign a number of large tombs were prepared as final resting places for his senior courtiers, as well as for himself and his wife, Nefertiti. The main section of burial chambers runs along the line of hills to the north of the city, and most are still relatively untouched by the ravages of time. No bodies were found in the main sepulchres, but we know who was to be buried where in most of them. Panehesy, Akhenaton's 'Great Favourite and Servitor of the Aton', commanded one of the largest and most highly decorated chambers, situated at the far southern end of the line. Strangely, the figures and cartouches of the Aton, Akhenaton, and Nefertiti were not defaced by visitors to this tomb, as they were in many other tombs. Something else, which is rather peculiar, was the arrival, some time in the early years of the first millennium AD, of what can only have been followers of Jesus. They must have made the arduous journey from Judaea to Amarna and established a presence in Panehesy's tomb. The timing of the arrival of the first pilgrims is not certain, and commentators talk of the tomb being 'later enlarged to become a Coptic Christian church'. As we will see, it was a very unusual church, if it can be called that, as there were none of the usual structures, of an altar or a place for focused worship, or apparently the figure of Christ or a plain cross.

In the Coptic period the pilgrims fashioned a 1.5m/5ft deep niche in the corner of an extensive open area, opposite a large detailed relief of Akhenaton riding his vibrantly coloured chariot, under the bright, glowing rays of the Aton. This niche was evidently used to hold a baptismal font. Above the apse the image of a bird with outstretched wings was decorated onto plaster. Having established their place of worship, one would have thought the pilgrims would have set about obliterating pagan imagery, as occurred in other places that were converted into churches. To the contrary, *there is clear evidence that they venerated the existing reliefs and even worshipped in front of them*. On images of Akhenaton and Nefertiti, adjacent to the apse, they painted the sign of the cross as a *chi* and *rho* in red paint and added the image of a small infant in the arms of Nefertiti. Around the head of the child, almost certainly meant to depict Jesus, they drew a perfect gold circle. On the right-hand side of the tomb they constructed slots allowing them to climb up the relief of Akhenaton and gouged out holes in which to place prayers in the horse-and-chariot areas of the huge relief.

Previous investigations by N. de G. Davies and Richard Lepsius, and others like Wilkinson in the early 20th century, and more recently by M. Jones,[5] indicated the work had been done in the Coptic period of the 2nd and 3rd centuries AD, but recent work by Barry Kemp, Gillian Pyke and Richard Colman,[6] has confirmed what I previously postulated, that the pilgrims arrived at a much earlier time. Although parts of the settlement continued to be occupied until the 6th century AD, it is now seen that the architectural features within the apse are without precedent and at odds with a holy area containing an altar.

The layers of paint in the apse demonstrate there was an earlier phase of decorative work. 'Detailed analysis of both the plaster layers and painted decorations has resulted in the identification of one decorative episode that probably predates the conversion of the tomb into a church, three significant decorative phases, one apparently in two episodes, and a final phase that seems never to have been executed.'[7]

The earliest phase seems to have comprised decoration using a dense hard white matrix containing medium yellow rounded sand and fine black particles. Red lines in the division between the rear wall and dome of the apse also seem to have been created at the same time as the red *chi rho* was painted onto the images of Akhenaton and Nefertiti.

At a later stage a six-winged creature with small birds was added to the top part of the arch of the baptismal font, with acanthus, pomegranate, candles, birds, a peacock and a saint in the surrounding frieze. Both Davies and Jones describe this creature as a 'soaring eagle', likening it to the six-winged seraphim mentioned in Isaiah 6:1–3, except Isaiah's creatures do not have outstretched wings.[8] There is, in fact, no known example in Coptic art of eagles with tri-partite wings. Beasts seen with evangelists are not uncommon in Coptic painting, often also appearing with the enthroned Christ; however, these scenes are usually bi-partite, with the upper section representing Christ in heaven, with four beasts and evangelists occupying the semi-dome or apse. An example of this appears in the nearby monastery of Kom el-Nana, within the precinct of El-Amarna, where we also see cherubim with six wings. Where the pilgrims got their ideas for a six-winged creature is not obvious. Isaiah's six-winged creature seems a possible source. Another possibility might relate to the cherubim of the Songs for the Sabbath Sacrifice.[9] What better image to reproduce in front of the throne-chariot of Akhenaton on the opposite side of the tomb?

The solitary representation of a beast/evangelist is without precedent and the lack of eyes on the wings is problematic. So is the inscription in the entrance portal of the tomb which includes the name Paul, written in Coptic. To quote from work supervised by Barry Kemp between 2007 and 2008:

> The presence of the church at the heart of the community
> confirms that these people shared the Christian faith. It is

difficult to see why the settlement should exist if this is not a monastic foundation, as it would not be a particularly attractive location, requiring supply from the Nile valley, and there is no particular evidence of quarrying or of other industrial activity that might require people to live here.[10]

Kemp and his team were unaware of the reasons I have put forward to explain why a settlement should exist within and around Panehesy's tomb. When I discussed with him the possible motivation being a link to the Qumran-Essenes in Judaea, at an annual meeting of the Egypt Exploration Society, he was sceptical, but admitted he knew almost nothing about Qumran. He was also not prepared to entertain digging for any of the treasures mentioned in the Copper Scroll, as he had a programme of excavations mapped out for the next ten years and would not consider deviating from the plan.

The reason I appear to be labouring the description of the apse in Panehesy's tomb is that it seems to be an original design, for a very special place, not reproduced elsewhere. The saint is the only human figure in the decoration scheme, and he stands alone. His yellow nimbus asserts his saintly role, and his tunic and cloak are consistent with the depiction of the apostles and saints, reflecting the secular dress of the middle and upper classes of the Roman Empire at the time of Christ![11] An article by Barry Kemp in *Journal of Egyptian Archaeology* suggests that the figure might be a representation of the founding father of the church and/or the community living within the northern tombs complex.

Why there should be no imagery of an adult Christ in the so-called church in Panehesy's tomb is a mystery, but the image of the infant Jesus may be the key to dating the arrival of pilgrims. The period of the church is estimated at 3rd to 4th century AD, but clearly there was a presence before then and at least two periods of occupation prior to that.

Coptic Church legend says that the Holy Family journeyed to Egypt at some time in the first few years of the millennium, and took a route that ended up almost exactly opposite Akhetaton.[12] This location was apparently the most important of any of their resting places. It was also the location where they stayed the longest.

All the evidence, then, points to an initial occupation in Roman times near to the time of Christ's crucifixion:

- The lack of any representation of an adult Christ;
- The lack of any defined altar;
- The lack of any representation of the Cross;
- The drawing of the *chi rho*, one of the earliest symbols of Christ;
- A figure dressed in costume consistent with Roman dress c50 AD;
- The architectural work pointing to a primitive place of worship, predating any known type of church;
- Pharaoh Akhenaton and Nefertiti were the central focus of the early visitors' worship, not Christ.

Whether Jesus himself was brought to Akhetaton is unknown, but it is certain that some of his followers came to Akhenaton's city and resided in Panehesy's tomb. Because of the lack of any clear representation of Jesus as the risen Christ, it seems most likely that they came before Jesus had been elevated, or recognized, as the Son of God. Why the pilgrims came is self-evident from all the other strong evidence that has been presented, showing Qumran-Essene awareness of Amarna's importance in their early history. That knowledge must also have been available to Jesus through his knowledge, and membership, of the community.[13]

Kom el-Nana

If a divine figure riding a chariot found on mosaics in Israel has caused endless confusion amongst scholars and theologians, the relatively recent discovery in a church at Amarna bearing images of three rows of saints and chariots has yet to be explained.[14] This building is particularly relevant to the mosaic chariots of Sepphoris and elsewhere in Israel.

A Coptic monastery at Kom el-Nana, in the southern part of Amarna, was constructed by Christian pilgrims some time in the 4th to 5th centuries AD and was sited within a small 18th Dynasty temple dedicated to Queen Nefertiti. It appears to have been her personal, private place of worship. The figures, nine in number, on the walls of the monastery are approximately two-thirds life-size, and although badly eroded, it is possible to see that some are depicted standing, with one arm raised in benediction (one with clenched fist and the curved fingers, the third and index finger, pointing upwards) and the other holding an object across the lower part of his body. Several are holding rolled scrolls, one with a red staff and another with a key – usually signifying St Peter. The figure with the staff is the only one wearing a white and gold cloak and is seen near a wheel, apparently being an image of Christ in a chariot.

The motif is very similar to that found in a larger, 6th century AD, monastery of Apa Apollo at nearby Bawit. Here in a niche apostles and two local saints are seen holding books and flanking the seated Virgin and Child on the upper part of the wall, with Christ riding a chariot on the curved ceiling above.

The figures at Kom el-Nana are seen wearing three-quarter-length cloaks, variously coloured gold, pink and green, over a gathered tunic with vertical blue lines and a wavy hem above the ankle – very reminiscent of the tunics worn by courtiers during the Amarna period. Coptic crosses are seen on both corners of the tunics. The names of the figures are indistinctly visible between the feet of the individuals, and one appears to be 'Andreas'. As well as various inscriptions, still being deciphered, there are palm fronds, a yellow gourd-type fruit dangling from a stem, pink flowers with red stamens and buds on woody stems with long leaves. Dark red and green fragments with a marble effect are thought to be decorative friezes separating the scenes. These resemble decorations in the Christian chapel within the tomb of Panehesy, which is almost certainly dated to a much earlier period than the more sophisticated monastery at Kom el-Nana. One highly significant, complex motif comprises a green-banded circle with a red and yellow centre and at least three grey rays radiating outwards, the upper one running over a perpendicular black-and-yellow-striped thick line.

Why Christ should be depicted riding a chariot and with other imagery so reminiscent of the Amarna period is not difficult to explain, once the idea of a conscious connection back to Pharaoh Akhenaton for Jewish, Christian and Muslim religions is taken on board. Christ's followers clearly saw him as taking on the mantle of Akhenaton and needing to emulate Akhenaton on his 'throne-chariot' – exactly as Akhenaton is seen in the mosaics at Sepphoris and other sites in Israel.

The Gospel Connection

A Christian presence at Amarna of what can only have been early followers of Jesus, if not Jesus himself and his family, has been demonstrated above. In addition, however, at the very beginning of the Christian scriptures, Matthew makes a special effort to establish Jesus' Egyptian credentials:

> When he arose, he took the young child and his mother by night, and departed into Egypt: and was there until the death of Herod: that it might be fulfilled which was spoken of the Lord by the prophet, saying, Out of Egypt have I called my son. *(Matthew 2:14–15)*

The question is: Why did Matthew feel such a strong need to tie Jesus to Egypt? It is my contention that both of the messiahs awaited by the Qumran-Essenes originated in Egypt, and therefore it is no surprise to find that the new messiah, Jesus of the Christian scriptures, was also to be associated with Egypt. The two messiahs the Qumran-Essenes looked to were, I maintain, King Akhenaton and his High Priest, Meryre I.

It could be argued, as the Dead Sea Scrolls seem to indicate, that a possible third 'Egyptian' messiah was awaited by the Essenes, and that this 'prophet like Moses', who clearly came out of Egypt, was the Egyptian antecedent to whom Matthew was alluding. The prophets Isaiah, Jeremiah, Ezekiel, Daniel, Hosea, Joel and Zechariah, however, whose words were to be fulfilled, refer to a restoration out of Egypt that is linked to the time of Joseph or the distant future End Days. Joseph lived at a much earlier time than Moses, and, of course, I equate Joseph and Jacob to the dates of Pharaoh Akhenaton and his high priest, Meryre.

The idea that David was the exemplar for the Qumranites, or the Bible for that matter, for a future messiah is, in my view, misconceived.

It is only possible to touch on some of the ways the New Testament corroborates knowledge of Akhenaton. The New Testament's concept of the messiah mentioned above, the need to identify Jesus with Melchizedek, discussed in Chapter 16, the significance of Abiathar to Jesus (discussed later), and the probable visit of the holy family to Akhetaton, already discussed, are clear examples of a continuous awareness.

Chapter 15

Clear Solutions to
Serious Questions

Armed with the information set out above, we can now return to the specific questions posed in Chapter 3 and start to answer each one in turn.

The Community of Qumran and its Texts

Question: *Who was the Plant of Righteousness?*
Answer: *Pharaoh Akhenaton.*

The Qumran-Essenes knew precisely when Akhenaton lived and dated their history from the time of his reign. An important group among the Dead Sea Scrolls are those known as the Early Chronology Texts, particularly the Book of Enoch and the Testament of Levi. The Dead Sea Scrolls versions of both of these were composed in the Hellenistic era of the 3rd century BC and appear to use blocks of 490 years as a measure of key events in the past and future. Thus, the Testament of Levi talks of the appointment of a high priest in the time of Jacob, with successive priests appointed over periods of 490 years. The choice seems to be based on a 70-'week' periodicity, measured as years rather than weeks, multiplied by the holy number seven.

The appointment of a high priest in the time of Jacob, well before the building of the First Temple in Jerusalem, is, of course, an impossibility for conventional biblical scholarship. The significance of this dilemma was initially brought home to me while discussing aspects of my first book, *The Copper Scroll Decoded*, with Esther Eshel. She was then working on an analysis of the Testament of Levi, and the repeated insistence of the texts on the appointment of priests several hundred years before there was an established temple had been a puzzle.[1] In considering the idea that Jacob might have been contemporary with an earlier temple – that of the Egyptian king Akhenaton – she suggested that the associations in the Testament of Levi might well be an important support to my theory. On the same theme, Józef Milik also pointed out that in the Testament of Levi, which he judged one of the most important of all the Dead Sea Scrolls, Egyptian names are present. It is, in fact, in reference to the Levites that the Hebrew scriptures mention most of those who bear Egyptian names.

How the Qumran-Essenes understood time, especially in relation to their own history, gives yet another set of indisputable evidence. The Book of Enoch from Qumran, and from external sources, speaks of 'blocks' of years measuring history from creation, with great events occurring at the end of each block of 490 years, in a similar manner to that seen in the Testament of Levi and the Book of Daniel. The blocks begin with creation and move successively forward. At the end of the seventh block, the most important event is said to have occurred – the establishment of the 'Plant of Righteousness' – presumably referring to the original reason for the establishment of the Qumran-Essene community. After the arrival of 'The Plant', the text relates that there would be only three more blocks of 490 years before the End Days arrived.[2]

As the philosophy of messianism evolved, the End Days were not just understood as the restoration of what had been lost, but were also envisaged as ushering in a reign of harmony and order and a paradise never before attained. The 'final week', or period before the End Days occur, is identified as 170–163 BC, when the Book of Daniel speaks of 'the anointed one' who is 'cut off' at the transition from the previous weeks. The 'cut off' of the anointed one is taken by most scholars to be the murder or death of the high priest of the Jerusalem temple, Onias III, who was stripped of his office in c175 BC and replaced by Onias IV. This identification is quite wrong. In fact, the translation of the critical verse in Daniel 9:26 from the Hebrew version reads: 'And after those 62 weeks, the Anointed One will disappear and vanish.' This phrase is entirely different from that appearing in most Christian translations of the Bible, which has even led to the equation of the anointed one to Christ.

That the Book of Daniel was of special importance to the Qumran-Essenes is demonstrated by the finding of eight scroll fragments of

Apocalyptic events in 490-year blocks

Event	Lapsed Years	Equivalent Date
1. Creation	0	4780 BC
2. Enoch	490	4290
3. Noah and the Flood	980	3800
4. Abraham?	1470	3310
5. ?	1960	2820
6. ?	2450	330
7. Abraham	2940	1840
8. Eternal Plant of Righteousness, Akhenaton	3430	1350
9. Solomon's Temple	3920	860
		586 Solomon's temple destroyed
10. End Days	4410	370
		177 Teacher of Righteousness*
		140 Essenes at Qumran
		110 Teacher of Righteousness dies
		70 BC Apocalypse†
Apocalypse	4900	120 AD

* 390 years after the destruction of the First Temple, the Plant of Righteousness (Teacher of Righteousness) comes, according to the Damascus Document.
† Expected end, according to Daniel.

Daniel amongst the Dead Sea Scrolls and the indications that they viewed Daniel as a prophet in his own right, rather than a relatively minor writer. We do not have a complete version of their record of Chapter 9 from Daniel, but it must have been of considerable importance to them as it appears to have been preserved in one scroll (4QDanc) specifically about Daniel's Prayer, as set out in this chapter.

A number of scholars also hold to Onias III as being the Qumran Teacher of Righteousness. Again this cannot be right. Part of the confusion may be caused by the misleading statements of Josephus,[3] who also confuses Onias III and Onias IV. Onias III was almost certainly murdered shortly after 172 BC (2 Maccabees 4:33–5) and therefore cannot possibly have been the Teacher of Righteousness who led his radical group to Qumran around 150 BC.

I identify Jason, Onias III's brother, as Onias IV the successor high priest, who becomes known as the Teacher of Righteousness – 'The Plant'. The reasons are not just because of the above logic of events, but also for many other testified pieces of evidence relating Onias IV to Qumran and because of his stay in Egypt where he built a temple which reflected aspects of Atonism.

The sect distinguished at least four periods in its understanding of the world's history leading up to the final apocalypse:

1 The past, before the sect's establishment;
2 Its own historical present and its preoccupation with clearing the way in the wilderness;
3 The approaching period of war to be fought by the forces of light against the forces of darkness;
4 The ultimate future of full peace.[4]

At the time of the death of the Teacher of Righteousness, thought to be c110 BC, the Essenes had calculated from the works of Daniel and Isaiah that the End Days would come in 70 BC – 40 years after his demise – a time block related to the length of time the Hebrews were wandering in the wilderness.[5] When 70 BC came and went, some recalculations were needed, as evidenced by the Essenes' Commentary on the Book of Habakkuk, composed about 50 BC. A further review of the Book of Daniel indicated that the beginning of the period of Final Judgment might now come in 70 AD, but from reviewing works of the prophets Hosea, Nahum and Habakkuk, a new, open-ended date, depending on the length of Roman rule, was determined. What that date was is not clear from the Dead Sea Scrolls fragments that deal with the subject, but it appears to be post-70 AD.

The next indication of the Qumran-Essenes' thinking on this post-70 BC date comes from the New Testament Book of Revelation. composed some time in the 1st or 2nd century AD. The content of Revelation is a mixture of early Christian theology intertwined with material identified from the Essenes' sectarian Chronology Texts and a visionary taste of the apocalyptic End Days.[6] Revelation does not mention the crucifixion of Jesus. Understanding its true meaning is a challenging task, as analogy and imagery are the fabric of its composition, but built into it is the revised date the Qumran-Essenes must have finally established as that for the end of time, or perhaps had established much earlier in their history.

Interestingly, the views of Paul in the New Testament on the timing of the End Days are peculiarly congruent with those of the Qumran-Essenes. This is perhaps not such a surprise if my conjecture is accurate that Paul's mysterious three-year absence in Arabia was time actually spent with an Essenic community. He first believed that the end of the world would come around 70 AD, but later modified his view, just as the Qumran-Essenes did (2 Thessalonians 2; Romans 12–13).[7]

According to Barbara Thiering, interpretation of the timescale set out in Revelation shows that the expected *eschaton* (final restoration) would come in 120 AD.[8] The significance of this date is indeed testified to by a dramatic series of events that occurred among the Jewish communities scattered within the Roman Empire. An unexpected, widespread, and apparently orchestrated, uprising of Jews in the diaspora and in their homeland is recorded in 115 AD, during the reign of Emperor Trajan.[9] This seems to support the contention that some outside knowledge was the driving force that encouraged an attempt to throw off the Roman yoke in anticipation that the messiah would return in 120 AD.[10]

One way or another, interpretation of these Chronology Texts has proved a nightmare for scholars and a fertile hunting ground for all manner of weird theorists to play around with possibilities and numbers – 666, the number of the beast, and the four horsemen of the apocalypse mentioned in Revelation being just two of the numbers that have caught the imagination of the public. Even Isaac Newton, among many others, spent an inordinate amount of time trying to analyze numerical aspects of the Book of Revelation. Much more sense of the written matter can be made, however, when it is viewed through a pair of Egyptian glasses.

According to the Essenes' own accounts, the most important event in human history took place at the end of the seventh block of 490 years. Working back from the final days, for which both the Essenes and the early Christians (as the Book of Revelation indicates) were preparing themselves, we now have an interesting interpretation of when this most important event must have taken place. The final days were to occur at the end of the tenth block of time, and this was expected to come around 120 AD. The end of the seventh block of time must therefore have occurred 1,470 years before the End Days. So in 1350 BC, 1,470 years before the End Days, the most important event in the religious history of the Qumran-Essenes is said to have occurred. If I seem to be labouring the point somewhat, it is because it is of such significance.

We know the dates of the early Egyptian pharaohs with a fair amount of precision;[11] 1350 BC was the date of the enthronement of Akhenaton as pharaoh. That he was the Plant of Righteousness is therefore confirmed in the Chronology Texts. His distant successor, the Teacher of Righteousness, was the leader who took his community to Qumran.[12] There can be no doubt that this successor to the Plant of Righteousness was the founder of the separatist Essene movement, and not some other biblical character or event, because the Teacher of Righteousness was referred to as the Shoot or Branch of the Plant of Righteousness. The exactness of the Qumran-Essene knowledge of a date when the most significant event in their history occurred being so close to the lifetime of Akhenaton can hardly be a coincidence.

In 1350 BC the Hebrews had not yet entered Canaan; they were still in Egypt. The associations that have already been made to the city of Akhetaton and its ruler Pharaoh Akhenaton now weight the historical evidence heavily in favour of the overall contention that the Qumran-Essenes had a direct connection to the Amarna of that period.

Question: *Who was the Teacher of Righteousness?*
Answer: *The High Priest Onias IV.*

The Teacher of Righteousness was the man who, the Dead Sea Scrolls aver, led the Qumran-Essenes into the desert wilderness of Judaea and charged them with a renewed religious spirit. The unanswered question, however, in many accounts is, who was he?

Historians are completely at odds with each other as to his true identity. Most see him as some anonymous unknown priest of the Hasmonean period. Many more-conscientious historians admit they just do not know who he was. Whoever he was, we do know, from quite detailed descriptions in the Dead Sea Scrolls, that he must have been a person of considerable standing, charismatic, highly learned, someone who inspired people – in fact, a major priestly figure of his time. Given these attributes, it is even stranger that scholars are so uncertain as to his identity. Such a person could hardly be invisible to history.

The view that the Essenes originated out of a devout group of Second Temple-period Jews, known as the Hassidim (or Hasidim: 'devout ones'), has long been held by some scholars.[13] We know little of the Hassidim's beliefs, except that they were strong supporters of Judas Maccabee – which might explain the disenchantment of the Essenes when Jonathan Hyrcanus was appointed high priest in 152 BC (if the Essenes are to be equated with the Hassidim). Other scholars see the Hassidim in an enlarged role, attributing to them the apocalyptic writings of Enoch and Daniel.[14] They are, to these scholars, the 'chosen righteous' and 'lambs' of the Enochic texts and the 'children of Jubilees' of Daniel.

Yet other scholars, in what is known as the Grøningen school, see the Essenes as quite distinct from the Hassidim, emerging before the Maccabean revolt. Professor Geza Vermes has similarly distanced the Qumran-Essenes from the Hassidim. It is a view that most scholars now accept as correct, and one I basically go along with, although of course I maintain that the roots of Essenism go much deeper. These scholars base part of their reasoning on a passage in the Damascus Document that declares:

> He [God] left a remnant to Israel and did not deliver it up to be destroyed. And in the age of wrath, three hundred and ninety years after he had given them into the hand of King Nebuchadnezzar of Babylon, He visited them and He caused a plant root to spring from Israel and Aaron to inherit His land and to prosper on the good things of His earth. And they perceived their iniquity and recognized that they were guilty men, yet for twenty years they were like blind men groping the way.[15]

It is worth looking closely at this quite specific chronology that the Qumran-Essenes spell out, because I believe it is of critical significance in the development of the case I have put forward relating the Essenes to Egypt and Akhenaton and the date of the appearance of the Teacher of Righteousness.

In the Damascus Document the reference to Israel being conquered by King Nebuchadnezzar of Babylon can only refer to the period of the destruction of the First Temple in 586 BC. Three hundred and ninety years after, we are told, in 'the age of wrath', the Seleucid rulers of Syria took control of Judaea and commenced a rule of disruptive Hellenization. This would, accordingly, be dated to 196 BC. The Damascus Document is spot on. The Greek successors of Alexander the Great began their rule of Judaea in 197 BC. The 'plant root' is in disarray as to how to deal with the new threat, and 20 years of groping like blind men pass until the Teacher of Righteousness takes command. It is now 177 BC.[16]

So from this quite specific information, can we not deduce who the Teacher of Righteousness was? For many scholars the information is too good to be true, so they choose to ignore it. They are quite happy to accept the 20 years of groping like blind men, but the figure of 390 'cannot be used for precise calculation. It was a round number of prophecy put to Essene use'![17]

In my view there can be no doubt, from other evidence and from this precise chronology given to us by the Qumran-Essenes, that the Teacher of Righteousness was Onias IV, known as Jason, the last of a Zadokite line of high priests. We know from other external sources, both Roman and Greek, that Onias IV took office in 176 BC.[18] Again, the Damascus Document gets the date exactly right.

Three years later, Onias IV was expelled from office by the 'Wicked Priest', who can be none other than Menelaus, who, as the new high priest, profaned and plundered the Temple. Onias IV and his retinue fled to Egypt, and there he did something quite remarkable. He got permission from Ptolemy VI, in 170 BC, to build a temple at Leontopolis, near Heliopolis[19] (not to be confused with another place called Leontopolis, located further north in the Delta and now known as Tell el-Muqdam). Onias IV was obviously a powerful persuader and wealthy enough to build a magnificent temple at the centre of a settlement near Heliopolis, now known as Tell el-Yahudiyah (Mound of the Jews). Building a temple in competition with the Temple at Jerusalem was in itself a surprising thing to do, and contrary to

Deuteronomic law. There were hardly any other legitimate buildings of worship at that time, apart from the Temple in Jerusalem, although a number of pre-Temple period synagogues have recently been discovered.[20]

Onias IV did something else that requires explanation. He replaced the *menorah* (seven-branched lamp stand), specified in biblical texts as an essential holy piece of furniture for the temple, with a single huge golden orb.[21] Why should he do that? Was the golden orb his attempt at representing the spherical golden sun of the Aton? There seems to be no other sensible answer, nor to my knowledge has anyone ever given any reasonable explanation for the action – what one might call a series of parallel universe black holes.

There are other curious links from Leontopolis to Qumran. Solomon Steckoll excavated extensively at Qumran in the late 1960s and unearthed a strange stone cube in the ruins of the Qumran buildings that was very similar to one found at Leontopolis.[22] He also noted a common practice of burying animal bones in jars: 'This practice of burying animal bones was carried out, a unique practice, to say the least, and significant, surely, by its use at the same period by Jewish Communities at both Leontopolis and Qumran, a circumstance which appears not merely one of sheer coincidence.'[23]

All these associations between Leontopolis and Qumran, knowledge of which has come from historical sources and from the statements found in the Qumran texts, tend to confirm that Onias IV and his followers had a presence at both locations, and that he was indeed the Teacher of Righteousness.

As he had been a high priest and came from priestly stock, some of his disciples would have had priestly attributes, and indeed priestly sentiments are seen at Qumran.

The Different Strands

The difficulty of the conflicting views on the origins of the Essenes is readily resolved if these origins are seen as coming from two distinctive priestly strands. There was, I maintain, a continuing legacy of Akhenaton-inspired separatist priestly followers who traced their lineage and knowledge back beyond the exodus. Now, with the positive identification of the ex-high priest Onias IV as the Essenes'

Teacher of Righteousness, there is a further possibility. Professor George Brooke posited in my previous book, *The Mystery of the Copper Scroll of Qumran*, that the knowledge the Essenes absorbed about ancient Egypt, and particularly about some of the secrets the Qumran-Essenes undoubtedly possessed, may have been derived from an interaction between Onias IV and residual knowledge in Egypt about Akhenaton.

As the Teacher of Righteousness, Onias IV could have reinforced his knowledge and learned more of the secrets of Akhenaton at Heliopolis itself, the centre of religious learning in Egypt and at one time a place where Atonism flourished. I have previously suggested that a submerged belief in Akhenaton's monotheism persisted there, as well as at Elephantine Island.[24] An alternative possibility is that Onias' knowledge could have come through contact with the Theraputae, a sect closely related to the Essenes, who were based near Alexandria, in the Valley of Natrun, and in the Delta region of Egypt. In this respect the influence of an Egyptian line of Onias priests related to the Boethians cannot be ignored.[25]

On his return to Judaea, the Teacher of Righteousness was therefore armed with a new depth of understanding to add to the store of secret knowledge available to him through the line of separatist priests. He then began the task of bringing his adherents back to the ancient traditions of the Mosaic and pre-Mosaic Laws and directing them towards a place where they could practise and develop the religious path he advocated.

If I am correct in identifying Onias IV as the Teacher of Righteousness, the reverse side of the coin implies that his contemporary was Menelaus, the Wicked Priest, who ousted him and took his place as high priest. If, therefore, the information we have from the scrolls about the Wicked Priest fits with the historical information, we would have a virtually watertight case for concluding that the Teacher of Righteousness was one and the same person as Onias IV. There are, in fact, three such references in the Dead Sea Scrolls.

The sectarian text of Habakkuk declares that the Wicked Priest: originally aspired to a 'trustworthy name', but abused his position; pursued the Teacher of Righteousness 'in his place of exile' at a time when he was occupied with a religious ceremony; met a horrible demise at the hand of his enemies (in a manner almost justified by his transgressions against the Teacher of Righteousness).[26]

Josephus records that Menelaus assumed the role of high priest after deposing Onias IV and then proceeded to abuse his position. If Menelaus was indeed the Wicked Priest, what previous more 'trustworthy name' could he have held than that of high priest?

Pursuing the Teacher of Righteousness 'in his place of exile' implies that the Wicked Priest went to an establishment outside Judaea. Onias' abode in Egypt was certainly outside his homeland, and he must have been worshipping in the temple he built at Leontopolis when confronted and attacked by the Wicked Priest and his retinue. If Onias IV and his followers were preoccupied with a religious festival (probably the Day of Atonement) and were caught unawares, why was Menelaus not observing the same festival?

The Qumran-Essenes' corroborated practice of observing festivals at times different from those followed at the Temple in Jerusalem explains the discrepancy. Onias IV, as the precursor and founder of the Qumran-Essene movement, was following a solar calendar, quite different from that of normative Judaism, and therefore his holy festival date would have had no significance for Menelaus, who would have been free to travel and seek out his enemy. This action attests again to Onias IV being the founder of the non-conformist Qumran-Essene movement.

The third fact we learn from the Dead Sea Scrolls is that the Wicked Priest died an unnatural death. Menelaus was, according to historical record, murdered.[27] Everything fits. The dates, characteristics and movements of the two main contenders, Onias IV and Menelaus, as spelled out in Dead Sea Scrolls texts, conform to external historical records. There are, of course, arguments both direct and indirect against Onias IV being the Teacher of Righteousness, but they as yet do not take into account the larger picture I have painted for the pro case.

Direct Arguments against Onias IV

The direct problem cited by scholars relates to part of the description of Onias IV, in 1 and 2 Maccabees[28] and in Josephus, as a Hellenizing high priest. These descriptions, especially in 1 Maccabees, portray Jason, as he was known (or more correctly Joshua, as his Hebrew name is recorded), as promoting Greek influences and therefore possibly betraying his ancient ancestry.

Hellenizing influences in themselves do not, however, conflict with the possibility of Jason being the Teacher of Righteousness. On the contrary, they reinforce the idea. It may well be that this description of the Teacher of Righteousness by the authors of the Maccabean books merely reflected the infatuation of a great thinker who would inevitably have been attracted to Greek ideas, particularly Pythagorean ones.

There are indeed some similarities between the behaviour advocated by the Pythagorean movement and that of the Essenic community that was later to settle at Qumran under the guidance of the Teacher of Righteousness.[29] In fact, it is quite apparent that Jason obtained some of his ideas from these Greek sources. Like the community of mystics founded by Pythagoras, the community at Qumran attached great importance to common meals, sharing of material and intellectual property, a scientific approach to religious-related healing, strict community rules (including binding their adherents with strange oaths), ritual purity, moral asceticism, and a belief in immortality and the reincarnation of the soul.

The Books of Maccabees were undoubtedly written with a strong pro-Hasmonean slant, and when Onias IV became an enemy of their movement, fleeing to Egypt and the protection of a feared Ptolemaic king, his role in the office of high priest inevitably came under attack. His building of a competitor temple at Leontopolis added to the need for his denigration: 'To keep you from the false worship of Onias IV's Temple at Leontopolis'.[30]

Not surprisingly, if, as I deduce, Onias IV was the Teacher of Righteousness, the Essenes would have had little regard for the hostile content of the Books of Maccabees. Although examples of texts from virtually every other book of the Hebrew scriptures and Apocrypha were present, not one single fragment of the Books of Maccabees has been found at Qumran; the Essenes would hardly want to keep in their possession books that were critical of their founder. As far as I am aware, no one has previously put forward this explanation for the rather surprising omission in the Qumran-Essene collection.[31]

Later, even Josephus discounted the Maccabean version of Onias

IV's behaviour. (The books were subsequently excluded from the Hebrew canon, although they do appear in the Catholic canon.[32])

Indirect Arguments against Onias IV

The indirect arguments against identifying Onias IV as the Teacher of Righteousness are those that relate to the alternative figures suggested, but when these are examined in detail, it becomes apparent that Onias IV is the most likely – if not the only – candidate. A convenient way of looking at the other suggested candidates is to list the known attributes of the Teacher of Righteousness, as indicated in the Dead Sea Scrolls, against the historical figures who have been proposed in his place (*see* table overleaf).

The idea that the Teacher of Righteousness was some anonymous person insignificant to history just does not hold water. Professor Charlesworth refers to him as 'a brilliant, highly educated and dedicated Jewish priest of the most prestigious lineage', but admits he does not know his identity.[33] For Hartmut Stegemann, the Teacher of Righteousness was 'perhaps once an officiating high priest'. Even in the Dead Sea Scrolls Thanksgiving Hymn, whose composition is generally ascribed to the Teacher of Righteousness, we find the author perceiving himself as the rejected high priest (a work that, by the way, is replete with allusions to the River Nile).[34] The characteristic of the Teacher of Righteousness as a one-time high priest is also suggested by his Hebrew sobriquet in the Dead Sea Scrolls – *Mare Hazeddek*, a traditional title applied only to the Temple high priest.

As previously mentioned, one of the most telling arguments that Onias IV was the Teacher of Righteousness involves his fleeing his homeland. None of the other candidates, except Ezekiel, fits this shoe, and Ezekiel's feet are too big on other grounds. The requirement for the Teacher of Righteousness to flee his homeland is deduced from the Psalms of Thanksgiving found at Qumran, and more precisely a psalm known as D. This is written in the first-person singular and is attributed to the Teacher of Righteousness himself:

> For [I] was an object of scorn to them and they did not esteem me when Thou wast strengthened in me! For I was driven from my country, as the bird from the nest.[35]

Figures Proposed as the Teacher of Righteousness, and Their Attributes

	Ezekiel	Onias III	Onias IV	Unknown priest			Hyrcanus II	Jesus	John the Baptist	James brother of Jesus
Date of Emergence	6th cent. BC	170	172	c160	150	100	67 CE	c30	c30	c33
High priest	x	√	√	x	x	x	√	x	x	x
Zadokite Lineage	x	√	√	?	?	?	x	x	x	x
Charismatic Leader	√	x	√	?	?	?	?	√	√	√
Group of Followers	x	x	√	?	?	?	?	?	√	√
Contemporary candidate for Wicked Priest	x	√	√	√	√	√	√	√	√	√
Went to Egypt	x	x	√	?	?	?	x	√?	x	x
Proposer	a	b	b1	c	d	e	f	g	h	i

a. Ben-Zion Wacholder, 'The Teacher of Righteousness and Expectations of the End Days', The Dead Sea Scrolls Fifty Years After Their Discovery, International Congress, Jerusalem, 20–25 July 1997.

b. George Athas, 'In Search of the Seventy "Weeks" of Daniel 9', *Journal of Hebrew Scriptures*, Vol. 9, Art. 2, 2010.

b1. Robert Feather, *The Mystery of the Copper Scroll of Qumran.*

c. J. Murphy O'Connor, *Paul and Qumran, Studies in New Testament Exegesis,* Chicago. Priory Press, 1968. James H. Charlesworth, ed.,

Jesus and the Dead Sea Scrolls, Doubleday, 1992. Charlesworth notes that J. Carmignac equates the Teacher of Righteousness with Judas the Essene ('Qui était le docteur de Justice?', *Revue de Qumran*, 10, 1980).

d. J. T. Milik, *Ten Years of Discovery in the Wilderness of Judaea*, SCM, 1959. In his analysis of the Habakkuk commentary scroll from Qumran, Milik notes that the Hebrew term '*masal*' could not refer to a Jewish king, and therefore 'The Wicked Priest must be a predecessor of Aristobulus I' (104–103 BC). In Geza Vermes, *The Complete Dead Sea Scrolls in English* (Allen Lane/Penguin, 1997), Professor Vermes uses as one of his arguments the fact that his choice of the Teacher of Righteousness was opposed to Onias IV because he did not follow him to Egypt. If my contention is correct, he would have been following himself! The contemporary opponent of the Teacher of Righteousness is suggested as Jonathan, son of Mattathias, the high priest from 152 to 142 BC (notably by Vermes and J. T. Milik); Jonathan's brother Simon, who led the country between 142 and 135 BC; and Alexander Jannaeus, king of Judaea from 102 to 76 BC.

    One of the objections to the more favoured theory of Vermes and Milik is that it would imply that the Teacher of Righteousness was the high priest from 159 to 152 BC, whereas the evidence from 4QMMT, a composition considered to be by the Teacher of Righteousness, testifies that a significant part of Judaea was not following either the author or the addressee of this composition. (See John Kampen and Moshe J. Bernstein, *Reading 4QMMT: New Perspective on Qumran Law and History*, Society of Biblical Literature Symposium Series, Scholars Press, 1996; also Hanan Eshel, *4QMMT and the History of the Hasmonean Period*, Bar-Ilan University, Ramat Gan, Israel.)

    Frank Moore Cross, *The Ancient Library of Qumran*. Cross sees the Teacher of Righteousness as being an anonymous Zadokite priest with Hassidic sympathies. He dismisses the 390 years after 586 BC as the date for his arrival as spelled out in the Damascus Document, apparently because it was a round number! See also L. H. Schiffman, *Reclaiming the Dead Sea Scrolls*, Doubleday, 1995; Roland de Vaux, *Archaeology and the Dead Sea Scrolls*, Oxford, 1973; Rainer Riesner, *Jesus, the Primitive Community, and the Essene Quarter of Jerusalem*; James H. Charlesworth, ed., *Jesus and the Dead Sea Scrolls*, Doubleday, 1992.

e. Michael O. Wise, 'Dating the Teacher of Righteousness and the Floruit of His Movement', *Journal of Biblical Literature*, 122(1), 2003. Wise doubts that the Essenes knew with any accuracy how long before the arrival of the Teacher of Righteousness the Temple was destroyed, or even when Persian rule ended, whereas from their own writings and 1 Maccabees, written in the period of the Essenes, it is clear they knew precisely the length of the reign of Alexander the Great and had a close timing for the end of Persian rule.

f. Greg Doudna, Orion 17, November 2001, www.mail-archive.com/orion.

g. J. Teicher, 'The Dead Sea Scrolls', *Journal of Jewish Studies*, 1957.

h. Barbara Thiering, *Jesus the Man: A New Interpretation from the Dead Sea Scrolls*, Doubleday, 1992.

i. Robert Eisenman, *The Dead Sea Scrolls and the First Christians*, Element, 1996.

Later in the same hymn, where the author castigates his enemies, there is yet another allusion to Egypt:

> But as for them, they are the wretched, and they form thoughts
> of Møth–Belial, and they seek thee with a double heart.[36]

Møth here must surely be the Egyptian vulture goddess, Muth, who terrorizes the people of the earth, set in phraseology that is typically ancient Egyptian.[37] Add to the conclusion of this analysis the date spelled out in the Damascus Document for the death of the Teacher of Righteousness as 110 BC and it becomes a racing certainty that the high priest Onias IV was the Teacher of Righteousness.

Chapter 16

Melchizedek:
Nothing is New under the Sun

This mysterious character crops up in the Hebrew Bible, the New Testament and the Dead Sea Scrolls,[1] as well as in the Talmud, and was an ongoing fascination for early Christian commentators and the Tannaitic rabbis from the 2nd century AD onwards. In the numerous learned papers, books, dissertations, and textual references about him almost everyone agrees he was of great significance. His attributes and qualities have been analyzed to the nth degree by dozens of scholars; conferences have been staged specifically to discuss Melchizedek; yet no one has any certainty as to who he really was.[2]

The first appearance of the name Melchizedek comes in Genesis 14. Here the Bible relates a battle between four kings – Ampraphel, Arioch, Chedorlaomer and Tidal – who attacked five other kings in what is assumed to be the land of Canaan. Abraham's nephew Lot becomes embroiled in the conflict and is taken hostage. Abraham rides to the rescue with 318 of his armed retinue, saves his relative and routs the four kings. Then comes the interesting part of the story. One of the five kings, by the name of Melchizedek, heaps praise on Abraham and, in dividing the spoils of the battle, Abraham appears to offer him a tithe of the plunder.

This is the first mention of tithes in the Bible and seems to anticipate the Israelite institution of donating one tenth of a person's earnings to the Temple; however, no Israelite temple existed at the time of Abraham. The other huge significance of this offer is that it implies Melchizedek is superior to Abraham, although the Hebrew (and Greek) sources of the Bible are ambiguous on this point and it could be the other way around, that Melchizedek offers Abraham the tithe. However, as Abraham did the capturing of the spoils it would make more sense if he was doing the offering, and the modern New Testament translations, in Hebrews 7:1–4, records that Abraham gave a tithe to Melchizedek.[3]

Whilst the usual biblical translation of this event describes Melchizedek as king of Salem, and it is assumed that Salem is the site of what is to become Jerusalem, this is by no means certain. The Hebrew stem letters SLM could well be read as something other than Jerusalem, and, in fact, there is every indication that the letters should be read as *shalom*, which means peace. As Genesis describes Melchizedek as the Priest of God Most High, Melchizedek would be the only person to access the altar of the temple, which, Deuteronomy 27:6 says, must be made of unhewn stone, implying wholeness and peace. The ambiguous description of Melchizedek could well be saying 'king of peace' rather than king of Salem.

Another biblical reference to Melchizedek (as a priest forever) comes in Psalm 110, considered to be one of the oldest psalms, though modern scholars do not understand its true meaning. They do, however, conclude that Melchizedek was not a Jewish priest, but was a priest before there were any Jewish priests! Quite a piece of mental juggling.

Other references to Melchizedek come in Dead Sea Scroll 11QMelchizedek, the Songs of the Sabbath Sacrifice, the Genesis Apocryphon, from Philo of Alexandria, Josephus, the Cairo-Genizah texts, 2 Enoch, Pseudo-Eupolemos, the Siddur Rabbah, the Gnostic texts tractate NHC IX 1, Second Book of Jeu and Pistis Sophia.[4]

The antiquity of Melchizedek is well understood by Dr Margaret Barker in her brilliant paper on the subject 'Who Was Melchizedek And Who Was His God?' To quote from her work:

> What both the Jewish and Enochic traditions are saying is that the Melchizedek priesthood was the priesthood of Enoch and the generation before the flood. The Book of Jubilees claims that many of the prescriptions of the Torah were far older than Moses, and had been given to Noah by his ancestors, the ancient priests (Jubilees 7 and 10). We cannot just dismiss this as fiction.[5]

These are all claims to a more ancient religion than that of Moses, an ancient religion represented in the biblical texts by the figure of Melchizedek.

In respect of my thesis it could hardly be put more succinctly. Unfortunately Dr Barker is unable to give an explanation that addresses the implications of her own statement.

Question: *Who was Melchizedek to the Essenes?*
Answer: *A composite kingly/priestly figure of Pharaoh Akhenaton and his high priest, Meryre I.*[6]

This prima donna is often referred to as a human/divine figure, but despite intense study, he has not been identified.

The information we have about Melchizedek from the Hebrew scriptures, and from numerous Dead Sea Scrolls references, is so detailed that it is curious he remains such a mystery. Those who wrote about him certainly had an image in mind of some biblical/historical character closely related to God.

For the Qumran-Essenes, the messiah they awaited embodied this as yet unidentified figure of Melchizedek – the priest of God Most High (11Q Melch., Song of the Sabbath Sacrifice), and even though, in the New Testament, Jesus' line of descent is claimed through the Davidic kings, he is also seen as Jesus the heavenly high priest. In fact, Jesus subsumes into his person all three types of messiahs awaited by the Qumran-Essenes: one king, one priest, and one prophet like Moses – as well as the mantle of Melchizedek.

Whilst, as we have seen, the name Melchizedek appears early in the Hebrew scriptures, for the Qumran community he is recast as a human/divine figure who will lead the 'sons of light' in the final eschatological battle and act in a priestly manner to expiate the sins of his followers. The expiation that Melchizedek, the divine mediator, is to bring about is related to the Day of Atonement.

To try and identify the Melchizedek of Qumran, we need to look at the attributes associated with this figure in the biblical and Qumran texts to see whether it becomes clear to whom they refer. Melchizedek is variously described as:

1 An angel identified with the divine name; an 'angel of the Lord'.[7]
2 A human figure as 'Son of God'.
3 A human form who sits on a divine throne.
4 A human figure who is mystically elevated to a divine status through seven heavens, having alternative names of Michael, Metatron, Adoil,

Eremiel, Wazir, 'the son of man'.

5 A visionary figure seen by Moses as sitting on a divine throne.

6 An angelic human who carries within him 'the name of God'.

7 A being associated with a dazzling, glorious heavenly chariot (Hebrew, *merkabah*).

8 A leader of the 'sons of light' in the final eschatological battle against the forces of evil, and in doing so one who brings expiation for the sins of humanity and a Day of Atonement.

Melchizedek as a Hebrew title means 'king priest' or 'righteous king'. It carries the sense of one person who combines the roles of king and high priest, but no one in conventional scholarship has been able to explain the origins of this mysterious being, despite intense speculation. If we go through the above-listed attributes of Melchizedek, it can readily be seen how they relate to Egypt and, more specifically, to the Amarna period. The roles enumerated are precisely embodied in King Akhenaton, in conjunction with his high priest, Meryre. Together, they comfortably fulfill all the characteristics of the 'angel of the Lord'. Melchizedek then is surely the memory of a combined kingly/priestly union of King Akhenaton and his high priest, Meryre.

Correlations of the Criteria to Amarna

1–3 Akhenaton, in the tradition of the pharaohs, was the earthly representative of the High God. As such he at times became indistinguishable from the High God, and even for students of Egyptology it is not always clear who was being worshipped by the people. Akhenaton perceived himself as God's representative on earth, and although he was a 'son of man', he had a special privilege of also being the 'Son of God'. His eventual place was to be beside God on a throne.

4 Seven heavenly stages are a characteristic representation in ancient Egyptian mythology of the route to eternal heaven. Understanding the choice of all these names that seem to derive from Melchizedek is not easy, however, and I have no full explanation. There could be an association between the rabbinic name Metatron and Aton. The name of God as Adon in the Bible, the Lord, can readily be equated to Aton, and there may be a linkage to the name Adoil or Ado-El, as it could be pronounced. Wazir might be equatable with the Egyptian name for the vizier, the right-hand man of Pharaoh, who, I maintain, was Joseph at the time of Akhenaton. Additionally, a number of names found in the Merkabah Kabbalistic literature adopt the suffix -on.[8]

5 To describe the visionary figure that Moses sees, Alan Segal analyses a descriptive word in Ezekiel the Tragedian as having the double sense of 'a venerable man' and 'a man of light.'[9] (Ezekiel the Tragedian was a Jewish playwright of the 2nd century BC, who included scriptural history in his works, fragments of which were found at Nag Hammadi near Amarna.) What better way to speak of Akhenaton, a man of greatness whose symbol of God was light? For the royal figure that Moses sees to be a king of Israel, mentioned in the text, does not make any sense, because even the first king of Israel, King Saul, came long after Moses. The Nag Hammadi text of Ezekiel the Tragedian must have been referring to a throned figure who preceded Moses, and that could only be a king of Egypt. The Nag Hammadi text goes on to speak of the throned figure handing Moses a sceptre and placing a diadem on his head – both prime motifs of Egyptian kings. That the central figures of Judaism and Christianity, Moses and Jesus, could take on this mantle of equivalence to the 'angel of the Lord' is apparently seen by the authors of these texts as essential for both the Hebrews and followers of Jesus.

6 The hieroglyph cartouche of the name Akhenaton contains within it the hieroglyph for the name of God, Aton – a semicircle over a rippling line over an open circle preceded (or followed) by a feather-like symbol.[10] The modern reading of Amenhotep IV – the enthronement name the pharaoh had before he changed it to Akhenaton – did not carry the name of a god, but when he changed his name his new title did carry within it the name of God – Akhen*Aton*.

7 The great similarity between the description of the heavenly chariot in the Dead Sea Scrolls, that were apparently unique to the Essenes, and those actually found in the tomb of

Tutankhamun and seen in reliefs at Amarna cannot be ignored. The pictorial representation at Amarna of Pharaoh Akhenaton riding his heavenly chariot is particularly colourful and dramatic and is unique to Amarna. No early royal chariots have ever been found in Israel, yet chariot experience features strongly in Jewish and Christian mystical traditions.[11]

8 That the adjectival Hebrew word for 'atonement' (*atonali*) has within it the root sound *aton*, can be no coincidence, nor perhaps now even a surprise. That the English word also carries the same root sound is more surprising. At Akhetaton, the time of atonement was the day when Akhenaton's return, as the divine mediator, would celebrate the name of God, whom he called Aton. In Exodus 23, the angel of the Lord embodies and carries the name of God as the Tetragrammaton (four-letter representation of the name of God).

As if to verify the contention that Melchizedek also incorporated the concept of Akhenaton's high priest, Meryre, new light on the New Testament Epistle to the Hebrews has been shed by the fragmentary 1st century BC document found in Cave 11 at Qumran, known as the Heavenly Prince Melchizedek (11Q Melch.). The description in Hebrews of Christ as the 'Son of God' and 'without beginning of days or end of life', now makes sense as reflecting the same image of Melchizedek portrayed by the sectarian Dead Sea Scroll. This interpretative understanding was taken still further in discussion at a recent international conference on the Dead Sea Scrolls at St Andrews in Scotland. A paper by Margaret Barker published in the *Scottish Journal of Theology* maintains that Jesus knew of and understood Melchizedek; that he may have patterned his life on the Qumranic conception of Melchizedek; and that his earliest followers built on that understanding.[12] In Hebrews, Jesus is also seen as 'a priest forever, according to the order of Melchizedek' (5:6). That this is the same high priestly figure of the Qumran-Essenes is underlined by a further reference to him as the superior priest. Suggestions that this priest is Aaron, or a Zadok of his lineage, is excluded by the insistence that Jesus, like Melchizedek, is in the Greek wording *agenealogetos*, 'without a genealogy'. As Professor Joseph Fitzmyer points out, 'Every priestly family was supposed to be able to trace its lineage from Levi via Aaron and Zadok. Aaron's lineage itself was known from Exodus 6:16–19, but Melchizedek's lineage was unknown.'[13] If, as I maintain, the name Melchizedek relates to the high priest Meryre, he would have been the first of his line and therefore without any previous priestly lineage.

Analysis of the Melchizedek that Jesus was to emulate, however, shows that this attribution, as explained by Deborah W. Rooke, was 'not merely of high priesthood but of royal priesthood'.[14] The relationship is spelled out in Hebrews, but although the royal association is assumed to be to King David, scholars are at a loss to explain why there is no specific Davidic categorization for this royal element.[15] David is not referred to by name in Hebrews. Instead, the king specifically mentioned is the king of Salem, who is related to the patriarchal period of Abraham, long predating the Israelite kings, and a royal figure who had nothing to do with David. Once again, there is no Israelite king that conventional scholarship can turn to, and the issue is stuck in the mire of preconceptions. Indeed, it is made crystal clear in Hebrews 14:18 that the Melchizedek Jesus aspires to emulate, is the King of Salem of Genesis: 'And Melchizedek king of Salem brought forth bread and wine: and He was the priest of the most high God.'

A number of scholars have noted that the Melchizedek of Hebrews can definitely be linked to the Melchizedek in the Qumran scrolls, and that this character is certainly not Davidic. Even if a royal association were tied only to the Genesis descriptions and not also to the Qumranic descriptions, we would have to ask why an apparently pagan king, the king of Salem, should be singled out as a prototype for a divine personage. Not only is he seemingly a pagan; he is not even a Hebrew![16]

The answer, I suggest, lies partly in the Amarna letters, where Jerusalem is singled out by Akhenaton as his holy city forever.[17] The appellation of King Melchizedek can then clearly be seen as a sacral name combining the royal aspect of King Akhenaton and his high priest, Meryre. The problem of why Abraham and Jesus should want to associate themselves with an apparently pagan figure is thus entirely explained by the fact that Akhenaton and Meryre were not pagan but, together with Jacob and Joseph, the first true monotheists. Thus,

Abraham acknowledges Melchizedek's God El Elyon (God Most High) as his own God in their encounter in Genesis.

For this high priestly figure to have no ancestors can only mean that he was the first of his class. Once again, the literal evidence points strongly in the direction of Meryre, the first high priest of Akhenaton's new monotheism, who was nevertheless an hereditary Egyptian prince.

The following summary of Melchizedek's characteristics demonstrates that he was not a Hebrew and, although a high priest, predated the Temple in Jerusalem:

- He acknowledged and appeared to believe in the same God that Abraham worshipped El Elyon – God Most High;
- He was not circumcised – a Hebrew requirement;
- As a king–high priest, he (or they) would officiate in a temple – but there was no temple in Jerusalem at the time;
- The name incorporated the role of king and high priest and was a combined personality comprising two separate people, reflected in the name being split as Melech Zedek;
- Without a genealogy, Melchizedek must have been the first of his line, as high priest of a line, preceding Aaron as high priest.

Tannaitic and Rabbinic Tradition on Melchizedek

We have already seen some of the Qumranic and biblical references to the figure represented by the name Melchizedek. It is quite apparent that these characteristics are a very good fit with the attributes of Akhenaton, conflated with the qualifications of his high priest, Meryre. When we come to the post–Qumran period, when the Essenes have been scattered in all directions by the Romans, their upheaval evinces even more hidden details about the persona of Melchizedek. The Tannaitic period followed after the destruction of the Second Temple and lasted about 300 years, during which time the rabbis were codifying the content of the Hebrew Bible and the Talmud. In her study *The Secret Doctrine of the Kabbalah*, Leonora Leet looks at the post–Second Temple period and concludes that a priestly strain of influence emanating from the residual Essenes of Qumran had a profound effect on the formulation of the Talmud. The secretive elements of this strain also emerged in the form of Kabbalah. She traces this hidden knowledge to common origins, including aspects of Pythagorean geometry, and to very ancient Egyptian sources. I believe she is basically correct in her deductions and that a central theme of the 'divine son' who is also the 'son of man' is an inherent part of this mystical teaching.[18]

Question: *What was the Qumran-Essene idea of the heavenly chariot modelled on?*

Answer: *The heavenly chariot driven by Pharaoh Akhenaton.*

There is no archaeological evidence of chariots in ancient Canaan, even though there are numerous mentions of chariots in the period of Hebrew rule. One has to assume that chariots were present in Canaan, but the Bible gives scant descriptions of indigenous models, despite the fact that King Solomon was supposed to have 1,400 chariots and built chariot towns across Israel (1 Kings 10:26). Descriptions of the heavenly chariot that appear in the Dead Sea Scrolls and Bible are of a golden vehicle adorned with gleaming jewels, flashing light in all directions – a powerful vision of a divine figure riding in the sky. That this imagery came from Egypt is strongly indicated by the reality of Egyptian chariots, drawn by two stallions with gorgeous trappings and nodding head plumes, for example as seen in the tombs of Tutankhamun and Tutmoses IV. I cite Cyril Aldred, one of the greatest authorities on Egypt and the Amarna period:

> When Akhenaten describes his epiphany at the ceremony of demarcating the city of Akhetaten, 'mounted in a great chariot of electrum like the sun-god when he rises on the horizon and fills the land with beneficence', he not only describes the dazzling appearance of such equipages, he reveals how deeply their imagery had entered into Egyptian consciousness, since from time immemorial the gods in Egypt had travelled over the waters of heaven in ships.[19]

That this imagery came more specifically from awareness of the Amarna period is almost certain, when we examine the closeness of biblical and Dead Sea Scrolls descriptions to our certain knowledge of the style of royal chariot used by Pharaoh Akhenaton, and to other impinging evidence. During his reign Akhenaton raised the status of the chariot as a ceremonial vehicle to a greater height than in any other period in Egyptian history. For him, it was the symbol of his 'going out to the people' and showing himself in state processions. We know from archaeological remains that very early followers of Jesus, and perhaps Essenes at an even earlier period, journeyed to the ruined and completely desolate city that was Akhetaton, and worshipped in front of a relief of Akhenaton riding his glittering 'heavenly chariot'. I have little doubt that this overwhelming experience, and the transmitted memory from the time of Akhenaton, was the basis for the chariot imagery we see in the Dead Sea Scrolls and Bible. The reluctance of the rabbis in later times to talk about 'heavenly chariots' can also be ascribed to a conscious or conveyed fear of having to discuss the hidden past and Egyptian origins.

It is noteworthy that the Egyptian word for chariot 'wrrt' dating to the 15th century BC, gives rise to the Hebrew word 'merkabah', and the earliest forms of Kabbalah are all about the riding of heavenly chariots. It is difficult to see where this imagery and obsession with chariots can have came from, if not from a mystical memory of Pharaoh Akhenaton's fascination with chariots and passion for parading his glorious bejewelled chariot through the streets in royal processions.

Question: *Why were they awaiting two (and possibly three) Messiahs?*

Answer: *They awaited the return of one kingly and one priestly messiah, based on their memory of Akhenaton and his high priest, Meryre I.*[20]

The kingly and priestly messiahs are extensively referred to in the Dead Sea Scrolls texts, and if there is any surprise, it is that the persons behind these quite explicit delineations have not been identified by most scholars. Both of the awaited messiahs are given various titles in different scrolls:

Kingly: Prince of the Congregation, the Sceptre; the Messiah of
Israel;[21] the King Messiah[22]
Priestly: Interpreter of the Law, the Star; the Messiah of Aaron,[23] who
was of princely descent

In addition, the Qumran community expected the third messiah – a prophet like Moses – to return alongside the kingly and priestly messiah as described in the Community Rules Scroll (1QS ix) and in Deuteronomy: 18: 15–17. The identification of the Prophet as a 'new Moses' is supported by inclusion of the Deuteronomic passage in the Dead Sea Scroll known as the Messianic Testimonia, found in Cave 4 (4Q175).

When Qumran-Essene texts refer to a kingly messiah, this is almost inevitably taken, by those studying the question, as being someone emerging from the Davidic line of kings commencing with King David himself. The tacit assumption, by most scholars, is that King David was the role model for this returning royal or kingly messiah. If King David was not the role-model messiah, ordinary scholarship has nowhere else to go. The assumption, however, is fraught with problems and almost certainly wrong. King David (who ruled around approximately 1000 BC) noticeably failed to live up to the righteous ideals demanded by the prophets of the books of Kings and Chronicles, Jeremiah, Ezekiel and Micah.[24] David's hands were stained with blood and he broke almost every one of the Ten Commandments. He had Uriah, an officer in his army, effectively murdered in order to marry Uriah's wife; he brought destruction on 70,000 Israelites for his evil doings.[25] In a castigation by the prophet Nathan, David is roundly condemned for his evil acts against God and told that his descendants will suffer as a result of his murderous deeds.[26] This is hardly a worthy pattern for a future messiah. In fact, formal messianism in Jewish scripture does not appear until the time of Daniel in the 2nd century BC,[27] so King David is even less likely to have been the role model the Qumran-Essenes were thinking about. One has to wonder, therefore, where the Qumran-Essenes obtained their very detailed descriptions and well-developed philosophy of these anticipated messiahs and messianism – which, in any event, appear to predate any of the royal kings of Israel.

The problem of identifying the two messiahs, one kingly and one priestly, alluded to in the Hebrew scriptures but distinctly specified in the Qumran-Essene literature, is so contentious that modern scholarship either ignores the problem or scratches around to try to find possible candidates, using very weak evidence. Nowhere does the Pentateuch or any succeeding text of the Hebrew scriptures suggest that, when the faithful in Israel worshipped at the Tabernacle or later in the Temple at Jerusalem, they looked to the Aaronic high priest as a foreshadowing of a future messianic high priest.[28] Yet the return of a high priest-like figure, in the shape of a messiah, is exactly what the Qumran-Essenes looked forward to. Almost in desperation, some scholars have even suggested Zerubbabel, the rebuilder of the First Temple, or Joshua, the post-exilic high priest, as contenders.[29]

The phrase 'Davidic line' is, in my view, only an indicator of a longer royal line predating King David. In fact, in Qumran texts, and in most biblical texts, the messianic king is deliberately not referred to as Davidic.[30] Although many of the motifs in the expectation of a future king may be drawn from Israel's experience of kingship, other motifs can clearly be traced to earlier periods of Israel's history.[31] Indeed, how can King David be the personification of a messianic figure when the same messianic figure is seen by Isaiah and Zechariah, and by Dead Sea Scrolls texts such as 4Q285, as a 'suffering servant' of God who is frustrated in his ambitions and killed for his efforts? None of these characteristics can be applied to King David. The eminent Kenneth Pomykala and others have postulated that any reference by the Qumran sect to a messiah of Israel should be regarded categorically as non-Davidic.[32]

Where there is mention of a kingly line, this is surely a memory of another previous line of royalty. In the same way as there is no reference to Jerusalem in the so-called New Jerusalem Scroll, a Davidic messiah scarcely appears in the sectarian Qumran-Essene scrolls. These limited and ambiguous references have not prevented most scholars from falling back on the assumption that David was the Essenes' role model for a future messiah, even given the fact that there are alternative explanations that have not yet been explored.

If the relevant Dead Sea Scrolls are read carefully, there are many clues about who the messiahs they awaited were. One of the community's fundamental texts, the Rule of the Community (1QS), refers to 'a Messiah begotten by God' and clearly this cannot be referring to Jesus. In the context of the other references to messiahs, it has to be a previously existing person and none other than the monotheistic King Akhenaton, who was 'the son of God' in Egyptian terms.[33]

The phrase occurs in Column II lines 11–12, and using the facilities at the West Semitic Research Institute, the author has been able to verify that the disputed interpretation of 'Messiah begotten by God', which depends on reading '*ywlyd*' at the end of line 11, is in fact correct.

Prince of the Congregation

Most controversial among the sectarian writings about a messiah is the apparent reference in Dead Sea Scroll 4Q285, fragment 5, to the Prince of the Congregation as being a suffering and executed messiah, who has been equated with Christ by certain sensationalists:

> [As it is written in the book of] Isaiah the Prophet, [the thickets of the forest] will be cut [down with an axe and Lebanon by a majestic one will f]all. And there shall come forth a shoot from the stump of Jesse [. . .] the branch of David and they will enter into judgment with [. . .] and the Prince of the Congregation. The Br[anch of David] will kill him [. . . by strok]es and by wounds. And a priest [of renown (?)] will command [. . . the s] lai[n] of the Kitti[m . . .].

In the opinion of Geza Vermes, the reference here is not to be related to a contemporary Jesus, but is a reference back to the messiah of Isaiah:[34]

> And he shall cut down the thickets of the forest with iron, and Lebanon shall fall by a mighty one. *(Isaiah 10:34)*

> And in that day there shall be a root of Jesse [the father of King David, who lived in Bethlehem], which shall stand for an ensign of the people; to it shall the Gentiles seek; and his rest shall be glorious. *(Isaiah 11:10)*

This explanation, it seems to me, deals with only half the picture; nor have many other obvious questions even been broached by the great number of scholars who have studied and written on the position.[35] Some commentators even speculate that the Dead Sea Scrolls passage refers to Jesus. Clearly the Qumran-Essenes were not writing about a contemporary experience of Jesus, but were looking back to a royal messiah and a priestly messiah whose descendants would bring the word of God not just to the elite few but also to the wider community. Any full explanation of this Dead Sea Scrolls fragment and other references in the Dead Sea Scrolls to messiahs needs to explain where these ideas of messianic figures originated, and to answer various questions.

Summation by way of 20 Questions and Answers

1 *Who were the royal and priestly messianic figures the Qumran-Essenes and Isaiah were referring to?*

The original two messianic figures whose return was fervently awaited by the Essenes were King Akhenaton and the high priest of his holy temple, Meryre.

2 *Why were the royal and priestly messianic figures alternatively referred to as 'the Sceptre' and 'the Star'?*

The royal and priestly messianic figures in the Dead Sea Scrolls were referred to as 'the Sceptre' and 'the Star', because the sign of the royal office of Pharaoh Akhenaton was a sceptre, and when the Pharaoh died, he became a star. The invisible God worshipped by Pharaoh Akhenaton and his high priest in many inscriptional representations found at Amarna in Egypt was portrayed as 'the Aton', a sun disk – the brightest symbol of light known to humankind. There seems no other sensible explanation for the use of these titles.

In the Cairo–Damascus Document and the related Dead Sea Scrolls fragments from Cave 4 at Qumran, there is the clearest possible reference to a 'Star' messiah who equates to the messianic Interpreter of the Law and Prince of the Congregation – a messiah who relates to the time of Jacob, whom I date as a contemporary of Akhenaton: 'A star shall come out of Jacob and a sceptre shall rise out of Israel.'[36]

This phrase also occurs in the Book of Numbers (24:17), but in the Damascus Document (Cairo–Damascus version) the star, as the Interpreter of the Law, is used to describe a figure who comes to Damascus (a place Barbara Thiering identifies as Qumran[37]). What the significance of this person's journey might be will be discussed later, but it has been suggested that when the Teacher of Righteousness fled into exile, another of his followers fled in a different direction – to Damascus.[38]

3 *Why was the priestly messianic figure often referred to as 'Prince of the Congregation' and also designated as a hereditary prince in his own right?*

The priestly messianic figure was designated a hereditary prince in his own right because the high priest Meryre was also a prince by birth, just as he is referred to in the Dead Sea Scrolls. The *shabti* figurine in the Metropolitan Museum, mentioned earlier, has robes and accoutrements strikingly similar to descriptions of the robes worn by the high priest in the Temple of Jerusalem. The two objects Meryre holds are what can only be the *urim* and *thummim* (objects used as casting lots when decisions of state were in question) which are described in Exodus 28, Leviticus 8:8 and in many other parts of the scriptures. Nor can it be ignored that the *shabti* is made from blue serpentine (a translucent mineral containing hydrated magnesium silicates), just as the descriptions in Exodus and Leviticus, from the Hebrew scriptures, required: 'And thou shalt make the robe of the ephod all of the Blue' (Exodus 29:31). (An ephod was a ceremonial outfit worn by the high priest.)

4 *Why were there constant associations of the messiahs to light and the stretching out of hands for a bread offering?*

The imagery of a messiah who 'will extend his hands to the bread offering', described in the Messianic Rule of the Dead Sea Scrolls, is unmistakably reminiscent of the extended hands of Pharaoh Akhenaton offering bread to the Aton. This pictorial gesture appears as a dominant theme in many reliefs found at Akhetaton, as does the vision of the extending hands of the Aton giving light, life and sustenance in return.

In the Manual of Discipline (often called the Community Rule), there is a long description of a last meal before the messiah comes. This description of an Essene ritual meal attended by ten men and presided over by a messiah is in manner and style reminiscent of the Last Supper description in the Christian scriptures (Matthew 26; Mark 14; Luke 22; 1 Corinthians 11):

> Fo[r he shall] bless the first [portion] of the bread and the wi[ne] and shall ext[end] his hand to the bread first. Afterwa[rds,] the messiah of Israel [shall exten]d his hands to the bread. [Afterwards,] all of the congregation of the community [shall ble]ss, ea[ch according to] his importance.

5 *Why did Isaiah, who lived c740 BC, prophesy that the tasks that God would perform at the time of the reconstituted messiah would include recovery of remnants of his people from Egypt and Cush (Nubia)? A supplementary question is: 'Why when the messiahs arrived was their first task to deal with evil in Egypt?*

There could hardly be a more definitive confirmation than in the Cairo-Damascus texts, of the messiah's connection to Akhenaton and Egypt. The first task specified in the Cairo-Damascus Documents for the Star Messiah to perform is not, as we would expect, to restore the Temple, revive the dead, cure the sick, bring peace to the world, attend to problems in Judaea or get rid of the Romans. The first task is to attend to problems in Egypt – to destroy Seth: 'And when he comes he shall smite all the children of Seth.'[39]

Any illusion that we are talking about anything other than an Egyptian-related Seth is destroyed by a quotation in a Dead Sea Scroll relating to Ezekiel, where we find: 'And I will slay the wicked in Memphis and I will bring my sons out of Memphis and turn favourably towards their remnant.' (4Q386)

Why Seth? Why Memphis? For conventional thinking, the only place to turn to is Seth of the Hebrew scriptures, the obscure third son of Adam. This assumption is obviously absurd, and most scholars avoid confronting the issue, or conclude that the text is referring to some inexplicable supernatural force. The real target can be none other than the traditional enemy of Akhenaton's monotheism, the fearsome, most powerful Egyptian god of chaos and evil – Seth.

Memphis was the administrative hub during the reign of Akhenaton and a centre of theology. It was there that the first temple to Aton was built; the city reverted to paganism after the pharaoh's death. Once again there is a preoccupation with settling old scores in Egypt, not in Israel.

The current absurd interpretation of Seth as the human third son of Adam is completely undermined by the view the Qumran-Essenes held on the origins of evil and 'the children of Seth' (Dead Sea Scroll 4Q417). In his masterly analysis, Professor John Collins shows that the idea of Seth as an 'evil inclination' is derived from 'a myth of cosmic conflict' – that is, a story that relates to legendary spiritual forces, rather than a human being.[40]

166

To put a final nail in this particular coffin, the notion of a powerfully evil Seth as the third son of Adam is untenable not only on logical grounds, but in Christian terms it is heresy. Chapter 3 of the Gospel of Luke lists Jesus' family tree all the way back to Adam, the son of God. His second most ancient ancestor was Seth.

6 *Why would the new messiah want to encompass a wider audience of 'the people' rather than just the special few?*

Because a principle of Pharaoh Akhenaton's new religion was that it was open to all people, not just for the privileged few. Secretive worship within an enclosed shrine was not promoted. In fact, the Great Temple itself at Akhetaton was mainly open to the skies and had a large main court to allow access to thousands of people.

7 *Why was the return of the messiah(s) always linked to an apocalyptic age that would herald the reestablishment of the kingdom of God, and what triggered these eschatological ideas?*

Because the earlier 'apocalypse' had been recognized as the demise of Akhenaton and his holy city and it was hoped the returning messiahs would reinstate the city and its central figure-heads, deal with the evil in Egypt first and restore the boundaries of the holy city. The imminent anticipation of this golden age was predicted from the texts of Enoch, Ezekiel and Daniel, and other prophetic writings.

8 *Why had the figure of the royal messiah suffered and been killed?*

Because the Qumran-Essenes believed that Pharaoh Akhenaton had been ill-treated and killed by his enemies. More light on the subject of the 'suffering servant' and the destruction of the city of Akhetaton will be shed in the discussion on Isaiah and what he knew about this period of the 18th Dynasty.

9 *Why was the community following a different form of Judaism to the normal population?*

Because they followed the basic laws of the Pentateuch, underpinned by the religious philosophy and practices of Akhenaton.

167

10 *Why did they follow a solar calendar, whereas the normative population, led by the Temple priests, followed a lunar–solar calendar?*

Because that was the form of calendar used at Akhetaton. The new festivals Akhenaton must have introduced are spelled out in the Temple Scroll and match the listings in the Great Hymn to the Aton, almost certainly composed by Akhenaton. Many of the community's scrolls, and the finding of a sundial at the Qumran site in 1954, testify to their adherence to a solar calendar. In following a solar calendar, the Essenes' festivals always fell on a fixed day, with Passover and the New Year always falling on a Wednesday. A detailed study published by Professor James VanderKam assesses the latest available translated material from Qumran and comes to the conclusion that the scrolls determinedly assign the use of the solar calendar to a very early, pre-Babylonian-influence period, dating back to at least the time of King David.[41]

11 *Why do the Dead Sea Scrolls frequently refer to the appointment of priests in the time of Jacob and Joseph, in a temple context, long before there was a tabernacle in Sinai or a temple in Jerusalem?*

Because priests were appointed to the Great Temple at Akhetaton, and Jacob and Joseph were witnesses to such events. Inscriptional evidence shows that Joseph was almost certainly involved in religious ceremonies in the Great Temple at Akhetaton, and a bound scroll was paraded in the place of worship just as it is in synagogues today.

12 *Why did they celebrate festivals at different times to the rest of the Jewish population?*

See answer 10 above.

13 *Why did they not celebrate Purim?*

Because it had no relevance to their cycle of festivals.

There may be other explanations, but this is the most likely one. Perhaps the Book of Esther, on which the festival of Purim is based, does not have God as the central theme and was therefore unacceptable to a highly devout community. No traces of the Book of Esther have ever been found at Qumran.

The Qumran-Essenes also did not celebrate Hanukkah, one of the major festivals of Judaism, celebrating the historic restoration of the temple and victory of the Maccabees. The conventional explanation is that God is not the major force described in the Maccabean recapture of the Second Temple.

A more plausible explanation is that the antagonism expressed in 1 and 2 Maccabees toward Onias IV, who, as I have argued earlier, was the Essenes' Teacher of Righteousness, had two effects. First, not even a fragment of any of the six books of Maccabees has ever been found at Qumran. Second, if Essenism was a major influence in early rabbinic Judaism, as I maintain, it would not be surprising to find that any work derogatory of their Teacher of Righteousness would be excluded from the Hebrew canon at this formative stage, as was the case.

14 *Why did they apparently celebrate festivals unknown outside their community?*

The answer to this question is linked to the answer to question 10 and relates to a basing of new festivals on seasonal events as designated in the Great Hymn to the Aton.

So what were the festivals being observed at Akhetaten? As far as we can tell, the festivals celebrated by Pharaoh Akhenaton were related to new crops, organized around the spring and autumn harvest products, and would have paralleled those described in the Temple Scroll. So is there any other evidence to tie in the four festivals mentioned in the Temple Scroll which advocates the celebration of three new, previously unknown festivals − of wine, oil and wood. In addition, the Temple Scroll elevates the Festival of Waving of the Sheaf to the status of a major festival.

Why they should adopt these new rituals is, I believe, spelled out in Psalm 104. Psalm 104 has long been noted by numerous scholars as being remarkably similar to, and almost certainly based on, the Great Hymn of Akhenaton found carved on the tomb wall of Ay at Amarna, which is dated to c1350 BC.[42] In each of them, we find a sequence of festivals of wine, oil, wheat and wood that is identical.

Perhaps even more extraordinary is the indication that the ceremony of Waving the Lulav, the most important of the First Fruits Festivals for the Essenes, which is observed to this day during Sukkot by Jews around the world, is almost identical to a ceremony seen in the Great Temple of Akhetaton and must therefore have originated in Egypt of the 14th century BC, long before the existence of a temple at Jerusalem. The plates section of this book shows processional courtiers in a ceremony waving a sheaf in the temple at Akhetaton.[43] The crucial evidence relates to the four binding rings wrapped around the long palm. These palm-leaf wrappings are not part of the palm, but are separate bindings added in exactly the same form and spacing as seen on palm fronds used in the Sukkot ceremony in synagogues today.

If there can be any lingering doubt that some of the festival ceremonies enacted in synagogues of today are rooted in ceremonies that were introduced at the time of Jacob and Joseph in the Great Temple of Akhetaton, a visit to the Museum of Luxor will completely dispel it. On the first floor, engraved on a long wall composed of reconstructed *talatat*, there are pictorial pericopes of activities in and around the Great Temple of Akhetaton. One of these scenes shows the figure of a priest parading a large scroll around the Temple in exactly the same manner as the Torah Scroll is carried around synagogues to this day. There are, of course, thousands of examples across Egypt, carved on temple and tomb walls, of papyrus scrolls being carried or *in situ*, but there are no other examples of a scroll matching that paraded in the Great Temple at Akhetaton, or being carried in the same manner.

Closer examination of the scroll cover shows that it might actually be inscribed with decorations of pomegranates (Hebrew *rimonim*) – a traditional Hebrew emblem for fertility – and a decoration on the robe of the High Priest (Exodus 28:33). The two cartouches on the cover appear to carry emblems related to the Aton.

I believe this kind of revelation does not devalue the authenticity of modern Judaism or of the Hebrew scriptures. On the contrary, it verifies the ultimate antiquity of its traditions and the reality of its central characters, like Jacob and Joseph. In effect, it confirms that many of the stories of the Hebrew scriptures are not, as some detracting minimalists claim, based on fiction and myth, but instead on hard, engraved fact.

15 *Why did they denigrate the Temple in Jerusalem?*

Because they abhorred the practices and design of the Jerusalem Temple and venerated a memory of the plan of the temple at Akhetaten

In many of their texts the Qumran-Essenes stress their preference for the Tabernacle over the Jerusalem Temple and their disquiet at the Temple's design. For them, the number of courts was wrong, the ceremonies were inappropriate, the furnishing were incorrect, the officiating priests were unholy – so many things were unacceptable that they refused to pray in or enter the Jerusalem Temple.

When Onias IV, their Teacher of Righteousness, built a temple at Leontopolis in Egypt, he modelled it on the proportions of the Great Temple at Akhetaton and instead of the usual menorah installed a huge golden globe. One can only imagine that this was his attempt to represent the Aton sun symbol that adorned the Great Temple in Pharaoh Akhenaton's capital.

16 *Why did the Temple Scroll, and the so-called New Jerusalem Scroll, speak of a city and a temple that were quite different from Jerusalem and its Temple?*

Because they were talking about the memory and record of the city of Akhetaton and its Great Temple.

17 *Why did Ezekiel of the Hebrew Bible, whom they revered, also speak of a temple quite different to the one at Jerusalem?*

A discussion on the importance of Ezekiel to the Qumran-Essenes and the significance of his descriptions in the Bible of how he was conducted around a huge temple and a city of enormous size is given in Chapter 14.

18 *Why has Akhetaton been identified as the most likely city the Qumran-Essenes are describing in their scrolls?*

A number of scholars, including Michael Chyutin and Shlomo Margalit, respectively an Israeli architect and a field archaeologist, have studied the similarities between the descriptions in the New Jerusalem Scroll and El-Amarna and come to the conclusion that they are directly related.

19 *Why was the largest room and probably the main prayer hall at Qumran built in almost exact geographic alignment with the Great Temple at Akhetaton?*

The closeness of the alignments is difficult to dispute. When confronted with this conclusion, most scholars do not challenge the accuracy of the statement, but question how the Qumran-Essenes could possibly know how to achieve the result. I do not have a complete answer to the 'how' of this question; the 'why' is answered by the huge volume of evidence already cited, but the fact that there is such a close alignment should be sufficiently remarkable in itself.

20 *Why is the name of the high priest at Akhetaton mentioned in the War Scroll as a leader of the forces of light in the war against the sons of darkness?*

The name of Akhenaton's high priest, who appears to be mentioned in the War Scroll as 'Merere', 'Meriri' or 'Meryre' is not found in the Bible. Of course, it is an interpretation of a name that would have originally been written in hieroglyphs, so it may not be exact. However, the name is sufficiently close to the generally accepted pronunciation of the Egyptian name to conclude that the Dead Sea Scrolls version has to be referring to the same person.

As I have proposed in my previous book, *The Mystery of the Copper Scroll of Qumran*, in which I make a firm connection between the Qumran-Essenes and Pharaoh Akhenaton of Egypt, there is an explanation forthcoming that fulfills all the criteria needed to answer these questions – namely, from within the messianic characteristics of Pharaoh-King Akhenaton and his high priest, Meryre, who was also a hereditary prince.

As Joseph Fitzmyer notes: 'It is a surprise to see a priestly figure become part of the Qumran community's messianic expectations, because there is little in the Hebrew Scriptures itself about a future "priest".' He finds no reasonable explanation for this phenomenon.[44] In fact, I believe both the name of Akhenaton, preserved in the text of the Copper Scroll, and a variation on the name Meryre, Merveyre, as a title for a leader of the Qumran community, reflect this priestly connection, among many other indicators. A stronger indicator is the recording of the name of Akhenaton's high priest in their War Scroll: 'And on the banner of Merari they shall write . . . God's offerings [and the name of the Prince of Merari].' *(4QM)*

If, as I deduce, the origins of monotheistic Judaism were Egyptian, and, more specifically, involved a blending of intellectual belief at a specific period in Egypt's history between Pharaoh Akhenaton and the biblical patriarch Jacob, through Joseph as intermediary, then a strain of priestly heirs — such as the Qumran-Essenes — might well have preserved original knowledge and secrets of this period. They certainly kept the secret name of Akhenaton within their texts, along with many allusions to Egyptian religious experience.

That persecution of the ancestors of the Essene sect dated back to well before 1200 BC is attested to by a pseudepigraphic Psalm of Joshua appended to, and contiguous with, a description of the messiahs of the future.[45] This psalm is about the Joshua who succeeded Moses as leader of the Hebrews, c1200 BC, before Israel had a king or a high priest, or a city, and yet this fragmentary Dead Sea Scrolls text talks in the past tense of events related to a king and to a high priest who are connected with persecutors of the sect and the destruction of a holy city – 'cursèd be men who rebuild this City'.

Chapter 17

Signposts from Amarna to Qumran

How a separate strain of Akhenaton-period inspired priests might have sustained their religious ideals and practices from Akhetaton to Qumran is, on the face of it, not easy to explain. The time span covers a period of some 1,150 years and the difficulty in bridging the gap has been a generalized criticism of the theory. That there are definite hard connections is impossible to refute, but that has not impeded critics from demanding a detailed explanation of the mechanism of transfer between the 'two islands of belief'. The demand for concrete sequential historical evidence of events that occurred between 3,350 and 2,000 years ago is a tall order.

Nevertheless, even if not one link in the chain can be proven, the theory remains intact because of the overwhelming similarities of the two base points. And, in fact, there are numerous links along the way that can be substantiated, and a mechanism of transfer described which is entirely feasible. Norman Mailer used to say: 'To get from one bank of a river to the other you only need a few stepping stones.' To expect a continuous bridge from one bank to the other is expecting something beyond reality. The many emails and letters from scholars and members of the public I receive often contain citations of linkages I was unaware of. I am absolutely certain that if biblical and Dead Sea Scrolls academia looked for evidence within their own area of expertise, they would find support for the Amarna–Qumran theory. Like James Bond in the 1973 film *Live and Let Die*, when he used crocodiles as stepping stones to traverse the infested water to reach the bank, it requires imagination and courage. It requires people to assume the theory might be correct and start seeking supportive evidence, rather than simply rejecting it as being impossible and looking for faults.

I argue that it is possible to establish the continuity of a specific priestly group, separate from the other tabernacle and temple priests, from the very earliest times of the Israelites. DNA evidence,[1] the record of the Old Testament and the direct connection between the Akhenaton–Jacob–Joseph axis and the Qumran-Essenes confirm that there was a separate strain of priests from before the time of the exodus. It is, I believe, possible to trace the probable history of that group and show how the knowledge and the religious convictions of Akhenaton–Jacob–Joseph emerged in the Old Testament, and more particularly to show how the special and often secret knowledge held within the group emerged at Qumran – for example, as knowledge of the treasures of the Copper Scroll, the geometry of Akhenaton's temple, the layout of Amarna, and the continual allusions to extremes of sun and light imagery.

Jan Assmann has re-evaluated the work of Sigmund Freud in the light of modern knowledge, and come to the conclusion that the monotheism of Moses can be traced to the monotheism of Pharaoh Akhenaton.[2]

An overview of the case for a separate strain of priests that extended from the time of Akhenaton-Jacob-Joseph is given in the table overleaf.

Israel testified in Egypt prior to the Exodus!

It is well accepted that the earliest written mention of Israel as a people can be found in the Merneptah stela, now in the Cairo Museum. I have previously argued that the exodus took place during and shortly after the reign of Pharaoh Merneptah, the immediate successor of Ramses II, or possibly during a period of upheaval that followed the death of Merneptah c1207 BC, in the reign of Pharaoh Setnakhte. There are many differing views on the dating of the exodus, but the Merneptah stela is the strongest evidence, amongst other contributing factors, for a 13th century BC dating, with there being no clear written record of Israel in Egypt prior to the Merneptah inscription, except that which I have submitted in my previous books and documentaries – *until recently*.

Re-examination of an Egyptian pedestal relief in the Berlin Museum, by Peter van der Veen and others, has demonstrated a strong case for the inscription to read 'Israel' in hieroglyphic script.[3] The word for 'Israel' (Hebrew *ys'r'l*) is almost identical to that seen on the

The Priestly Lineage from Amarna to Qumran

Akhenaton – Jacob + Joseph
Akhetaton (Amarna)
1350 BC

Refugees including priests flee to

On (Heliopolis)

Yeb (Elephantine)

Moses
1210

Mixed company of Hebrews, Moses' armed guards, Egyptian priests

Exodus

Sinai

Ten Commandments and holy texts in Ark of Covenant, housed in portable Tabernacle

Aaron appointed High Priest; priests appointed to Tabernacle, from Levites

Rebellion of Korah; Dathan, Abiram and On priests against Moses and Aaron

Joshua
1160

Canaan

Tabernacle at Shiloh in North, near Mount Gerezim

Judge Samuel[1] anoints Saul[2] as King

Period of Judges

Saul massacres many Shiloh priests for supporting David

1000
David King[3]

David moves capital from Hebron to Jerusalem.
Appoints two High Priests: Abiathar from Shiloh (N)[4]
and Zadok from Hebron (S)

Solomon King, builds First Temple at Jerusalem

970 Solomon demotes Abiathar and expels him to Anathoth in South

Solomon dies

Kingdom divided
930

South (**Judah** + Benjamin)
Ruled by King **Rehoboam**[5]
Keeps Jerusalem as his capital

North (**Israel**)
Ruled by King **Jeroboam**
Makes Shechem his capital;
establishes alternative centres of worship
at Dan and Beth-el[7]

Ostracized Levitical priests of Shiloh, claiming
descent from Moses, now centred at Anathoth,[6]
continue to record 'E' version of scripture

Aaronid priests control Temple at Jerusalem,
maintain 'J' version of scripture

722
Assyrians destroy Northern Kingdom,
exile ten tribes of Israel northwards

700 King Hezekiah, reformer with Atonist links[8]
Aaronid priests control Temple at Jerusalem,
maintain 'J' version of scripture

680 'E' and 'J' versions combined,
'P' version[9] enhances Aaron's role within 'J' and 'E' versions

622 Book of Deuteronomy, 'D' version, revealed,
written by 'E' priests at Anathoth, directed by **Jeremiah**[10]

587 Babylonians conquer Southern Kingdom, destroy First Temple at Jerusalem,
exile bulk of Israelites and elite, including Ezekiel to Babylon; Jeremiah flees to Egypt

538 Persians conquer Babylonians
Allow exiles to return and rebuild Temple at Jerusalem,
now under Aaronid control

Ezra, an Aaronid priest, and **Nehemiah** return
from Babylon with a complete version of the Five Books of Moses

323 Greek Ptolemaic rule from Egypt after Alexander the Great dies

198 Greek Seleucid rule from Syria

175 **Onias IV**, an 'E' sympathizer becomes
High Priest of Second Temple in Jerusalem

172 Onias IV ousted by **Menelaus**, 'The Wicked Priest',
and flees to Egypt where he builds a Temple at Leontopolis

and installs a huge golden orb

167 Maccabean revolt ousts Greek Seleucids, restores Jewish State
Onias IV returns from Egypt

150 Onias IV, 'The Teacher of Righteousness',
leads separatist 'E' priests to Qumran

1 Samuel, a prophet, priest and judge from Shiloh, and a descendant of Korah.

2 Saul came from the tribe of Benjamin.

3 After Saul's death at the hands of the Philistines, the kingdom was temporarily divided, with the South ruled by Ishbaal, Saul's son, and the North by David. When Ishbaal was assassinated, David, from the tribe of Judah, became king and reunited the kingdom.

4 Before David died, two of his sons contested the throne. Adonijah was supported by the High Priest Abiathar and the priests of Shiloh, and Solomon, David's son by Bathsheba, was supported by the High Priest Zadok and the priests of Hebron. David chose Solomon to succeed him, who, when king, had Adonijah killed, and banished Abiathar to Anathoth in the South.

5 Rehoboam was Solomon's son.

6 A village near Jerusalem.

7 Jeroboam used golden calves as alternative iconography to golden cherubs in the Jerusalem Temple.

8 'E' sources of the Old Testament are so called because they usually refer to God as Elohim; 'J' sources use the term Jahwe. The 'P' version flows through all first four Books of Moses; the 'D' version appears to be independent.

Significantly, as Richard Elliot Friedman points out, 'The overall picture of the E stories is that they are a consistent group, with a definite perspective and set of interests, and that they are profoundly tied to their authors' world' (Friedman, *Who Wrote the Bible*, Harper, San Francisco, 1987). The 'E' group concentrated on Moses and the Tabernacle, from which one can deduce they were closely associated with guarding its contents, and they were not at all interested in the Temple – just as the Qumran-Essenes had little interest in the Jerusalem Temple and denigrated it.

9 According to Friedman, 'P1' was written in the time of King Hezekiah (c715–686 BC) and 'P2' in Second Temple times.

10 Probably set down by a Shilonite scribe, Baruch.

Merneptah stela, except that the 's' sound has a different sibilance. In the case of the Berlin inscription it is a hard *ⱳ* (Hebrew *'sin'*), whereas on the Merneptah stela the 's' has a soft *ⱳ* (Hebrew *'shin'*). From other comparisons, especially the Amarna letters, and from the archaic style of associated words for Ashkelon and Canaan on the relief, the sibilant form on the Berlin pedestal name ring indicates an earlier date for this newly deciphered captionm and the preferred date by Peter van der Veen and his co-authors, is mid-18th Dynasty: in other words the Amarna period of Pharaoh Amenhotep III and his son Akhenaton.

This latest discovery seems to be further evidence that Hebrews were in Egypt during the 18th Dynasty and more particularly in the Amarna period.

Chapter 18

Isaiah Knew about Akhenaton

Before Ezekiel there was another prophet who forms a vital link in the chain back from Qumran to Akhetaton, and that prophet was Isaiah. A number of critics of my work find it difficult to comprehend that such a link could ever exist. However, they have never considered the proposals in depth, invariably have not bothered to read my books, and have never even been to El-Amarna, or considered the real significance of Israel's Egyptian ancestry.

Even a casual look at Isaiah, Chapters 2, 19, and 20, reveals that when the prophet is talking about 'the last days', he is referring to purging the evil not just of Israel but primarily of Egypt. The land that has strayed, he relates, is full of silver and gold, chariots and idols.[1] This can only be referring to a country other than Canaan, notably Egypt, and his examples of restoration are of a people who walk in the light of the Lord, the House of Jacob, as it flourished in Egypt:

> Behold, the Lord rideth upon a swift cloud, and shall come into Egypt: and the idols of Egypt shall be moved at his presence, and the heart of Egypt shall melt in the midst of it . . .
>
> In that day shall five cities speak the language of Canaan, and swear to the Lord of hosts; one [almost certainly a reference to Akhetaton] shall be called, the city of destruction. In that day shall there be an altar to the Lord [as there was in the time of Jacob in the temple of Akhetaton] in the midst of the land of Egypt, and a pillar at the border thereof to the Lord [exactly as Akhenaton had set up at the borders of his holy city] . . .
>
> Blessed be Egypt my people, and Assyria the work of my hands, and Israel mine inheritance. *(Isaiah 19:1, 18–19, 25)*

Isaiah, like some of the Dead Sea Scrolls, is fixated with retribution and restoration primarily in Egypt, and Egypt is equated with Israel and Assyria. This thread of belief in the physical restoration of past glories is crystallized in the thinking of the Qumran-Essenes, who define a kingly messiah and a priestly messiah for whom they wait. The Qumran-Essenes' vision of the temple in their New Jerusalem and Temple Scrolls is undoubtedly related to that of the biblical prophet Ezekiel, and a distantly remembered structure that is clearly identifiable with the Great Temple at Akhetaton. Wrapped up in this vision of restoration is the dream of rebuilding the holy kingdom and re-creating its holy boundaries.

Isaiah is also preoccupied with the theme of light and the sun, the two indicator elements of Aton and Egyptian symbolism. Isaiah 60 commences with a good example (especially when it is recalled that in Egyptian translation the 't' is interchangeable with 'd'):

> Arise, shine, for your light has dawned; the Presence of Adonai
> has shone upon you! Behold! Darkness shall cover the earth,
> And thick clouds the peoples; But upon you Adonai will shine,
> And God's presence be seen over you. And nations shall walk
> by your light, Kings by your shining radiance.

As previously mentioned, one of the specific questions I am sometimes faced with is: 'How can you make a jump of a thousand years to connect Pharaoh Akhenaton to Qumran?' Sometimes I am told, by those with a smattering of knowledge of Egypt, that Akhenaton disappeared from history, so how would the Qumran-Essenes know anything at all about him? I do not claim to know absolutely every detail of what happened between the Second Temple period and 3,350 years ago, and I understand the extreme problems of academic scholars and those of orthodox religious persuasion, who fear their entire life's teachings will be put in jeopardy if they start to acknowledge, or even investigate, the evidence. These are not adequate reasons to avoid confronting the facts.

My answer is to suggest that the questioner studies my work, in written and documentary form, and then puts some evidenced challenges forward. I believe the totality of the facts here presented is so overwhelming for anyone who bothers to study it in depth – not only my work but the work of people like Sigmund Freud, Eric Hornung, Roger and Messod Sabbah, Joseph Davidovits, Harold Ellens and Sarah Israelit Groll – that any reasonable person would come to similar conclusions, in principle, if not in exact detail. Isaiah and Ezekiel come into the category of essential reading in this mission

A common denominator for people whose studies confirm much of my work is that they are knowledgeable about Ancient Egypt. Sarah Groll falls into this category, though I was not familiar with her work before I completed my first book. It is one of my regrets that I was not able to meet and discuss the subject of Akhenaton with this brilliant lady. She founded the Department of Egyptology at the Hebrew University in Jerusalem and published a number of ground-breaking books, particularly related to the Ramesside period in Egypt.[2] She unfortunately died in December 2007, but her legacy lives on and is worthy of close study. Her paper 'The Egyptian Background to Isaiah 19:18' makes fascinating reading and underlines an awareness of Akhenaton, not only by Isaiah, but right down to the time of the Essenes.[3]

To quote Professor Groll:

> According to Isaiah 19, God will bring upon Egypt civil war, natural and economic catastrophe and overall political chaos. There will be fear in Egypt, fear of the 'Judaic God', which will induce the people of Egypt to begin worshipping that God.

Much of the thrust of this passage and Isaiah's preaching is directed towards Egypt, and 19:22 further clarifies his stance: 'The Lord will first afflict and then heal the Egyptians; when they turn back to the Lord, He will respond to their entreaties and heal them.' In other words, the Egyptians who have strayed from God will return to a belief in Him. We now know the period of these events. There is only one period in Egyptian history when the inhabitants believed in God, and that was during the monotheistic period of Pharaoh Akhenaton!

Again in Isaiah 27:13, predicting the Day of God's retribution: 'And in that day, a great ram's horn shall be sounded; and the strayed who are in the land of Assyria and the expelled who are in the land of Egypt shall come and worship Adonai on the holy mount, in Jerusalem.'

The earliest writings of Isaiah are considered to date to the 8th century BC, so he would have been aware of the invasion by the Assyrians and capture of many Israelites from the northern territories and their removal to the area of the Euphrates in that century. However, when he talks (27:12) of recovery of the people from 'the Wadi of Egypt' and 'the expelled who are in the land of Egypt', he cannot be talking about those who left Egypt in the exodus, who were now in the Promised Land. So who are they and where were they being 'expelled from? The only logical answer is that he was referring to a remnant of Hebrew people who were expelled from somewhere in Egypt, but were still in Egypt. My conclusion is that Isaiah was referring to the settlement of pseudo-Jews at Elephantine Island in the far south of Egypt, and that he was aware of their history.[4]

The significance of these verses was not lost on the Qumran sectarians, as they homed in on them in a text, known as 4Q246, which were of obvious importance to them, but completely misunderstood by today's scholars. The fragment, written in ancient Hebrew, provides more detail than Isaiah on events related to Egyptian history and the City of the Sun. I will return to this Dead Sea Scroll fragment after looking at Professor Groll's analysis.

According to Professor Groll, Isaiah was an educated Judaean aristocrat, well acquainted with the Egyptian language and culture, and had a knowledge of ancient Egyptian words, and even those that had fallen out of use by his time. Isaiah mentioned the five cities in the land of Egypt as: עיר ההרס יאמר לאחת. The Hebrew letters are syntactically Egyptian and, to quote Professor Groll:

> [This] is a reference to El-Amarna, the home of Egyptian monotheism which exercised so great an influence on the formation of Israelite monotheism (or vice versa). I thus follow a number of commentators who accept the reading ציר החרס 'the city of the sun' of a few manuscripts, although I do not accept the prevailing opinion that it is a reference to Heliopolis (biblical On). The reading of the majority of the Hebrew manuscripts, עיר ההרס translated as 'the City of Destruction', however, is not surprising: it would seem that Isaiah deliberately chose the rare vocable חרם (horos) for 'sun' instead of the common שמש (shemesh) precisely because of its phonetic similarity to the word רהס 'destruction'. Here we find profound sarcasm vis-à-vis the materialistic values which were so despised by Isaiah. The city was thought to have been destroyed because it was

physically in ruins, yet Isaiah singles it out because he sees that the spiritual power and influence of El-Amarna as the source of Egyptian, and ultimately Israelite, monotheism had survived.

Professor Groll's findings here are in complete agreement with my conclusions from other sources. She reinforces my case better than I ever could.

The book of Isaiah is now considered to have been written by several different people: first, at an early stage in Israelite history, around 800 BC: and second by the so-called Second Isaiah, around 400 BC. From her analysis Groll concludes: 'Isa. 19:18 should therefore not be treated as a late addition; rather, one should attempt to comprehend the prophet's sensitivity to and subtle conception of the international affairs of his time.'

The implication of Professor Groll's work is that my finding of the name Akhenaton in the Copper Scroll, dismissed by some sceptics as 'impossible', is now shown to be entirely feasible. The links I make from Qumran to Amarna are strengthened enormously by her pronouncements, and the signposts in the route from Akhetaton to Qumran come more sharply into focus. In this, and my previous book *The Secret Initiation of Jesus at Qumran*, I include a timeline showing the priestly lineage from Akhetaton to Qumran, which now can be supplemented by two further torch bearers of the truth that came out of Amarna – Professor Groll's 'First Isaiah' and Professor Ben Zion Wacholder's 'Ezekiel'. A key feature of the transmission was identified as the High Priest Abiathar who was demoted by King Solomon around 970 BC and banished to live in Anathoth (1 Kings 2:26). Here, he and his retinue began the succession of Levitical Benei Zadok-1 priests who would guard and cherish the secret understanding of monotheism's genesis, until their descendants finally carried it physically and orally to Qumran.

As I maintain that Jesus and John the Baptist were both members of the Qumran *Yahad* at some period in their earlier lives, it would not be surprising to find that they had taken on board the magnitude of Abiathar's role. In 1 Chronicles 15:11, Abiathar and some Levites are addressed by David as 'The heads of the father's houses of Levites'. The importance of Abiathar is not lost on one of the New Testament writers – in Mark 2:26 Abiathar is cited as the high priest at the time King David came into the house of God and ate the bread of presence. The puzzle is that the passage has Jesus saying:

> Haven't you ever read what David did when he was in need and he and his companions were hungry? How he entered into the house of God when Abiathar was high priest and ate the sacred bread that is not lawful for anyone but priests to eat, and also gave it to his companions?

This verse has caused endless problems in theological circles. Why is Jesus suddenly mentioning Abiathar, especially as he is not understood now as being high priest during David's reign? Did Jesus make a historical mistake? Perhaps the answer is that Jesus, being privy to the inner secrets of the *Yahad* community, knew more about the significance of Abiathar as being in the line of a High Priest Forever and referred to him as such, emphasizing his disdain for the chronology.

This passage is quoted by Professor George Brooke in his contribution to a book on Temple Scroll Studies, but he does not realize why this relatively obscure character in biblical history is taken so seriously, or even mentioned, by Mark. Nor, it seems do Matthew and Luke as they omit this identification. Some scholars, such as V. Taylor, erroneously believe: 'The statement about Abiathar is either a primitive error or a copyist's gloss occasioned by the fact that, in association with David, Abiathar was better known than his father.'[5] This comment fails to understand Abiathar's role in preserving the legacy of the original Plant of Righteousness and his significance at Qumran where the role of the successors to the High Priest Forever stretching out hands to the bread offering is spelled out in the Messianic Rule of the Dead Sea Scrolls.

The messiah of the Qumran banquet is not, in my view, Jesus, as some sensationalists would have it, but a picture of a messiah associated with the period of Akhenaton. The phrase 'extend his hand to the bread first', found in the Qumran text, is a vivid recollection of the wall reliefs that can still be seen today at Amarna. These show the rays of Aton tipped with outstretched hands receiving the bread and wine offering from the extended hand of the offerer, kept on the table in front of the altar.

Chapter 19
And Along Came Kabbalah

It might be a puzzle as to what Kabbalah could have to do with the connections that have been made back to Egypt and Akhenaton for the Hebrews. However, there is almost certainly awareness within its hidden depths of legends from the Amarna period, which are of relevance to the discussion. Mystical knowledge has been a parallel progression alongside development of the Hebrew religion from the earliest times. I do not intend to venture too deeply into the murky caverns of this subject, but, nevertheless, there are nuggets of information within Kabbalah which, I believe, reveal a secret knowledge of Akhenaton's Egypt carried down to us today through legend, myth and ancient texts by rabbinic sages, who in some instances may not even have been aware of the source, or significance, of what they were recording and embellishing.

In *The Secret Initiation of Jesus at Qumran* I concluded that the '*Ka Ba Ahk*' of Egyptian mythology were the original ideas behind the basic concepts of early Kabbalah. The current suggestion, repeated in almost every book on Kabbalah, assigns the derivation of the word as meaning 'tradition' or 'to receive'. In my understanding both these assumed meanings of the word are quite wrong. Even a cursory study of the Egyptian *Book of the Dead* which sets out the function and definition of the '*Ka*', the '*Ba*' and the '*Akh*' shows that these concepts are exactly matched by the parallel themes in ancient and modern Kabbalah of '*Nefesh*', '*Ruach*', and '*Neshemah*'. A reflection of the same acknowledgement of the mysterious side of existence can be seen in the naming of the 'Ka-Ba' stone in Mecca, and the ultimate goal of Muslim pilgrims to reach up to God, 'Allah'.

Part of my interest in Kabbalah was allied to the importance Akhenaton placed on the role of the ceremonial chariot and its significance to the earliest forms of Kabbalah. Again, I identify the earliest formulations of Kabbalah *Merkabah* chariot mysteries as a direct reflection back to Egypt and in this instance to the 'heavenly chariot' imagery of Akhenaton.

Even to this day there are warnings by rabbis that study of Kabbalah can be dangerous, and should not be undertaken by anyone under the age of 40, and then only in the company of an initiate. I conclude that this inhibition is mainly due to the perceived likelihood that it will inevitably lead back to Egyptian sources, which are considered pagan. Of course, if the sources are in fact related to the Amarna period, there is actually nothing to fear from a monotheistic point of view, except, perhaps, the knowledge that Judaism may have originated as an Egyptian–Hebrew synthesis, rather than have been exclusively Israelite.

Lead Codices

My interest was re-ignited when my opinion was sought on a discovery of lead codices by Bedouin in the northern region of Galilee. This amazing collection of what may well be the earliest ever examples of a codex, which carry cast and engraved lettering and images, initially defied understanding. I took samples of the material to Dr Peter Northover, at the Materials Characterisation Laboratory, Oxford University, for metallurgical analysis and mass x-ray spectroscopy. Dr Northover's conclusion was that the lead material was consistent with examples of Roman lead from the 2nd century AD, but nevertheless could be an ancient forgery. Deciphering the content and meaning of the codices has proved extremely difficult, and the various expert opinions that have been sought have not been definitive. Professor André Lemaire of the Sorbonne considered the written content to be representative of the 2nd century AD and, in some instances, identical to writing on coins of the Bar Kochba period.[1] Having physically examined only two of the numerous objects found by the Bedouin, Professor Lemaire reserved his position as to the authenticity of the collection. Another expert in decipherment, Brian Colless, of Massey University, thought the material might reflect an even earlier compilation period and was able to elicit a number of key phrases in the text.

From my knowledge of the location of the find, and other information given to me by Hassan Saida (one of the Bedouin who discovered much of the material), and by piecing together the translations of phrases by various experts, I also came to the conclusion that some of the artefacts were indeed from the Bar Kochba period. I believe that they could well be the work of Rabbi Shimeon Bar Yochai, who was the spiritual leader of the Jewish revolt against the Romans.

An interim report on the findings was published in the largest-circulation Israeli newspaper *Yedioth Ahronoth* on 5 March 2010, and it is intended that a fuller version will be produced in book form in the near future, after further studies have been completed.[2]

However, my further research has determined that much of the lead material is almost certainly fake. It appears that whilst a few items may possibly be genuine, others in the collection have been forged to create items of potential value. This development unfortunately throws doubts on even the very few that have indicated an ancient date under metallurgical examination. One favourable outcome has been that it has led me to research some esoteric medieval texts which have considerable relevance to the present study, including the strange '*grimoires*'.

The Sixth and Seventh Books of Moses

Alongside the earliest mystical references, a large number of Kabbalistic texts have emerged, extrapolating and extemporizing on images and ideas in the earlier formats. Often these texts are confusing and their meanings obscure, but if they are examined carefully, there are pieces of information, the significance of which the authors may not even have been aware of, which shed light on the origins of the texts. Among these are the Sixth and Seventh Books of Moses. Printed versions are available from the 18th and 19th centuries AD, undoubtedly transmitted from much earlier times. These contain magical incantations and images of seals used in creating spells to achieve objectives and the summoning and dismissal of spirits and other transient entities. Talmudic and biblical Christian names and passages are cited to control the natural elements, or people, or conjure up the dead, and the books clearly contain Kabbalistic features.

In the Seventh Book of Moses the seal of 'The Breastplate of Aaron' carries the following remarkable inscription, which can be read as: 'SADAJAI AMARA ELON HEJIANA VANANEL PHENATON EBCOEAL MERAI'. This is translated by Johann Scheibel as: 'That is, a Prince of Miens, the other leads to Jehova. Through this, God spoke to Moses.'[3]

189

Indeed, many of the seals mentioned in the *grimoires* are said to relate to the time of Moses and ancient Egypt. However, I believe that the reading is rather different, and what it is saying is: 'Shadai [God related to the Sun] at Amarna God of Akhenaton and Meryra support and keep us.'

The three key words of the blessing on the seal are immediately identifiable and a connection back to the Amarna period is self-evident. Although at the time of Pharaoh Akhenaton the name of his city was Akhetaton, its nomenclature as Amarna stretches back to ancient times, and no doubt it was known by that name after Akhenaton's name was stricken from Egyptian record.

The phrase is reminiscent of the priestly blessing believed to have been recited by the High Priest in the First and Second Temple in Jerusalem. It is still recited in synagogues today, often at the end of a service, and is also used in many Christian churches. The modern verse can be read as:

> May the Lord bless you and keep you.
> May the Lord make his face to shine upon you and be gracious
> unto you.
> May the Lord lift up his face unto you and give you peace.

This formula of a three-line priestly blessing is very similar in structure, sense, and feeling to the three-line blessing uttered by the high priest in the Great Temple of Akhetaton.[4]

> The beams [rays: *setut*] that give health and sustain all that is created.
> The beauty [*neferu*] of the light giving the power to see and enjoy life.
> The love [*merut*] from the warmth giving beneficial qualities of well-being.

The possibility that all of these are related cannot be discounted.

Clearly, then, Kabbalah and its subsidiary texts carry within them a distant memory of Akhenaton and confirm Sarah Groll's assertion that his name was not lost to history, but continued to be referred to in Hebrew memory, wittingly and unwittingly.

Chapter 20

The Controversial 'Son of God' Fragment

We can now turn to one of the most alarming pieces of text found amongst the Dead Sea Scrolls – the 'Son of God' fragment – and consider how it relates to Isaiah 19:18. Alarming on at least two counts. Firstly because it uses a phrase previously thought unique to the New Testament, and secondly because no one has had much idea of what it is talking about. As will become apparent, the same themes that are expressed in Isaiah 19 and 20 are seen here in 4Q246 – purging of evil primarily in Egypt; a land that has strayed; turmoil and destruction, and then restoration with God reinstated in his holy placement. Again there is only mention of Egypt and Assyria; however, this time we have more detail, which is what one would expect from a group who had much more intimate knowledge of Egypt and the origins of God's works.

Few pieces of Dead Sea Scrolls material better exemplify the dictum that everyone carries 'baggage' from their previous learning into a new encounter, and the so-called 'Son of God' fragment is no exception. Even Józef Milik, doyen of the Ecole Biblique translators, was nervous about its contents, as the history of its consideration shows.[1]

Of all the controversial material found at Qumran, the Son of God fragment stands out as one of the most illuminating. This tiny piece of leather found in Cave 4, with its ancient Aramaic writing, talks in apocalyptic terms of a prince and a fallen ruler. It is worth quoting to appreciate its significance. Note that brackets [ ] here indicate editorial interpolations; parentheses ( ) indicate alternative translations:

[The spirit of God] dwelt on him, he fell down before the throne. O [K]ing, wrath is coming to the world (you are angry forever), and your years . . . is your vision and all of its coming to this world . . . great [signs] a tribulation will come upon the land . . . a great massacre in the provinces . . . a prince of nations . . . the King of Assyria and [E]gypt . . . he will be great on earth . . . will make and all will serve . . . he will be called (he will call himself) [gr]and . . . and by his name he will be designated (designate) himself.

The Son of God he will be proclaimed (proclaim himself), and the Son of the Most High they will call him. But like the sparks (meteors) of the vision, so will be their kingdom. They will reign for only a few years on earth, and they will trample all.

People will trample people, and one province another province until the people of God will arise and all will rest from the sword. Their kingdom will be an eternal kingdom, and their paths will be righteous. They will jud[ge] the earth justly, and all will make peace. The sword will cease from the earth, and all the provinces will pay homage to them. The Great God will be their helper. He Himself will wage war for them. He will give peoples into their hands, and all of them He will cast before them. Their dominion will be an eternal dominion, and all the boundaries of . . .[2]

One can only imagine the confusion these three short columns have caused among biblical scholars. The phrases 'Son of God' and 'Son of the Most High' occur in Luke 1:32–5 and seem to indicate reference to Jesus the Messiah. The puzzles in 4Q246 are:

- Who is the dethroned ruler?
- What is the civil war being described?
- Who is the new king who appoints himself Son of the Most High?
- Which provinces will pay homage to those who vanquish the new king and reinstate peace?
- Why are Assyria and Egypt mentioned?
- Is there a reference to Jesus?

Add to this the fact that the various translated versions differ in wording and it can easily be seen that the complications multiply. The general thrust of the story, however, is readily discernible from the quoted version and is similar in other translations. Explanations of the identity of the anti-hero in the text range from the Syrian tyrant Antiochus IV, to Emperor Augustus,[3] to the Seleucid ruler Alexander Balas.[4] Some, such as Florentino García Martínez, have argued for an apocalyptic interpretation, with the 'Son of God' being the 'Prince of Light', or a future Davidic messiah.[5] The explanations are extremely varied, but none fits more than a few of the circumstances of the passage. In fact, they amount to no more than speculation within the constraints of conventional understanding – or one might say misunderstanding. John Collins is one of the few scholars to begin to take up the challenge thrown down by Professor Schiffman to look further afield than the dusts of Judaea for explanations of difficult Dead Sea Scrolls texts.[6]

In my opinion there is only one scenario in the history of the Hebrews that fits this specification. It is when Joseph, Jacob and their Hebrew families are at the court of the monotheistic Egyptian king Akhenaton and the king is killed, possibly together with his high priest, Meryre I, who is also a hereditary prince.[7] Consequently, within a few years, Akhenaton's great temple and his holy city are destroyed. His followers and the Hebrews are dispersed as civil war breaks out. Place the distant ancestors of the Qumran-Essenes in the historical context of witnesses to the events surrounding Akhenaton's death and every perplexing phrase in 4Q246 becomes explicable through their knowledge and handed-down memory of these events. By tracing the priestly strain of Qumran-Essenes right back to the monotheistic Pharaoh Akhenaton – whom they viewed, I contend, as their vision of God's representative on earth, their Melchizedek – we find the circumstances that surrounded his life fit every essential detail of 4Q246. In addition, anyone who has even a cursory knowledge of the ancient Egyptian texts of the Amarna period will recognize the style of phraseology used in the 'Son of God' fragment.

From what we know of the historical record, King Akhenaton's reign in his newly established holy city of Akhetaton came to an abrupt end when he was almost certainly killed, probably by Ay, his trusted aide. Akhenaton may well have been struck down before his own throne. Civil war then broke out throughout Egypt, and Akhenaton's followers were massacred throughout the provinces, or *nomes*, of Egypt.

In the words of Nicholas Weeks, director of the Amarna Royal Tombs Project, 'The situation rapidly deteriorated into mayhem and widespread religious persecution.'[8] There was a brief intermediate pharaoh, Smenkhkare, and then Tutankhamun succeeded to the throne, but he was too young to govern. Ay was effectively in control of Egypt, and he almost certainly also killed Tutankhamun and appointed himself king. This self-elevation of a non-royal was virtually unknown in Egypt, as the direct family descendant invariably became ruler.

The terms 'Son of God' and 'Son of the Most High' are typically Egyptian of the period and appear in many ancient Egyptian texts. The phrases allude to the pharaoh's direct connection with the highest god, Amun, supported by Khons, Ra and all the other lesser gods. Akhetaton was destroyed within 20 or 30 years of Ay assuming power and re-establishing Thebes as the capital of Egypt. In doing so, he appropriated the traditional pharaonic title of 'Son of God'.

The text of 4Q246 then moves to a vision of the future, anticipating the 'people of God', the followers of Akhenaton, regaining power by sweeping away and 'trampling' the followers of the treacherous usurper. When they succeed, 'their dominion will be an eternal dominion and all the boundaries of . . .' Akhenaton's city and temple would be reconstituted.

The dream of Akhenaton's followers would inevitably have been that the people of God would eventually triumph and that he would one day be restored to power with the 'provinces again paying tribute' to him – a typical Egyptian custom.

Reference to Assyria and Egypt in 4Q246 as being under the hegemony of the anti-hero king can only be a reference to an Egyptian king. Egypt was the only power ever to be exclusively referred to as the controller of both these regions. The only time in ancient history when any country controlled both Egypt and Assyria was pre-1200 BC, and that controlling country was Egypt itself. At the time, the people of Mesopotamia were being referred to as an Assyrian empire and as vassals of Egypt. Subsequent to the 8th century BC, the region was controlled by the Babylonians, and then successively by the Persians, Greeks and Romans. Their empires were vast, but were never spoken of as being controlled by a king exclusively controlling Egypt and Assyria.

The idea suggested by some scholars that the reference might be 'broadly speaking' to the domination by the Romans of Assyria and Egypt just does not fit. The northern region of Asia was no longer called Assyria and had not been since pre-Babylonian times, and Rome also dominated most of the countries bordering the Mediterranean. There would be no sensible reason to single out Egypt and Assyria.

All the conventional explanations of 4Q246 are forced, but put on a very ancient polished pair of Egyptian glasses and read the passage again. All the elements of Akhenaton's story are there, a story known fairly accurately from historical records: a king who faces disaster and possible treachery – 'a tribulation will come upon the land' – and is almost certainly slain, betrayed and killed by a close friend, and becomes a messianic figure for his people of God. Civil war breaks out 'throughout the provinces' of the country; the traitor appoints himself king of Egypt and Assyria and proclaims himself the new 'Son of the Most High', incarnate on earth, as all previous pharaohs were accustomed to do; he is the anti-God; the people of God dream of their redeemer, a kingly messiah (Akhenaton), returning and taking revenge on the peoples of the anti-God; 'the people of God' restore 'all the boundaries' of Akhenaton's holy city.

All the related Dead Sea Scrolls texts, and the phrases that keep cropping up in them, fit this interpretation of 4Q246. This was the messiah the Qumran-Essenes were waiting for, a king who carried a sceptre – the emblem of kingship in Egypt. The second priestly messiah, the Prince of the Congregation,[9] was Akhenaton's high priest, Meryre,[10] while the priestly leader of the Qumran community was called Mervyre.[11] Light was the overriding motif of Aton, Akhenaton's One God, with the 'hands' of life, bounty, food and goodness radiating outward from a central winged sun image – an image that continued to appear in Egypt after Akhenaton and keeps popping up in excavations across ancient Canaan, modern Israel. We even find two of the Akhenaton motifs combined in the Essenic phrases by the hands of the Prince of Lights and 'Prince of Light'[12] seen in other Dead Sea Scrolls material. The War Scroll describes a banquet where the Prince will extend his hands to offer bread, reminiscent of the way Akhenaton is seen, in wall reliefs at Amarna, extending his hands towards the Aton with bread offerings.

The War Scroll is even more specific. It unequivocally names Akhenaton's high priest, Meryre, as a leader in the final battle of the 'Sons of Light' against the 'Sons of Darkness': 'On the standard of

Merari they shall write the votive offering of God . . . And the Prince of Light Thou hast appointed from ancient times'.

Josephus recorded a number of descriptions that identify the sect and even gives an oblique indication that he also knew of the name Aton as that of God. In Book 2 of his *Antiquities of the Jews*, he refers to the need for caution in discovering the four-letter name of God.

Read in conjunction with the so-called Pierced Messiah fragments found in Cave 4 (4Q285),[13] the thread of the story is continuous. The phrases found in these fragments can plainly be identified with Egypt and Akhenaton. The future dream of the people of God, now in the hands of the Qumran-Essenes, speaks of God shining his face toward his people and giving them life and bounteous fruit and food in plenty (4Q285, fragment 1). Rays of light with hands giving life and food are the defining symbols of Akhenaton's vision of his One God, Aton.

In a recent study C. D. Elledge opposes, as I do, 'much recent scholarship that views the "Prince" in Qumran literature as a Davidic Messiah', and concludes that 'this figure should be considered a "quasi – or proto-messianic figure"'.[14] When all the characteristics of this quasi or proto-messianic person are analyzed, it becomes patently obvious who the figure really is. The identity of a messiah who embodies the titles 'Son of God' and 'Son of Man' can readily be equated to Pharaoh Akhenaton, from the diverse historical sources we have describing his distinctiveness, and numerous hieroglyph descriptions of him from Egyptian sources. Stela 324, in the British Museum, is a good example. Here, the cartouches show the double nature of the king as divine son and earthly regent. This is a recurring laudation of the two natures of the Father-God, along with the divine human son, characterizing the pharaoh in Egypt as the 'Son of God'.[15]

Considering that the two hugely controversial fragments discussed above almost certainly espouse one theme – a slain religious leader and his high priest – the overall conclusion is that the Qumran community was writing about messiahs in the far distant history of its movement, none of whom was Jesus, but that the original characteristics of Jesus might have fulfilled many of these expectations. It would not therefore be surprising to find that a strand of the Qumran-Essene community would become followers of Jesus as a messianic figure, and might have spread his message to other Essenes outside Qumran.

Chapter 21

A Chance Meeting:
The Elephant on the Move

After the gathering in of copious amounts of scroll material, the Jordanian authorities, in whose territory Qumran and the caves lay after 1948, sanctioned the formation of a team, including foreign scholars, to commence the gargantuan task of studying, safeguarding and classifying the finds. Under the auspices of the Ecole Biblique, part of a Dominican monastery in East Jerusalem, the team included eight new recruits who were also to acquire publishing rights in much of the material they were allocated. This turn of events would hamper release of the scrolls to a wider audience for the next 40 years.

Initially, the publishing programme looked promising as the first volume of the official publication *Discoveries in the Judaean Desert of Jordan* came out in 1955 and dealt with findings from Cave 1, but things soon slowed down.[1] By 1968 only five volumes had been published, comprising perhaps some 15% of the available material. After this, the pace ground to a complete standstill. Why? What happened to stall the publishing process?

Much of the classification and translation of the scroll fragments had taken place in the Palestine Archaeological Museum in East Jerusalem, renamed the Rockefeller Museum under an endowment from John D. Rockefeller. After the Six-Day War of June 1967, the Israelis took over control of Jerusalem and the territories encompassing Qumran and the caves. Feelings between the Ecole team and the Israelis became fraught when the Israelis changed the ground rules and the team no longer enjoyed *carte blanche* to progress their private projects. One of the first acts of the new controllers was to forbid any further exhumation of bodies from the Qumran cemeteries. This was illegal under Israeli law, and still is. Somewhat surprisingly, the Israeli authorities did not insist

197

on Jewish members being recruited onto the translation team. Nor did they apply any pressure to have women brought on to the team, despite the then current all-male membership exhibiting evidence of misogynism.

Perhaps relations with the Catholic Church and the Jordanians were at a sensitive stage, and there were ownership issues in relation to the scrolls and Qumran materials. Matters were thus perhaps too sensitive to meet head on, and perhaps they did not want to jeopardize the status quo. Some material, including the Copper Scroll, was already in the possession of the Jordanians. Political factors also entered the equation with Christian- and Arab-controlled buildings suddenly coming under Israel's jurisdiction.

All these external pressures on the Ecole group added fertilizer to the insidious seeds being harboured within the team. I will return to this issue in the last chapter.

The then head of the editorial team, Father Roland de Vaux, came to an arrangement with the Israelis that they would be allowed to continue their work unhindered, but it was another ten years before the next volume of *Discoveries in the Judaean Desert,* Vol. 6, appeared. This was not good enough for the increasingly frustrated, excluded body of scholars, who were being fed scraps of a meal that had already revolutionized understanding of the Bible and early Christianity. (Public interest was equally unsatiated, and in 1991 Michael Baigent and Richard Leigh would capitalize on the unhappy situation by bringing out a book, *The Dead Sea Scrolls Deception*, that accused the Vatican of orchestrating a cover-up.[2] Their reasoning was that there were things in the scrolls that would seriously damage the Catholic Church.)

In 1977 Geza Vermes commented that the delays constituted 'the academic scandal *par excellence* of the twentieth century'. On the initiative of the Ecole's then director, Father Jean-Luc Vesco, and Father Jean-Baptiste Humbert, a team was set up to implement publication of the Qumran excavations, which were still only available in a preliminary form, much to the irritation of outside scholars keen to finalize their work. They appointed Professor Robert Donceel, of the Institute of Archaeology at the Catholic University of Louvain-la-Neuve, to conduct the analysis of de Vaux's original notes. He headed up an interdisciplinary team comprising his wife, Pauline Donceel-Voûte – a specialist in mosaics and the Roman period – seven other scholars from his university, and Christian Augé of the CNRS, Paris, a numismatist; and Françoise de Callatay, of the Cabinet des Medailles, Royal Library of Brussels. An appeal for funding by the Ecole was published in *Revue de Qumran*, but not much happened by way of publications. A few brief reports appeared in 1992 and 1993, but it soon became apparent that a serious rift was affecting the relationship with the new team. The damage was initially done by a broadcast in 1991 when Pauline Donceel-Voûte referred to Qumran, in the early Roman period, as an opulent summer residence. The Ecole team took fright at the thought that they were entrusting de Vaux's previously confidential excavation notes to people who did not believe Qumran was a religious centre.

The Belgian–French team's observations that some of de Vaux's excavation material carried no inventory numbers or stratigraphic information also cast doubts on the quality of his archaeological work. Much of the coin hoard was found to be missing, throwing more doubt on the chronology of the settlement. The Donceels' final conclusion was that Qumran was a *villa rustica*, a view firmly rejected by most of current scholarship apart from one notable exception, Zdzislaw J. Kapera, editor of *The Qumran Chronicle*. He refers to Qumran as a kind of Jewish *villa rustica*, but concedes that the unexpectedly large cemetery near the settlement cannot be explained by this theory.

If anything, the move to try and speed up the flow of information exacerbated the impatience of an expectant academic community and the public in general. Conspiracy theories continued to abound, and the delays continued. Already, however, a conference had been convened in London in 1987 to review the situation and see what could be done.

Various excuses have been put forward on behalf of the Ecole team to try and explain the delays – the task of sorting through some 85,000 fragments was too daunting for the small team, manipulation of the fragments before any translation could even be attempted was painstakingly difficult, funds were short, key members of the team were suffering ill-health or died, etc., etc. These excuses, and Baigent and Leigh's claims of a Vatican-inspired cover-up, were undoubtedly partly valid, but there was something else lurking in the background. That something, which few people cared to broach or knew about, was the main reason for the delays right the way through from the earliest days. The other factor, which has never been fully described, was the remedial mechanism which enabled the delays to be overcome, apparently facilitated through an unknown source of funds. Various references in the literature are made to an 'anonymous donor', but who was this mysterious person, or organization?

Clues appear in the later volumes of *Discoveries in the Judaean Desert*, where acknowledgements to various sources of funding are given. In the volume on Cave 4 Greek manuscripts, for example, we find the following statement:

> Endowments from: National Endowment for the Humanities, a US Federal Agency; Catholic University of America; the University of Notre Dame, Department of Theology; Princeton Theological Seminary; Yarnton Fund for the Qumran Project of the Oxford Centre for Postgraduate Hebrew Studies.

In the second part of my conversation with Professor Geza Vermes, details of which follow, I asked him about the source of funding, but he was reluctant to disclose much information. In fact, he would not divulge the source, only saying that it was 'anonymous', but he did confirm that it came through 'Yarnton' (the Oxford Centre for Hebrew and Jewish Studies, a part of Oxford University, located at Yarnton, near Oxford). When I told him that I thought I knew the source, he would neither confirm nor deny the organization I mentioned.

Since my conversation with Professor Vermes discusses various leading members of the translation team I list here the editors in chief, and the number of volumes of *Discoveries in the Judaean Desert* published under their auspices, to assist in understanding this.

Editors-in-chief of the Ecole translation team

Editor	Dates	Vols. published
Father Roland de Vaux	1948–71 (died)	5
Father Pierre Benoit	1971–87 (died)	2
John Strugnell	1987–90	1
	(forced to resign)	
Emanuel Tov	1990–2010 (retired)	31
		(1 pending)

Interview with Professor Geza Vermes, Part 2

Continuation of an interview with Professor Geza Vermes at his home in Oxfordshire, in March 2010.

RF: The delays in the publication [of the Scrolls] were discussed in 1987 at conference convened in London. I believe you were there as was [John] Strugnell, and by a strange coincidence I met someone who was with the Wolfson Foundation who was also there.

GV: Which Wolfson?

RF: No, one of the employees of the charitable foundation. His name was Franks. You met with him and Strugnell?

GV: We might have happened to be in the same group.

RF: The conference was convened to try and speed up the process of publication. Did it have any positive results? Did it come to any active decision to do anything?

GV: Incidentally, yes. The man who is referred to as the 'anonymous donor' decided that money should be put in.

RF: So that money was donated so that things would be freed up a bit, via Strugnell?

GV: Money continued to be put in. In fact.

RF: It went through to Emanuel Tov?

GV: It never went to Strugnell.

RF: It never went to Strugnell!?

GV: This was in 1987. In 1990 it started, so there had been some money, financial support until Strugnell disappeared.

RF: And then it stopped?

GV: No, it continued going to Emanuel Tov through Yarnton.

RF: How long did that go on for?

GV: More or less until quite recently.

RF: Really. That's curious; I mean it's not actually public knowledge is it? Perhaps it shouldn't be?

GV: Yes, we are dealing with an anonymous person. If you look in the volumes [of *Discoveries in the Judaean Desert*], there is usually something in the credits; there is some reference to the anonymous support.

RF: But no reference to the donor as such.

GV: No, there is not.

RF: So it's gone on right up until the final publication, so it's stopped now? Nothing to support.

GV: Yes. I don't know the exact date, but until relatively recently in the thousands. There was still being held a one-yearly meeting to decide to do something.

RF: So there was an annual allocation of money. In a way it's odd because one of your most well-known statements is this scandal *par excellence* over the delays, and in a way you have been instrumental in undoing the delays.

GV: Well, I don't think it is all my doing. The delays were entirely due to the chaos which remained until the demotion of Strugnell.

RF: You don't think there was any Vatican involvement, plots, conspiracies?

GV: [Vigorous shaking of head in a negative fashion.]

RF: What about another possible effect. When I was in Milik's flat, he allowed me to look at his papers and I was able to look through his working papers, and I saw a letter from Benoit, written in 1977.

GV: By '77 . . . Benoit wrote to all of them in '72.

RF: Oh yes, you are right, '72. Benoit had written a letter to the Jerusalem team . . . implying that he was favouring the Arab interests in the scrolls, the Jordanians, rather than the Israelis.

GV: They all did.

RF: Why did they do that?

GV: That's how it was. With the exception of Frank Cross; I don't know exactly what Milik's position was, but they were all totally pro-Arab and anti-Israeli.

RF: Anti-Israel, not anti-Jewish?

GV: It's always difficult to distinguish, in principle. There is a new book by Weston Fields, a very detailed history of the Dead Sea Scrolls, volume one is out, volume two is still to come, and he asked Gerry Murphy-O'Connor to write a sort of pre-review of the book, and in 2009 or 10 when it was written, he is still talking about an Israeli invasion, and it's the old Biblique, and he is not even French, he's Irish.[3]

RF: That's a real mind-set. There were other instances, of course, other instances of anti–Semitism, particularly with Strugnell. The other instance of them acting together was the letter to *The Times* condemning John Allegro. Milik's signing that letter against Allegro was partly against his will. He said he had to do it as part of the group, but he wasn't keen, he wasn't happy. Milik kept his faith, although he came out of Catholicism. I never sensed any anti–Semitism from Milik.

GV: When there was the '87 conference, he was the only one who didn't come. All the other editors came out.[4]

RF: Cross is still alive, isn't he?

GV: He had some heart problem, and then his wife died. Most of them are dead now.

RF: Strugnell, of course, was anti–Semitic.

GV: Not just anti–Semitic, yes. He would not date his letters from Jerusalem.

RF: Were any of the others? De Vaux?

GV: Anti–Semitic, I don't know, but certainly anti–Israeli.

RF: Maybe they were so immersed in their scrolls that they resented anything that interfered with their work, rather than they were Jewish people.

GV: There wasn't much love. If they had wanted to make a stand to show it was not anti–Jewish but just anti–Israel, they could have pretty easily found a Jewish scholar.

RF: They kept Jews off the team. Although Strugnell was the first to bring them on?

GV: Yes, but so late, and Qimron was a soft choice.

GV: I used to be very friendly with him [Strugnell] in the '60s and '70s until he lost his sense.

RF: He went off the rails, didn't he?

GV: Well, it was drinking.

RF: I am sure you are right. When he was forced out, he said he would fight Tov's appointment, implying because he was a Jew rather than an Israeli. The other one, of course, was Allegro. I don't think he was anti–Semitic in the early days, and he was, strangely enough, a great friend of Milik's. That notorious letter that they sent to *The Times*, Milik said to me he didn't really want to sign it; they were great friends. They both read to each other Wodehouse, P. G. Wodehouse, and they both had a great sense of humour.

GV: Well I don't know about that. When you read those letters now, Allegro's, to his various correspondents . . . Totally carried away.

RF: Oh well his books, the magic mushroom book . . .

GV: By that time it was academic suicide.

RF: And he also said some nasty things about Judaism. Judaism was a violent religion. Do you think Starcky, Barthélemy, all of them . . . ?

GV: Barthélemy pulled out. He was involved in Cave 1 and then left. But Starcky, I don't know.

RF: Did you ever meet Lancaster Harding?

GV: No, and of course after '56 he was out of it.

RF: Where did you stay when you first went to Jerusalem?

GV: Yes, at the Ecole.

RF: You had no problem at that monastery, but I believe you experienced something different earlier on when they wouldn't accept you at a Dominican monastery.

GV: That was when I was still a Catholic. The Dominicans and Jesuits had in those days rules, no Jews, thank you very much. I was later allowed into an Order of the Fathers of Zion and became friends with others of a Hungarian background, Paul Demann, and in Paris met Renée Bloch, so we worked against the distortion in Catholic education of all things related to Jews. It took ten years of hard work, but with the Second Vatican Council the Church's attitude changed from one of conversion to collaboration and understanding between Christians and Jews.

RF: What was your reason for leaving the Catholic Church in the end?

GV: I simply met someone and got married and left in 1957.

RF: That is somewhat similar to Józef Milik's experience, although I think he had become disillusioned before his marriage to Yolanta.

GV: Well, I had problems, but they wouldn't necessarily have led to my decision. I don't know exactly what his position was, but suddenly he cut all his contacts.

RF: He never really explained his reasons, but he did volunteer during our conversations, that 'he could no longer believe in the historicity of Jesus', and part of it was related to his study of the Dead Sea Scrolls, which opened up ideas he had not considered before . . . and of course his desire to marry. Do you think the Dead Sea Scrolls had any influence on your feelings?

GV: Not really, not as such, but of course they made many aspects of study more understandable.

RF: You know I am doing a biography of Milik, jointly with Zdzislaw Kapera. Did you meet him in 1952?

GV: Yes, I met him a number of times whilst I was there and in Paris, up until 1957, then we sort of lost touch until he began to pop up, unannounced, at Oxford, and then after the eighties he was quiet.

RF: In the late nineties I visited him in his flat in Paris, and he was still working on a draft book on Nabatean inscriptions. I was finishing off my book on the Copper Scroll, and he was very helpful in giving me pointers and his view of the translations and origins, and so on. Some of his views were not what people normally associate with him. He is generally quoted as thinking that the Copper Scroll was a fiction and a myth, and he did believe that in the early days, that's true, but later he came round to the conclusion that it was a genuine document, it was too matter of fact and too detailed, and once you adjusted the weights of the talent, the '*kikkar*', and used a different formula for the calculation with a different value, you got a more realistic result. I consulted him mainly about the Copper Scroll, and interestingly he changed his mind about the reality of the scroll over the period I talked with him. I went to his flat right up until a few weeks before he died.

GV: He died in January 2006 . . . When did you think he started to change his mind about the Copper Scroll?

RF: That's an extremely interesting question. It's like the question of when did he start thinking about leaving the Catholic Church. I'm still not too clear on the answers. I think when one of the students of Schiffman in New York, Lefkovits, brought out a book, although his came out after mine, suggesting that the talent in the Scroll, the '*kikkar*' that they were translating as a biblical talent, was not correct and suggested it was a Persian '*karsch*' of a smaller weight.

Although it was actually Allegro, who had originally suggested it was not the talent of about 35kg but something perhaps one sixtieth of that value. I had already suggested, before Lefkovits, that the term was not a biblical talent but an Egyptian '*kite*', which was about 10.1 grams, rather than about 72 pounds. Which means all the weights come down to realistic levels. Instead of 65 tonnes of silver and 25 tonnes of gold, you get kilograms of silver and gold. And the weight of the jewellery, rings and so on, comes down from impossible levels to weights someone could actually wear. When all this information began coming out as an acceptable idea, then he (Milik) started to accept it might be a genuine document, so some time in the late nineties.

GV: So, by the time he had stopped publishing.

RF: Absolutely. I think part of his frustration was that they had taken a lot of his scrolls away from him. It hurt him a lot.

GV: Yes, yes, unfortunately it was necessary . . . he had no indefinite rights.

RF: In these later visits we talked about John the Baptist and Jesus, and their possible presence at Qumran. It was then that he told me that he had excavated a headless skeleton, which had not been reported in the literature. It was a very curious revelation, and I know you are not amenable to Jesus and the Baptist being members of the community.

GV: Well, if you have to have one, John would be the more likely.

The Source?

My reference in my conversation with Professor Geza Vermes to the 'anonymous' source of funding being connected to the Wolfson Foundation was based on a personal encounter and further research. In the early part of 2009 I had a chance meeting in London with an acquaintance of mine, a solicitor by the name of Gerry Franks. On learning of my activities in the areas of Dead Sea Scrolls and biblical research, he mentioned that his father was fascinated with ancient history and biblical matters and might like to meet me. A message soon came back that his father would love to see me, and I was invited to his home in Maida Vale.

The tall, distinguished-looking, elderly man who opened the door to welcome me turned out to be a retired lawyer who had acted for the Wolfson Foundation, a charitable trust that gave, and still gives, millions of pounds to deserving causes right across the field of human endeavour. The charity was founded in 1955 by Isaac Wolfson (later Sir Isaac Wolfson), his wife, and his son Leonard (Lord Wolfson), who made their money through Great Universal Stores, a group of companies including furniture manufacturers, retail shops and mail order businesses. By 2010 over £600 million had been awarded in the form of grants to medical and scientific research, education, arts, and humanities projects across a wide range of learned institutions and to individuals working on worthwhile projects.

When Yigael Yadin recovered the Temple Scroll in Bethlehem, during the 1967 War Israel fought against its Arab neighbours, he approached the foundation for help in paying Kando, who had possession of the scroll. A reported sum of $105,000 was paid to Kando with the help of the Wolfson Foundation. Since that time the foundation has had an ongoing interest in the Dead Sea Scrolls project and the Shrine of the Book Museum in Jerusalem, where many of the major scrolls are housed.

Although still associated with the foundation, since formal retirement John Franks had busied himself with his favourite pastime of studying and writing on a wide range of biblical and historical subjects. As we talked, the topic of the Dead Sea Scrolls inevitably came up, and I was riveted to hear him say he had met Yigael Yadin and other Dead Sea Scrolls scholars. Through a connection with Oxford University and the Yarnton centre, one of the beneficiaries of donations by the foundation, he had become friendly with Professor Vermes, and when the 1987 conference on the scrolls was convened in London, John Franks went along as an observer.

A salient factor that emerged during the conference was the lack of funding that the publications team faced. Joe Zias, curator of the scroll material kept under the auspices of the Israel Antiquities Authority, retrospectively highlighted the situation in email correspondence:

> As I was the curator in charge of the scrollery where the scrolls were kept (1972–97) I more or less knew all the reputable

scholars and one thing they shared in common was their lack of funds to pursue research on the manuscripts. It was unfortunate that many of these world-class scholars had to literally beg for research funds which were one of the main obstacles to their being published on schedule.[5]

Several people have been credited with prior status for 'freeing up the Scrolls', notably Herschel Shanks of the *Biblical Archaeology Review* magazine, and Bill Moffett, librarian at the Huntingdon Library, but the true hero of the story is a relatively unknown modest motivator we have already met – John Franks.

The parlous state of productivity in publishing the scrolls, and complaints by the delegates, was one of the main themes that emerged from the 1987 Conference, and in his capacity as a trustee of the Wolfson Foundation, John Franks sat listening, and had an idea. After the meeting he told me he sat down with Professor Vermes and John Strugnell, then editor-in-chief of the Dead Sea Scrolls publishing team, and they discussed the problems Strugnell faced. John Strugnell argued that one of the main difficulties he and his team had was lack of funding and that this deficit, amongst other less serious factors, had seriously hampered the progress of their work. A battle plan was soon hammered out whereby John Franks would use his influence with the foundation to make adequate money available to, as Franks puts it, 'free up the release of the scrolls'. Working with Professor Vermes, Franks arranged for a grant from the foundation to be channeled through the Yarnton centre, and on to Strugnell for, in theory, onward distribution by him to other members of the publishing team in most need of finance. Shortly after that, a regular stream of money, amounting to tens of thousands of pounds a year, headed in the direction of John Strugnell. How much of the money actually got through to the intended recipients is difficult to determine. All apart from Frank Moore Cross were dead at the time of my researches, and he was silent on the issue. Franks himself expressed the opinion that perhaps some of the money had gone into sustaining Strugnell's alcoholic predilections. However, there is evidence that Strugnell offered financial help to Józef Milik, sending him a cheque in April 1988, which was not cashed, and a letter dated 25 May 1988, which was not responded to.

The level of funding appears to have been initially $350,000 and continued until quite recently under Emanuel Tov, who took over from Strugnell as editor-in-chief after Strugnell's dismissal in 1990. Availability of this funding is also indicated by a circular letter sent out at the beginning of Tov's editorship in January 1991. A copy of this five-page circular was enclosed with a letter to Józef Milik dated 6 May 1991, and it was addressed 'to all those involved in the texts from the Judaean desert'. Essentially it dealt with the administrative conditions for achieving the publishing aims, the current state of publications and ended with an offer of possible financial assistance. According to Weston Fields, between 1988 and 2005 at least $4 million was spent on publishing the scrolls.[6] As Fields claims there are still dozens of biblical fragments languishing in private hands and he has been unable to raise funds from any source to try and purchase them over a period of four years from 2005 onwards, one has to conclude that the only funds readily available for publishing purposes came from the Oxford source.

The Dénouement

The provision of funding, however, soon began to have an effect on the rate of publication in the official journal, *Discoveries in the Judaean Desert*, and continued for a number of years up until the mid-1990s. The 'amongst others' reason for the delays was something that John Franks did not learn about till later on when he became better acquainted with John Strugnell. It was then that he learned from Strugnell that:

> the reason why publication had ground to a halt shortly after 1967, and had always been sluggish, was that there was an underlying anti-Semitism within the Ecole team. After 1967 a collective decision was taken not to cooperate with 'the Jews'.

The main reason behind the procrastination in the release of the Scrolls was not, therefore, the variety of reasons previously cited, or a Vatican conspiracy, as claimed by Baigent and Leigh, but resentful anti-Semitism, and anti-Israel, pro-Arab sentiment.

Weston Fields's *The Dead Sea Scrolls: A Full History* confirms that latent anti-Semitism was present in the scrolls team. As noted in a review of the book by Charlotte Hempel: 'Sadly absent, however, was any dialogue between non-Jewish and Jewish scholars. Some of the most unfortunate quotes in the book relate openly anti-Jewish sentiments.'[7]

When we look at the record of actions and statements from members of the Ecole team right from its inception, the pattern becomes clear. It was a glaring oversight that initially no Jews were invited onto the team, although from the earliest examinations it was obvious that the Scrolls were clearly Jewish documents, found near a Jewish settlement and mainly written in Hebrew. Roland de Vaux was quoted in an interview conducted in 1968 by writer/journalist David Pryce-Jones as referring to the Israelis as 'Nazis'. According to Magen Broshi, then Director of the Shrine of the Book Museum in Jerusalem, de Vaux was a rabid anti-Semite.[8]

Another example of the Ecole group's negative feelings towards the Israeli authorities can be seen in a letter from Father Benoit, written from Jerusalem on 9 November 1972 and addressed to key members of the inner Ecole Biblique clique. Five years after the Israelis had taken control of the Scrolls project and were formally in charge of procedures, a previous allegiance to the Jordanian authorities was still being pursued.[9]

The Acidic Abyss

The acidic abyss of procrastination was reached during the period of the so-called 'battle for possession of the scrolls'. The scrolls were 'freed up', in terms of availability in photographic form, in the autumn of 1991, after intense pressure from academics and the press. A lawsuit followed against Michael Wise and Robert Eisenman for appropriation of the work by two of the official team, John Strugnell and Elisha Qimron, on a controversial fragment known as 4QMMT – the Halachic Letter thought to have been composed by the Teacher of Righteousness himself. The work had actually been described in 1955, but it was withheld from general scholarship until 1990. The alleged breach was related in an attack by 19 signatories of the inner circle in *The New York Times* of 13 December 1992 and repeated at a conference held in New York on 14–17 December 1992.[10] Commenting on the events at the New York conference, Professor Norman Golb said:

The present state of malaise in Qumran studies revealed by this intemperate outburst, coming from Qumranologists allied with the official committees, began with the struggle over the freeing of the scrolls during the past few years. I refer to the innuendos, half truths, calumnies, fallacious claims and misuse of authority that seemed to characterize the actions of members of those committees as the struggle developed over the freeing of the scrolls, which all of us striving for mutual collegiality among Qumran scholars hope to have come to an end with the freeing of the scrolls and the editor-in-chief's welcome announcement of November 1991 acknowledging the rights of scholars to publish their own editions of Qumran manuscripts without regard to assignments made to others.

Professor Eisenman, together with Dr Michael Wise, came in for further flack as a result of their joint authorship of a book entitled *The Dead Sea Scrolls Uncovered: The First Complete Translation of 50 Key Documents Withheld for Over 35 Years.*[11] A group of attendees at an international conference at the New York Academy of Sciences condemned the authors for 'unethical appropriation of previous transcriptions and translations', and suggested that the authors' claims of having done independent and original work were 'laughable and manifestly dishonest'. In another conference, organized by the Society of Biblical Literature Conference in San Francisco, Professor Lawrence Schiffman called the volume:

> . . . fulfillment of the worst predictions of those who opposed the opening of the scrolls to the general scholarly community. It does not, as it claims, publish 50 unpublished texts. One half of those texts published here were fully published before the volume came out.[12]

The 'tempest' slowly subsided after Dr Wise offered an apology for effectively not acknowledging the previous work of his peers.

Efforts by Professor Ben Zion Wacholder and Martin Abegg to reconstruct the scrolls from a concordance were also characterized by the official team as a 'violation of international law' and 'thievery', whilst Professor Golb was portrayed as a 'revolting argumentalist, a polemicist and trouble-maker', who had 'filled the world with his dirt and of whom the world will be free when he is dead'.[13]

The Elephant Appears

One has to wonder if a factor in these malicious attacks on certain scholars by the official group may not have been partly motivated by the 'elephant in the room' dynamic that charges into view in this chapter. The after effects of this period of confrontation have served to erect barriers between numbers of scholars that still remain.

Even up to the time of the writing of this book, accredited Jewish scholars are not allowed easy access to examine the artefacts lying in the storage vaults of the Rockefeller Museum. Christian scholars are allowed much more ready access, but even they are not allowed to examine the original notes of Roland de Vaux's explorations. It is true that Joseph Zias, a Jew, was curator at the Rockefeller Museum from 1972 to 1997, but he did not permit access for anyone other than 'special visitors', nor did he provide a comprehensive description of the material being held in the Rockefeller Museum or at the Ecole Biblique. Even Zias was not allowed free entry to the Ecole repositories, as an article by him in *Dead Sea Discoveries*, published in early 2000, reveals. In a footnote to the article he states:

> I also wish to thank the anonymous colleagues who alerted me to the fact that additional human remains from Qumran, despite years of vigorous denial, were being stored in the Ecole Biblique. This is unfortunate for Qumran scholars, particularly since earlier publications were incomplete due to the omission of the material. As I was finally able to briefly view this material, I have included the findings in this study.[14]

Zias maintains that some of the bone material from the Qumran cemetery, excavated in 1953 and allegedly lost, was housed in the Ecole Biblique and then transferred to the Rockefeller Museum in Jerusalem. This information has great import in relation to my previous work on the missing bones of John the Baptist.[15]

How many of the Ecole Biblique team held anti-Semitic views is debatable, but some of the senior members certainly did. Most of the team held decidedly pro-Arab convictions, and after the 1967 War were reluctant to continue their work under Israeli auspices.[16] Roland de Vaux rejected offers by the Israelis to help his team and persisted in referring to Israel as Palestine. Other members of the tightly knit team also had a scorn of the political and religious nature of Judaism.[17]

The surprising thing is that the Israeli authorities, after gaining control of Qumran and East Jerusalem in 1967, assured the team that there would be no interference in their mode of work, and did not insist that Jewish scholars or women should be brought on to the team or outside scholars given full access to the scrolls. Control of the translations remained in the hands of the mainly Catholic members right up until the late 1980s. In addition, virtually all of the outside institutions that the Ecole called in to help with their research and work were Catholic-dominated, or the people that they consulted were Catholic. Ironically, one of the team's most outspoken anti-Semites, John Strugnell, was the first editor-in-chief to appoint Jews to the team. (He brought in Elisha Qimron, Devorah Dimant, the first ever woman on the team, and Joe Baumgarten, as the most qualified scholars living near Jerusalem.)

Strugnell was, in the early days, one of the most active of the Ecole team. An Englishman, recruited from Oxford University as a young man in 1954, he was appointed head of the scrolls team in 1987, following the death of the previous incumbent Father Pierre Benoit. Although Strugnell brought in several Jewish scholars to the team after his appointment, his anti-Semitic views are well documented, and three years later he was forced to resign for making derogatory remarks in public about Judaism.

The 9 November 1990 edition of the Israeli newspaper *Haaretz* published an interview Strugnell gave to a journalist by the name of Avi Katzman. Some of the things he said included: 'Judaism is a horrible religion; the answer to the Jewish problem is mass conversion to Christianity; Christianity should have been able to convert the Jews; Judaism was originally racist.'

Later in 1994 Strugnell gave another interview to *Biblical Archaeology Review* magazine where he made the excuse that his remarks were largely due to his ongoing manic depression and the fact that he had a drink problem.[18] He also implied that part of the reason Jewish scholars were kept off the original translation team, in relation to the possibility of finding connections to Jesus, was because they would be even more unable to offer an impartial view than Christian scholars, as the scrolls were closer to their religious philosophy than to Christianity.

When asked if he characterized himself as an anti-Judaist, he responded by saying:

> A lot of people talk about how my position is supersessionist. I have a much more positive viewpoint. I'm looking for largeness in Christology, I'm looking for making higher claims for Christ [and the consequences of these for the Jews].

Emanuel Tov took over as the new editor-in-chief, after Strugnell, but he, too, initially refused to make the scrolls public. At the time Associated Press reported Strugnell as saying: 'He would fight Tov's appointment', which he called 'an alarming attempt by Israeli scholars to claim credit for the research', and that he threatened legal action.

In relation to the delays in publication, Strugnell maintained they had to go at the speed of the editors, and he encouraged the team to keep to their targets, but was nevertheless not willing to throw them out, or to throw out their work – or make any photographs available to others.

Strugnell claims that he extracted from Józef Milik a half to a third of his allocated texts without any hard feelings, saying, rather conflictingly: 'It was like pulling teeth from a cat.' He considered the loss of Milik the most despicable act of the (Israeli) advisory committee, and the failure of Frank Cross, professor emeritus at Harvard, to defend him as a little shameful. Milik was not pushed out. He wasn't expelled, but he was harassed out. When I spoke to Milik about the subject in 2001, he expressed his resentment at the way his texts were forcibly removed from him and the criticism by Jonas Greenfield of his translations, which contributed to undermining his position.[19]

In the *Biblical Archaeology Review* interview, Strugnell also talked about the Israeli committee set up to try and expedite the rate of translation. The committee comprised Shemaryahu Talmon and Jonas Greenfield, both of Hebrew University, and Magen Broshi, curator of the Shrine of the Book. Strugnell compared Talmon and Greenfield to the leech in the Book of Proverbs. 'It says there that the leech, the blood-sucking animal, *ha-aluqah*, has two daughters crying, "Give! Give!"'

After his dismissal John Strugnell went back to Cambridge and was subsequently appointed a professor at Harvard University. He died on 30 November 2007, aged 77.

As previously discussed, by the early 1970s most of the Dead Sea Scrolls texts that remained unpublished were those in fragmentary form and publication virtually ground to a halt, until the cataclysmic events of the early 1990s. The breaking of the embargo by Martin Abegg and Ben Zion Wacholder, and immediately after by Robert Eisenman and Hershel Shanks, at last made most of the material available to a wider audience. Nevertheless, the rate of flow of official publications remained relatively slow. In effect, members of the second generation of the translation team were more determined, secretive hoarders than their predecessors, and a degree of resentment against those who had broken the embargo ensued. This culminated in the suing of Shanks and Eisenman by Elisha Qimron for claimed infringement of the copyright of his and Strugnell's work in relation to their version of a piece of text known as 4QMMT. It is ironic that Shanks, a person running a charitable organization, should be sued, when the material should have been freely available to everyone. This was made all the more poignant in the light of what we now know about the funding of Strugnell's work by the Wolfson Foundation, and one assumes Qimron's work would also have benefitted from this charitable funding.

John Marco Allegro

The one member of the team who developed and subsequently openly displayed extreme anti-religious and, eventually, anti-Jewish sentiments was John Marco Allegro. Joining the Ecole team in 1953, he was a key player in the unravelling of the Copper Scroll and at first a well-liked member of the team. However, his Methodist beliefs soon weakened, and he blotted his copybook by giving a number of radio broadcasts for the BBC in 1956, in which he claimed he saw a connection to the crucifying of Jesus in the scrolls. His peers roundly denounced him, and in a letter to *The Times*, published on 16 March 1956, five of his colleagues accused him of reading much more into his texts than was there. He responded with his own defence in a letter published in the same newspaper, dated 20 March 1956. But his membership of the team was finished and his academic career went slowly downhill. As time passed, his true attitudes emerged from the content of several books he wrote denigrating Christianity and Judaism and making personal attacks on Jesus.[20]

His anti-religious stance included ongoing attacks on Judaism, and one has to wonder how far back and how widely these prejudices reached, in an environment of anti-Israeli feeling within the Ecole Biblique and the team's pro-Arab feelings. Allegro was certainly closer to his Arab contacts than most of his colleagues, and his true feelings towards Judaism were subsequently revealed in his book *The Chosen People*, published in 1971.[21] This work focused on bloodthirsty aspects of Jewish history and portrayed Judaism as being closely allied to pagan fertility cults, and tars Judaism with the same hallucinatory brush that he besmirched Jesus and early Christianity with. In an otherwise learned treatment of the history of the Jews he nailed his colours to his rotting ideological mast in the following passage:

> If this tragic saga of the Chosen Race has any lesson for us today, it must be that religious emotionalism, however stimulated and for whatever motives, is an extremely dangerous and unpredictable force. Moral and patriotic idealism that springs from a racialist religion is a perilous philosophy that can soon burst through the bounds of rational control. Modern heralds of the New Era, from whatever gods they claim their authority and wherever they raise their prophetic voices – the Jerusalem Knesset, the Meccan kiblah or the platforms of Carnegie Hall or Wembley Stadium – should appreciate the power of the spoken word to unleash the mighty forces of religious fanaticism . . .

Ironically, Allegro was also the subject of scurrilous attacks on his character by Christian academics. When I visited Joan Allegro, his wife, at her home on the Isle of Man, she showed me evidence of claims by some of his colleagues that cast aspersions on his father as a 'Jew' and that his lineage was said to be one of the reasons for his anti-Christian stance. Mrs Allegro rejected the accusations and added that when she first met him he was training to be a Methodist minister and was fully committed to Christianity.

Chapter 22

Beyond Reasonable Doubt:
The Elephant Appears

A survey of the principal protagonists in the arguments about the origins of Khirbet Qumran, and what the community based there was doing, shows wide disagreement. A detailed analysis of the internal and external evidence has led to a decisive answer to the problems. The resultant conclusion is that the majority view, that the site was essentially established and operated as a religious enterprise, is correct.

A corollary to this conclusion is that, whilst not all the scrolls found in the nearby caves came from Qumran, many were copied by and some originated from within the *Yahad* community.

The great number of black holes in the understanding of the Dead Sea Scrolls texts, and biblical texts, is reflected in there being almost no agreement on the identity of numerous unnamed personalities written about in the scrolls. Also numerous crucial passages in the Dead Sea Scrolls, and biblical texts, are simply not understood and have no convincing conventional explanation.

Critical examination of these black holes against a backdrop of a connection back to the time of Pharaoh Akhenaton and his holy city at Akhetaton provides coherent interwoven answers to most of these problems. That the Qumranites had an awareness of the town layout, buildings and temple design, ceremonials, beliefs and teachings of the Amarna period is certain. To ignore this possibility is to deny the vast amount of internal and external evidence.

An inference from this conclusion is that Jews, Christians and Muslims are heirs to the same monotheism enunciated by Pharaoh Akhenaton, together with Jacob and Joseph, and that the line of priests that brought about the establishment of the *Yahad* community at Qumran had a special 'secret' knowledge of the origins of their religion.

217

This is incontrovertibly demonstrated by the accurate information they were party to about the geography, geometry, imagery and practices that pertained at Akhetaton.

As a corollary to illumination of the black holes in the Dead Sea Scrolls, the group of so-called minimalist scholars who maintain that the Hebrew Bible has almost no historical content and cannot be used as an historical document prior to about the 6th century BC are severely challenged. A summary of some of their views is given in the table on pages 220–1, although the analysis is subjective and is purely a broad categorization of a spread of views for different periods of Israel's history; some of those included have also expressed differing views at different times.

Most of the minimalist views commence with an extreme scepticism on the historicity of the exodus from Egypt, graduating into disbelief in the authenticity of the biblical record much before the united kingdoms of Saul, David and Solomon.

Some even claim that none of the Bible was composed much before the 3rd century BC and that much of the content was made up anyway. The general weakness in the claims put forward by the minimalist schools is summed up by Hans Barstad, commenting on the position of Niels P. Lemche.[1] Barstad: 'Not one single argument in Lemche's article can be said to support a dating to Hellenistic times.'[2] Others, like Jens Bruun Kofoed, conclude: 'Lemche's ideological crusade against conservative scholarship and his usage of confused heuristic terminology to discard the biblical text as a primary source for the history of ancient Israel thus appears to be an axiomatic and methodological boomerang that missed its target.'[3] James Barr is even more dogmatic, saying Philip Davies' views are 'too absurd to be taken seriously', and Keith Whitelam's arguments are 'without any factual evidence'.[4]

Donald Redford, a leading authority on Egyptian history, comments on the position of minimalist Gösta Ahlström and others who see a Canaanite/Mesopotamian mythology at work in Exodus and later historicization of this myth, saying: 'This is a curious resort, for the text does not look mythology . . . more ingenious than illuminating.'[5]

All this does not imply that I take every word of the Bible as sacrosanct, or the extreme position of the ultra maximalists, like

Kenneth Kitchen, who takes much of the Bible as recording history and meaning what he thinks it means. My position is what I call one of being a 'cautious maximalist'. Because there is virtually no archaeological evidence for the monarchy period of Saul, David and Solomon, or the vast empire that the Bible says they established, I nevertheless resist the main thrust of the minimalists' claims that everything in the Bible prior to this period was therefore mainly made up, and written down much later, in the Persian or Hellenic periods. For them the presence, or even existence, of the Hebrew patriarchs prior to the exodus, is largely fiction. I maintain that hard archaeological evidence proves the presence of the Hebrews at the court of Pharaoh Akhenaton, and the almost certain existence of Joseph and Jacob in this environment. (In a later book I intend to provide absolute proof of the existence and role of Joseph and his father.) I also maintain that the exodus, led by Moses, took place, and that the entry into Canaan, as broadly described in the Bible, was a historical fact of the 13–12th century BC. I do not maintain that the entry to the Promised Land was effected in the style of a kind of Blitzkrieg, as described in the Bible, but a partly peaceful settlement of the incoming Hebrews and their entourage, mainly in the hillside areas of Canaan. I do maintain that Moses was a real person and transmitted a form of the Ten Commandments to his followers, and that there is hard new archaeological evidence for this event, which I intend to provide in my next book.

In the light of the sustained and powerful criticism and the hard evidence revealed by the Dead Sea Scrolls that I have put forward here, the main thrust of the minimalist case is now confined to the rubbish tip of history as a set of defunct theories. The foundations this group rely on are now cut from under their feet.

Possible Remedies – An Amarna Seminar?

With all the criticism of individual theorists and the parlous state of some areas of scrolls research, it would be invidious not to offer some suggestions on how to try and improve matters. Very often individual theories are re-hashed over and over again at various conferences and meetings around the world, but very little progress is made towards resolving the disagreements that ensue. Entrenched academics and

Minimalists and Maximalists on the Historicity of the Bible

Minimalists	Maximalists
Jean Astruc[1]	William Halo[22]
	William Foxwell Albright[23]
H. B. Witter[2]	
J. G. Eichorn[3]	
W. M. De Wette[4]	
Herman Gunkel[5]	
Albrecht Alt[6]	
Martin Noth[7]	
	Anson Rainey[24]
	Bryant Wood[25]
John Bright[8]	Yigael Yadin[26]
Thomas Paine[9]	
Thomas Thompson[10]	William Dever[27]
Philip Davies[11]	
James K. Hoffmeier[28]	
Israel Finkelstein[12]	Hugh Williamson[29]
	Amihai Mazar[30]
Niels P. Lemche[13]	Eilat Mazar[31]
Keith Whitelam[14]	Jonathan Tubb[32]
Mario Liverani[15]	
	Robert Feather[33]
	Donald Redford[34]
	Samuel Loewenstamm[35]
Bernard Batto[16]	James Barr[36]
J. M. Modrzejewski[17]	
Gösta Ahlström[18]	Eric Cline[37]
Van Seters[19]	Ian Wilson[38]
Neil Asher Silberman[20]	Jens Bruun Kofoed[39]
	Hans Barstad[40]
	Eric & Carol Meyers[41]
Stephen Fry[21]	

The relative positions in the table are a rough indication of the intensity of individual views at one time in their careers

1. Jean Astruc 18th century (1684–1766), French physician to King Louis XV.
2. 18th century German minister.
3. German biblical scholar.
4. German biblical scholar.
5. German biblical scholar.
6. German biblical scholar.
7. German biblical scholar.
8. Union Theological Seminar, Richmond, Virginia.
9. Thomas Paine, US Founding Father.
10. University of Copenhagen.
11. Sheffield University.
12. Tel Aviv University.
13. University of Copenhagen.
14. Sheffield University.
15. University of Rome.
16. DePauw University, Indiana.
17. Papyrologist.
18. University of Chicago.
19. University of North Carolina.
20. American archaeologist who trained at the Hebrew University of Jerusalem.
21. British actor, comedian.
22. Yale University.
23. Johns Hopkins University.
24. Tel Aviv University.
25. University of Toronto.
26. Hebrew University, Jerusalem.
27. Tucson University, Arizona.
28. Trinity International University, Deerfield, Illinois.
29. Oxford University.
30. Hebrew University, Jerusalem.
31. Shalem Centre, Jerusalem.
32. British Museum.
33. Institute of Materials, London.
34. Canadian Egyptologist/Archaeologist Pennsylvania State University.
35. The Hebrew University of Jerusalem.
36. Oxford University.
37. Washington University.
38. British religious writer, Magdalen College, Oxford. He erroneously places the exodus in the 15th century BC (*The Bible is History*, Weidenfeld & Nicolson, 1999).
39. Dansk Bibel-Institut, Copenhagen Lutheran School of Theology.
40. University of Oslo.
41. Duke University, Durham, North Carolina.

scholars continue to plough their own viewpoint regardless of criticism, nervous of open challenges from their peers. These contentious disagreements need to be resolved, so that the whole discipline can move on to investigating and resolving new issues. One suggestion is to adopt a 'Jesus Seminar' type of approach, where groups of experts get together to try and resolve specific issues, one at a time.

Launched in 1985 by the Westar Institute, the Jesus Seminar is dedicated to discovering and reporting a scholarly consensus on the historical authenticity of the sayings and events attributable to Jesus. A third phase has resulted in a profiling of Jesus, based on the discussions in the first two stages. Seminars are convened twice a year in which delegates deliberate and vote on precise issues raised by members to try and reach a consensus.[6]

A similar organization could help to repair the current splintered nature of Dead Sea Scrolls and biblical understanding, bring dignity and respectability to the field of Qumranology, and present a unified voice to the media and the public in general.

A Qumranology Seminar might be the answer.

Delays and the Discordant Concordance

There are clearly two strands of interconnected reasons for the delays in publication of the scrolls: those due to the holding back of access of material to scholars; and those due to the holding back of official publications. This final section concentrates on delays in the official publications.

Various explanations and excuses have been put forward over the years, mainly by those external to the work, for the inordinate secrecy and delays in publication of translations and photographs, and restricted access to material recovered from the 11 Dead Sea Scrolls caves. They relate to:

- Fear of findings that might be detrimental to Christianity;
- Complexity of the task;
- Overwhelming volume of the material;
- Incompetence and laziness amongst the translation team;
- Deaths and illnesses amongst the translation team;
- Selfishness and personal aggrandizement;

- Lack of money;
- Vatican-inspired conspiracy.

An explanation of 'the conspiracy' and current thinking of scholars on the reasons for the delays comes from Professor Florentino García Martínez and Julio Trebolle Barrera, two leading second-generation translators of the texts, writing in 1995:

> The real explanation for the delays in the publication of the texts is many and varied [*sic*]. There was a tangled political situation and premature death of the first two directors of the editorial team (Roland de Vaux [in 1971] and Pierre Benoit [in 1987]); also several of the editors (Patrick Skehan, Yigael Yadin and Jean Starcky) died before finishing their work [in 1980, 1983, 1988 respectively]. These are some of the factors which have influenced the present situation. However, the most important factor is the actual condition of the still unpublished texts, hundreds of minute fragments, with pathetic remains of incomplete works.[7]

Another series of explanations comes from Weston Fields, who tries to refute 'that there was a small shadowy group of selfish men who had been keeping the scrolls all to themselves, conspiring to hide their contents, presumably to protect their own fame and fortune, or to protect Christianity or in other permutations, to protect the Vatican'.[8] His contrary argument is that the translation team did the best they could under the circumstances, were not part of any conspiracy and can hardly be blamed for the difficulties of the tasks.

These explanations and excuses from the establishment fall rather flat when it is considered that *a concordance of most of the scrolls and fragments was prepared as early as the 1950s!* Only concerted pressure and the determination of a few activists broke the embargo, and the 1990 spring issue of *Biblical Archaeology Review* carried information about a secret publication of a concordance on the 4Q fragments, which comprised some 15,000 items of the most critically important and potentially controversial texts.[9]

Most of the translations the outside world was clamouring for, but were told were not yet available, had therefore actually been completed

Dates of Publication of Dead Sea Scroll Texts

DJD	Authors	Date of Publication
1.	Barthelemy, Milik	1955
2.	Benoit, Milik, R. de Vaux	1960
3.	Baillet, Milik, R. de Vaux	1962
4.	Sanders	1966
5.	Allegro, Anderson	1968
6.	R. de Vaux, Milik	1977
7.	Baillet	1982
8.	Tov, Kraft	1990
9.	Skehan, Ulrich, Sanderson	1992
10.	Qimron, Strugnell	1994
12.	Ulrich, Cross	1994
13.	Attridge, Elgvin, Milik, Olyan, Strugnell, Tov, VanderKam, White	1995
14.	Ulrich, Cross, White, Crawford, Dunca, Skehan, Tov, Barrera	1995
19.	Broshi, E. Eshel, Fitzmyer, Larson, Newsom, Schiffman, Smith, Stone, Strugnell, Yardeni	1995
18	Baumgarten	1996
22.	Brooke, Collins, Flint, Greenfield, Larson, Newsom, Puech, Schiffman, Stone, Barrera	1996
23.	Martínez, Tigchelaar, Van der Woude, Van der Ploeg, Herbert	1996
15.	Ulrich, Cross, Fuller	1997
20.	Elgvin, Kister, Lim, Nitzan, Pfann, Qimron, Schiffman, Steudel	1997
24.	Leith	1997
27.	Cotton, Yardeni	1997
25.	Puech	1998

some 30 years before they were 'extracted', 'like pulling teeth from a cat', by the wider community of eagerly awaiting scholars.

In the 1950s and early 1960s, a concordance of the non-biblical Dead Sea Scrolls was compiled by Joseph Fitzmyer, Raymond Brown, William Oxtoby and J. Teixidor, who had access to the scrolls in Jerusalem. The concordance was kept secret except for a privileged set of scholars. Shortly before 1990 the cards on which the concordance was written were prepared for printing by a German scholar, Hans-Peter Richter, supervised by Professor Hartmut Stegemann of the University

26.	Alexander, Vermes, Brooke	1998
11.	H. Eshel, E. Eshel, Newsom, VanderKam, Brady	1998
29.	Chazon *et al.*	1999
34.	Strugnell, Harrington, Elgvin	1999
35.	Baumgarten *et al.*	1999
16.	Ulrich, Cross, Fitzmyer, Flint, Metso, Murphy, Niccum, Skehan, Tov	2000
36.	Pfann *et al.*	2000
38.	Charlesworth *et al.*, VanderKam, Brady	2000
21.	Talmon, Ben-Dov, Glessmer	2001
28.	Gropp, Schuller	2001
30.	Dimant	2001
31.	Puech	2001
33.	Pike, Skinner, Szink	2001
39.	Tov	2002
17.	Cross *et al.*	2005
37.	Puech	2008
40.	Newsom, Stegemann, Schuller	2008
5a.	Bernstein, Brooke	Not yet published
32.	Flint, Ulrich	Not yet published
41.	Concordance	Not yet published

Several more volumes as revisions of previous volumes may also be published.

The *DJD* series does not include the major texts from Cave 1, which were published by ASOR (American Schools of Oriental Research); Eleazar Sukenik (1955); Yigael Yadin and Naham Avigad (1956).

of Göttingen. One of the printed versions came into the possession of Professor Ben Zion Wacholder, who, together with Martin Abegg, was able to develop a computer programme that reconstructed fragmented sections of the scrolls, making the full content of the scrolls accessible and leading to the release of the original manuscripts, which had been withheld for years. It was this breach in the protective armour of the inner circle that broke the embargo.[10]

A list of volumes published to date is given in the table above. The *DJD* series was not exclusively confined to material found in the 11

Qumran caves, but also included a few volumes of material from closely related sites. It can also be seen from the table that the programme of publication did not run chronologically, as planned. After the 1967 War the rate of publication dried up to a standstill for another ten years, for reasons discussed in the previous chapter and below. There was another gap of five years from 1977 to 1982 and then an even larger gap of eight years before publications resumed in 1990. The pumping in of funds from the Wolfson Foundation, which started a year or so after the 1987 London Conference (*see* the previous chapter), can be seen to have soon had an effect with a flood of volumes released in the early 1990s. It is also noticeable that more man- and woman-power was brought in after 1995.

Allegro's volume, published in 1968, was already in proof form, before the embargo on work came into effect. To his credit, the much-maligned John Allegro was the only member of the team to publish all his text within a reasonable space of time.

Whilst all the problems previously listed by others contributed to the secrecy and delays, we now know that most of the texts were in fact available at a much earlier date. All the various reasons postulated for the delays, discussed in previous chapters, may have been contributory factors, but cannot have been the main reasons. The main reason for the delays in publication was a deliberate collective decision taken by the key members of the translation team to hold back their work and, in some cases, bring it to a virtual standstill.

This previously unrecognized reason now makes the succession of events quite clear. Just as John Franks was told by John Strugnell, the then head of the translation team, publication was deliberately ceased from 1967 onwards for a period of nearly ten years. This was not because: the translation team suddenly became frightened of findings that might be detrimental to Christianity; the task suddenly became impossibly more complex; the volume of the material suddenly became overwhelming; the fragments were in too poor a condition; the translation team suddenly became incompetent and lazy; they all died or fell ill; selfishness and personal aggrandizement suddenly set in; there was absolutely no money available; the Vatican issued a 'Papal Bull' to stop any further work!

The real reason, and Strugnell's revelation, is clearly confirmed by the above table and other evidence cited earlier on. After the 1967 War all the team stopped sending material for publication – even though most of it was available as early as the end of 1960, as confirmed by the existence of a concordance, which can only have been compiled from relatively finished material.

Sadly, the motivation for this decision was an antipathy to the Israeli authorities from 1948 onwards, and a positive resentment of them after the 1967 War. Coupled with this prejudice was a pro-Jordanian attitude, running from 1947 and the first scrolls discoveries right up until today. That this stance was simply anti-Israeli or was fuelled by an underlying anti-Jewish feeling, can be determined from the sentiments expressed by certain members of the translation team, and for some there was a definite anti-Semitic prejudice.

Many scholars and scrolls commentators were aware of a bias towards the Jordanians and resentment of the Israeli authorities, but no one has highlighted their corrosive effects, and that of the insidious underlying layers of anti-Semitism, as the main cause of the delays in publication – factors which restrict free access to Dead Sea Scrolls material to this day.

Notes

Preface

1 R. Azariah Figo, Giddulei *Terumah* (Hebrew - המורת ילודג) Vendramina, Venice, 1643. *See also* Robert Feather, 'Through a Glass Darkly', paper presented at Conference on Qumran, The Site of the Dead Sea Scrolls: Archaeological Interpretation and Debates, Brown University, 17–19 November 2002.

2 Some students of Kabbalah have noted that the acronym 'PaRDeS' has the root letters for the Hebrew word for 'Paradise'. They then read into this conclusion the idea that this process of studying Torah leads to 'Paradise'.

3 Measuring approximately 52 x 26 x 26cm, *talatat* were manufactured from sandstone, and their uniform size and ease of handling enabled faster and more effective construction of structures. A recent find at Sheikh 'Ibada (Antinopolis) north of Al Minya, in central Egypt, reported a *talatat* block, re-used in the construction of a Christian church, with a portrait of Queen Nefertiti (*Journal of Egyptian Archaeology*, Egypt Exploration Society, 2009).

4 Donald B. Redford, *Studies on Akhenaten at Thebes*, 1. 'A Report on the Akhenaten Temple Project at the University Museum, University of Pennsylvania', *Journal of the American Research Center in Egypt*, Vol. 10, 1973.

5 Hans Barstad, *History and the Hebrew Bible: Studies in Ancient Israelite and Ancient Near Eastern Historiography*, Forschungen zum Alten Testament, 61: Tübingen: Mohr Siebeck, 2008. William G. Dever was Professor of Near Eastern Archaeology and Anthropolgy, University of Tucson, Arizona. Philip Davies is Emeritus Professor at Sheffield University, and his comments are set out in 'The Search for Ancient Israel', *Journal for the Study of the Old Testament*, Supplement Vol. 148, 1992.

Interview with Professor Geza Vermes

1 Professor Vermes's publications include: *The Complete Dead Sea Scrolls in English*, Penguin, 1962; *The Dead Sea Scrolls – Qumran in Perspective*, SCM Press, 1977; *Jesus the Jew*, SCM Press, 1983; *The Dead Sea Scrolls: A Selection of Original Manuscripts*, The Folio Society, 2000; *The Religion of Jesus the Jew*, SCM Press, 1993; *The Changing Faces of Jesus*, Allen Lane, 2000; *The Authentic Gospel of Jesus*, Allen Lane, 2004; *Scrolls, Scriptures and Early Christianity*, T. & T. Clark, 2005; *Who's Who in the Age of Jesus*, Tantor Media, 2006; *The Resurrection*, Penguin, 2008; *The Story of the Scrolls: The Miraculous Discovery and True Significance of the Dead Sea Scrolls*, Penguin, 2010; *Searching for the Real Jesus: Jesus, the Dead Sea Scrolls and other religious themes*, SCM Press, 2010; *Jesus Nativity – Passion – Resurrection*, Penguin, 2010. Many of Geza Vermes's books

have been translated into numerous foreign languages, as well as being revised and reprinted, and he has contributed papers to a large number of learned conferences and symposia. He has also appeared in numerous TV documentaries.

Chapter 1   **Persistent Textual Problems**

1 The letter was dated 16 March 1956 and signed by five of the senior translation team in Jerusalem. On 20 March 1956 *The Times* published a response by Allegro. Contents of the two letters are included in Robert Feather, *The Secret Initiation of Jesus at Qumran*, Watkins, 2006.

2 Robert Cargill, interview on the Landmine Show, Israel National Radio, August 2010.

3 The last publication in the *Discoveries in the Judaean Desert* series will be Volume 32 dealing with the Isaiah scrolls. This was announced in 2009, but is not yet published. To correlate revision of nomenclature and references in previous volumes, Professor Tov produced Volume 39 in the series, in 2001, and, to update the record further, has recently published *Revised Lists of the Texts from the Judaean Desert*, Leiden, Brill, 2010. With completion of his work on the *Discoveries in the Judaean Desert* series, Professor Tov has now retired and future inventory work on the scrolls has been taken over by the Orion Center, at the Hebrew University of Jerusalem. Future revised material on earlier editions of the series will include a critical edition on the Cave 4 material of Volume 5. Information on the Schøyen collection of Dead Sea Scrolls fragments, housed in Oslo and London, will be updated in a new publication by Torleif Elgvin, due to be published by T. & T. Clark.

4 Professor Lawrence Schiffman, Skirball, University of New York, in a radio interview on the Landmine Show, Israel National Radio, August 2010. He went on to suggest that one of the main future tasks for scholars was to make the scrolls more understandable to a Christian audience in the study of the New Testament and the background of Christianity. In modern Jewish studies acknowledgement of the importance of the Dead Scrolls was, according to Professor Schiffman, minimal. Modern publication of the *Mishnah*, the *Halacha* (Jewish law) and other Jewish biblical works 'contain very few references to the Dead Sea Scrolls'. According to Professor Schiffman, the scrolls can enrich our knowledge of these subjects and can help explain rabbinic and scriptural texts, and need to be studied by Jewish scholars much more intensively than at present.

5 Wise, Abegg, & Edward Cook, *Les Manuscrits de la Mare Morte*, Perrin, 2003. Wise, Abegg, & Cook, 'The Discovery and Publication of the Dead Sea Scrolls', *Rosicrucian Digest*, No. 2, 2007. Michael O. Wise is Professor of Ancient Languages, Northwestern College, St Paul, Minnesota; Martin Abegg is co-director of the Dead Sea Scrolls Institute at Trinity Western University, British Columbia; and Edward M. Cook is Associate Professor of History, University of Chicago.

Chapter 2   **Confusion in the Role of Qumran**

1 Ben Stevens, *Daniel the true date of authorship,* ja-jp facebook.com/topic.php.

2 June Austin, juneaustin.co.uk.

3 Edna Ullmann-Margalit, 'Spotlight on Scroll Scholars: Dissecting the Qumran-Essene Hypothesis', *Biblical Archaeology Review*, March/April 2008.

4 Yizhar Hirschfeld, *Qumran in Context*, Peabody, Hendrickson Publishers, 2004. Reviewed by Professor Eshel in *Journal of the American Oriental Society*, Vol. 125, 2005. Tragically, Hirschfeld and Eshel are both now dead.

5 Among them James VanderKam, John A. O'Brien Professor of Theology, Notre Dame University, George Brooke and Geza Vermes.

6 For example, Martin Abegg, Peter Flint, Eugene Ulrich, *The Dead Sea Scrolls Bible*, T. & T. Clark, 1999.

7 Alison Schofield, *From Qumran to the Yahad: A New Paradigm of Textual Development for the Community Rule (Studies on the Texts of the Desert of Judah)*, Brill, 2008.

8 Described in a lecture by Professor André Lemaire of the Sorbonne, in November 2009.

9 Professor Ferdinand Röhrhirsch was part of a team of scientists based at Eichstatt, Germany, entrusted with the re-examination of some of the remains from the Qumran cemeteries in 1998. Joseph Zias is part of the Science and Antiquity group at the Hebrew University, Jerusalem, and was previously curator of Archaeology and Anthropology for the Israel Antiquities Authority, working at the Rockefeller Museum in Jerusalem.

10 See H. Frankfurt and J. D. S. Pendlebury, *The City of Akhenaton – Part II,* Oxford University Press, 1933. N. de G. Davies, *The Rock Tombs of El-Amarna*, Egypt Exploration Fund, 1906.

11 See for example the scaled map of El-Amarna in Jacquetta Hawkes, *Atlas of Ancient Archaeology*, McGraw Hill, 1975.

Chapter 3 **The Black Holes**

1 'Rewritten Bible and Scriptural Interpretation', 4 July 2011, Session on Qumran and the Dead Sea Scrolls, Society of Biblical Literature. International Meeting 2011, King's College, London, 3–7 July 2011.

2 Alexander Andrason, 'Biblical Hebrew Wayyiqtol: A Dynamic Definition?', *Journal of Hebrew Scriptures*, Vol. 11, 2011.

3 Michael Chyutin, 'The New Jerusalem Scroll from Qumran – A Comprehensive Reconstruction', *Journal for the Study of the Pseudepigrapha*, Supplement 25, Sheffield Press, 1997. Shlomo Margalit, an Israeli archaeologist, also confirms the finding that Akhetaton was the best fit of any city in the ancient Middle East for that described in the New Jerusalem Scroll,. Correspondence between S. Margalit and the author, summer 1997.

4 Review by Daniel Machiela, McMaster University, Hamilton, Ontario, in *Journal of Hebrew Scriptures*, Vol. 10, 2010, of a paper by Emile Puech, 'Qumran Grotte 4 XXVII: Textes Aramée deuxième partie', *DJD*, XXXVII, Clarendon, Oxford, 2009. Eibert Tigchelaar, 'The Imaginal Context and the Visionary of the Aramaic New Jerusalem', in Flors Florentino, *Dead Sea Scrolls and Other Early Jewish Studies in Honour of Florentino García Martínez*, Brill, 2008.

5 Summary of Songs of the Sabbath Sacrifice Seminar, 18 March 2005. Qumranica. com website of the University of St Andrews, Scotland. *See also* Robert Feather, *The Mystery of the Copper Scroll of Qumran* and *The Secret Initiation of Jesus at Qumran*.

6 See for example: Jean Duhaime, *The War Texts: 1QM and Related Manuscripts*, T. & T. Clark International, 2004; Brian Schultz, *Conquering the World: the War Scroll (1QM)*

Reconsidered. Leiden & Boston, 2009; Florentino García Martínez and Eibert J. C. Tigchelaar, *The Dead Sea Scrolls: Study Edition*, Brill, 2009.

7   Whilst there is agreement amongst scholars about the translation of most of the phrases and words in the Copper Scroll, there are many individual words that have not been previously encountered and are given different translations by different scholars. Because there are no vowels in the Hebrew texts, place names and these unusual configurations of letters are open to a variety of possible readings. One example is the word כהלת which may appear in Columns 1, 2, 4 and 12 of the Scroll. Geza Vermes (*The Complete Dead Sea Scrolls in English*) translates it as '*Kochlit*' but John Marco Allegro (*The Treasure of the Copper Scroll*, Routledge & Kegan Paul, 1960) reads the word as 'stored Seventh Year produce'. Florentino García Martínez and W. E. Watson (*The Dead Sea Scrolls Translated: The Qumran Texts in English*, Brill, 1994) also read the word as '*Kochlit*', but do not say what it means. In another section of the Scroll, M. R. Lehmann reads 'seventh year treasury' ('Identification of the Copper Scroll Based on Technical Terms', *Revue de Qumran* 5, 1964).

8   Michael Wise has stated that engraving on copper in Second Temple times was quite common, and has given examples of its so-called use in Roman correspondence. All the examples he quotes turn out to be engravings on bronze, and he, like some other commentators, seems unaware of the difference between copper and bronze (*see* Robert Feather, *The Mystery of the Copper Scroll of Qumran*).

9   Professors John Tait and Rosalie David confirm the possibility. H. Snyder has come up with an interesting idea for some of the Greek letters in the Copper Scroll. He suggests a reading of '*Aken-aten hodiotre -s-*' which could be translated as 'Akenaten, the one [who is] sustained by [a] deity'.

10   Hartmut Stegemann, *The Library of Qumran: On the Essenes, Qumran, John the Baptist and Jesus*, W. B. Eerdmans, 1998.

11   Interview given by Professor Eisenman to Andrew Gough, on Gough's Arcadi, March 2011. www.andrewgough.co.uk/17q_eisenman.html.

Chapter 4   A General Theory of Amarna–Qumran Relativity

1   A collection of Hebrew, Aramaic and Greek manuscripts recovered from a synagogue in Old Cairo in the late 19th century. *See* Glossary.

2   Erik Hornung, *Idea into Image*, Timkin Publishers, 1992. Hornung is a professor at Basel University; Jan Assmann, Professor of Egyptology at the University of Heidelberg; Joseph Davidovits (*La Bible Avait Raison*); Roger and Messod Sabbah (*Le Mystère de l'Exode* – *see* chapter 6); Ahmed Osman, *Out of Egypt*, etc.; Minna and Kenneth Lonnqvist (University of Helsinki), *Archaeology of the Hidden Qumran* – *The New Paradigm*; Hugo Kennes (Belgian lecturer and consultant in computer studies); Professor Kris Thijs (University of Hasselt, Belgium); Michael Joyce (Randolph Distinguished Visiting Professor at Vassar College, Poughkeepsie, New York). George Brooke is a professor at Manchester University and Harold Ellens a former professor at Michigan University.

Chapter 5   Tout ce que j'avais rêvé

1   'Everything I have dreamed of': saying attributed to Napoleon Bonaparte, 1803.

2   Zdzislaw J. Kapera & Robert Feather, *Doyen of the Dead Sea Scrolls*, Enigma Press, 2011.

3 Some of these authors' works of special interest include: Christiane Desroches
   Noblecourt, *Ramsès II – La Véritable Histoire, Lorsque la Nature Parlait aux Egyptiens*;
   Christian Jacq, *Nefertiti et Akhénaton*; Maurice Bucaille, *Moïse et Pharaon – Les Hébreux
   en Egypte*; Alaine Zivie, *La Prison de Joseph*; Mireille Hadas-Lebel, *Le people hébreu –
   Entre le Bible et l'Histoire*; Messod and Roger Sabbah, *Les Secrets de l'Exode*; Joseph
   Davidovits, *La Bible avait raison.*
4 Davidovits, *De cette fresque naquit la Bible*, Editions Jean-Cyrille Godefrey, 2009.

Chapter 6   The Amarna Connection to the Dead Sea Scrolls

1 These include Professor Ben Zion Wacholder (Hebrew University, Cincinnati),
   Professor Richard. E. Friedman (University of California), Professor Eduard Meyer
   (Berlin University), Professor Sarah Israelit Groll (Department of Egyptology at the
   Hebrew University) and Lucia Raspe (Freie University, Berlin)
2 Translation by Professor García Martínez. Martínez and Tigchelaar, *The Dead Sea
   Scrolls: Study Edition.*
3 Yigael Yadin, *The Temple Scroll: The Hidden Law of the Dead Sea Sect*, Random House,
   1985.
4 Notably Ben-Zion Wacholder (Hebrew Union College, Cincinnati), Dwight D.
   Swanson and Philip R. Davies (Sheffield University).
5 Joseph Angel, 'The Traditional Roots of Priestly Messianism at Qumran', *The Dead
   Sea Scrolls at 60*, 7 March 2008, Skirball Department, New York University. The
   Aaronic bias in Ben Sira does not apply at Qumran as, unlike Ben Sira, they were
   castigating the Temple priesthood. Another interpretation comes from Michael E.
   Stone (International Symposium of the Orion Center, Jerusalem, 12–14 January
   1997), who believes the text shows that its subject, Qahat, is the 'Great High Priest'
   and has a royal connotation. This implies he is in the line of the first high priest Meryre,
   who was a royal prince. The Aramaic Levi Document is supplemented and clarified
   by a fragmentary manuscript from the Cairo Genizah and some Greek extracts from
   Mount Athos. According to Aramaic Levi, Qahat is exalted: he was born on the first
   day of the first month, at the rising of the sun. This is a particularly significant date
   according to the solar calendar. According to some scholars the solar calendar started
   in the morning, as for the daily order of sacrifices in the Temple. Qahat is born on
   the morning of the first day of the year. This is a portentous beginning! Aramaic Levi
   relates the naming of Qahat in the following way: '[And I cal]led his name [Qahat
   and I sa]w that he would have an assembly of all the people and that he would have
   the high priesthood for Israel.' This is clearly a '*midrash*' (interpretation) on the name
   Qahat, which the author relates to the Blessing of Jacob in Genesis 49. The author
   takes the strange word 'thqy' in this blessing to be connected with the name Qahat.
   He explains the name Qahat by the meaning 'assembly'. This meaning is attested by
   Aquila's translation, as well as by the Midrash *Bereshit Rabbah* 99 (Theodor-Albeck,
   1280) J. Theodor and C. Albeck (eds.), *Midrasch Bereschit Rahhah* (4 vols., Berlin:
   Akademie, 1912–36). *Bereshit Rabbah* explains 'thqy' as 'wyl': 'he to whom the nations
   of the world gather'. The Athos Greek text of Aramaic Levi differs from the surviving
   Qumran Aramaic manuscripts in a number of readings. One is an additional phrase:
   'the great high priesthood' and 'he and his seed will be an authority of kings, a
   priesthood for Israel'. 'Authority of kings', could mean 'beginning of kings'. In either

case, the phrase indicates that Qahat will have both royal and priestly attributes. It calls him 'chief of kings' and 'priesthood', while the preceding phrase attributes to him 'the great high priesthood'. His line stands as one both of kings and priests. This is an extraordinary prediction, although its possible Hasmonean reference is precluded by the dating of the oldest Qumran manuscripts of the work.

6 Jonas Greenfield, Michael Stone, Esther Eshel, *The Aramaic Levi Document*, Brill, 2004.

7 The `Instructions of Amenhotep', a hieratic papyrus dating between the 6th and 7th centuries BC, sets out numerous ancient wisdom texts dating back to the early dynastic periods of Egypt. Line by line comparison with the Book of Proverbs shows a remarkable correspondence between the two; many scholars also refer to the Wisdom of Solomon as the wisdom of Egypt.

8 www: historel.net

9 Hanna Vanonen, Helsingin Yliopisto-Helsingfors Universitet, '"The Battles is Yours!": The Message and the Composition of 1QM 10-12', Society of Biblical Literature, International Meeting, 3–7 July 2011, at King's College, London. Session on Qumran and the Dead Sea Scrolls. *See also* Gaalyah Cornfeld, *Archaeology of the Bible: Book by Book*, Adam & Charles Black, 1977.

10 The location of this city is considered to be at Kalah Sherghat, on the west bank of the Tigris and was founded by Bel-kap-kapu around 1700 BC. The capital was moved to Ninua, known as Nineveh in the Bible, now known as Koyunjik, on the eastern bank of the Tigris.

Chapter 7 **The Amarna Connection to the Bible**

1 'Fieldwork 1997–8', *Journal of Egyptian Archaeology*, Volume 84, 1998.

2 Translation from Michael Chyutin, *The New Jerusalem Scroll from Qumran – A Comprehensive Reconstruction*, Sheffield Academic Press, 1997.

3 Niels Peter Lemche, *Ancient Israel*, Sheffield Academic Press, 1988.

4 Ben-Zion Wacholder sees Ezekiel as the founder of the Essenes, 'Ezekiel and Ezekielianism as Progenitors of Essenianism', in Devorah Dimant, Uriel Rappaport and Yan Yitshak Ben-Tsevi, eds, *The Dead Sea Scrolls, Forty Years of Research*, Brill Academic Publishers, 1992. He notes that Ezekiel assiduously avoids naming King David as the head of the restored lineage of the new order, and Jerusalem as the place where a reconstituted temple would be built at the time of the coming of the messiah. He merely refers to the location as the place in which 'the Lord is there', echoing Akhenaton's statement that the Lord resides in his holy city at Akhetaton.

5 U. Bouriant, G. Legrain, G. Jéquier, 'Monuments pour servir à l'étude du culte d'Atonou en Egypte', *MIFAO* 8, 1903.

6 *The Pharoah's Holy Treasure*, BBC1 Documentary, first shown 2002.

Chapter 8 **Confirmation from the Koran?**

1 Sura 14, 'Abraham', 44, 49–51: 'And warn mankind of a Day when the doom will come upon them, and those who did wrong will say: Our Lord! Reprieve us for a little while. We will obey thy call and will follow the messengers. (It will be answered): Did ye not swear that there would be no end for you? . . . Thou wilt see the guilty on that Day linked together in chains. Their raiment of pitch, and the Fire covering their faces, That Allah may repay each soul what it hath earned. Lo! Allah is swift at

reckoning.' *The Meaning of the Glorious Qur'an*, explanatory translation by Mohammed Marmaduke Pickthall, Dar Al-Faihaa, n.d.

The translation of the Koran that is quoted in this chapter is from the 'Musaf' copy of the Koran prepared by Al-hajj Muhammad Shakarzâat at the command of Sultan Mahmû of Turkey in 1246 AH.

2 Michael Lodahl, *Claiming Abraham: Reading the Bible and the Qur'an Side by Side*, Brazos Press, 2010. See Fig 22.1 'Flow chart showing evolution of the Christian Church, the Essenes and associated religious movements', Robert Feather, *The Secret Initiation of Jesus at Qumran*, Watkins Publishing, 2006, p. 114.

3 Robert Feather, *The Copper Scroll Decoded*, Thorsons, 1999.

4 Michael Lodahl, *Claiming Abraham: Reading the Bible and the Qur'an Side by Side*, Brazos Press, 2010, citing *Avodah Zarah* I.2.

Chapter 9   Anomalous Artefacts in and around Israel

1 Robert Deutsch, 'Lasting Impressions: New bullae reveal Egyptian-style emblems on Judah's royal seals', *Biblical Archaeology Review*, July/August, 2002.

2 'Archaeology and Media, Archaeology and Politics', Conference at Duke University, 2009. An audio record is available on ASORblog.org/?p=252.

3 Haarertz.com, 19 April 2009. 'Simcha Jacobivici has appeared in a series of TV documentaries where, as the Naked Archaeologist, he puts over his distorted view of Israelite and Christian history. Vendyl Jones claims to have found items described in the Copper Scroll, but none of his finds has been authenticated.' Jim Barfield claims to have solved the riddle of the Copper Scroll, but presents no proof of his findings (*see* www.bibleinterp.com/opeds/copper.shtml).

Chapter 10   The Ruined Fortress

1 N. Golb, 'The Problem of Origin and Identification of the Dead Sea Scrolls', *Proceedings of the American Philosophical Society*, 124, 1980.

2 Norman Golb, *Who Wrote the Dead Sea Scrolls?: The Search for the Secret of Qumran*, Diane Publishing, 1995.

3 Norman Golb, *Fact and Fiction in Current Exhibitions of the Dead Sea Scrolls*, The University of Chicago, 1 June 2007. Norman Golb, *The Dead Sea Scrolls as Treated in a Recently Published Catalogue*, The University of Chicago, 22 October 2007.

4 Yizhar Hirschfeld, *Qumran in Context: Reassessing the Archaeological Evidence*, Hendrickson Publishing, 2004. Hirschfeld believed Qumran was occupied by wealthy inhabitants. The book cover shows two wooden hair combs presented as if they had been found in the ruins of Qumran. In fact, as Stephan Goranson points out in a review on Amazon.com, they were not. These two combs were found far away in a cave in Wadi Murabba'at.

5 Yigael Yadin, *Masada: Herod's Fortress and the Zealots' Last Stand*, Sphere Books, 1971.

6 Hanan Eshel, 'Qumran: The Site of Dead Sea Scrolls Artificial Caves in Qumran', paper presented to conference at Brown University, 17–19 November, 2002. See also, Yizhar Hirschfeld, 'A Community of Hermits above Ein Gedi', *Cathedra*, 96, 2000.

7 Robert Feather, *The Mystery of the Copper Scroll of Qumran*. See also Robert Feather, 'Through a Glass Darkly', paper presented at Brown University, 17–19 November, 2002.

8 Measurement of the ratio of bromine to chlorine in ink from a Qumran Cave 1 manuscript concluded that the ink was prepared with water from or near the Dead Sea. Ira Rabin, Oliver Hahn, Timo Wolff, Admir Masic, and Gisela Weinberg, 'On the Origins of the Ink of the Thanksgiving Scroll (1QHodayot a)', *Dead Sea Discoveries*, 16 February 2009. The authors concluded that the carbon-based ink also contained extracts of gall nuts (nodules from oak trees rich in tannic acid, used in ink manufacture). *See also* Ira Rabin, 'Archaeometry of the Dead Sea Scrolls', Society of Biblical Literature, International Meeting, King's College, London, 3–7 July 2011.

9 Q&A Interview with Dr Risa Levitt Kohn on the controversy of the Dead Sea Scrolls, *National Post*, March 2009.

10 Apparently, Raphael Golb used his status as a graduate of the university to try to maintain his anonymity.

11 Ofri Ilani, 'Dead Sea Scrolls scholar defends son arrested for impersonating rival', *Haaretz*, 12 March 2009.

12 Robert R. Cargill, *Who is Charles Gadda? Or the Jerusalem Bobst Libraries Theory*, www.bobcargill.com, April 2009.

Chapter 11 How Potty Can You Get?

1 Yitzhak Magen and Yuval Peleg, *The Qumran Excavations 1993–2004: Preliminary Report*, State Office of Archaeology, Jerusalem, 2007. Yitzhak Magen and Yuval Peleg, 'Back to Qumran: Ten Years of Excavation and Research, 1993–2004', in K. Galor, J.-B. Humbert and J. Zangenberg, eds, *Qumran, The Site of the Dead Sea Scrolls: Archaeological Interpretation and Debate, Proceedings of a Conference held at Brown University, 17–19 November 2002*, Studies on the Texts of the Desert of Judah 57, Leiden, 2006. *See also* Hershel Shanks, 'Qumran – The Pottery Factory', *Biblical Archaeology Review*, 32, 2006.

2 Marta Balla, *Provenance Study of Qumran Pottery by Neutron Activation Analysis*, Budapest, 2005. *See also* J. Gunneweg and M. Balla, 'Neutron Activation Analysis: Scroll Jars and Common Ware, in Khirbet Qumran and "Ain Feshka II"', in J.-B. Humbert, J. Gunneweg, eds, *Studies of Anthropology, Physics and Chemistry*, Academic Press, Fribourg, Vandenhoeck & Ruprecht, Göttingen, 2003.

3 Frederick F. Zeuner, 'Notes on Qumran', *Palestine Exploration Quarterly*, 1960. *See also* Galor et al., *Qumran, The Site of the Dead Sea Scrolls*.

4 Eyal Regev, *Sectarianism in Qumran: A Cross-Cultural Perspective*, Walter de Gruyter, 2007.

5 Ronny Reich, 'Miqwar'ot (Ritual Baths) at Qumran', *Qadmoniot*, 30, 1997.

6 Joseph E. Zias, 'The Cemeteries of Qumran and Celibacy: Confusion Laid to Rest?', *Dead Sea Discoveries*, 7, No. 2, 2000.

7 Olav Röhrer-Ertl, Ferdinand Röhrhirsch and Dietbert Hahn, 'Über die Gräberfelder von Khirbet Qumran, insbesondere die Funde der Campagne 1956', *Revue de Qumran*, 73, June 1999.

8 E. L. Sukenik, *Megilot Genuzot*, Bialik Foundation, Jerusalem, 1948.

9 A Syriac letter sent by Timotheus I, Patriarch of Seleucia (726–819 AD) to Sergius, Metropolitan of Elam (who died c805 AD). Elam was east of Babylonia, in the modern Iranian province of Khuzestan. Its capital was Susa, the Shushan of the Book of Esther. The letter refers to the finding by an Arab, of Hebrew and other scrolls in

a rock-dwelling near Jericho. According to the letter's contents, many Jews came out from Jerusalem to study the documents and found them to be ancient books of the Hebrew Bible, together with some 200 psalms. There is no known reference in Jewish literature to the find, which, considering their potential importance, is rather surprising. *See also* O. Essfeldt, *Theologische Literaturzeitung*, No. 10, 1949, translated by G. R. Driver as *The Hebrew Scrolls from the Neighbourhood of Jericho and the Dead Sea*, Oxford University Press, 1951.

10 Hanan Eshel, Qumran: *The Site of Dead Sea Scrolls Artificial Caves in Qumran*, Brown University, Rhode Island, 17–19 November, 2002. *See also* Yizhar Hirschfeld, 'A Community of Hermits above Ein Gedi', *Cathedra*, 96, 2000.

11 Hanan Eshel, 'Qumran: The Site of Dead Sea Scrolls Artificial Caves in Qumran', Brown University conference, 17–19 November, 2002. *See also* Yizhar Hirschfeld, 'A Community of Hermits above Ein Gedi', *Cathedra*, 96, 2000.

Chapter 12   Sadducean Mysticism

1 Rachel Elior, *Memory and Oblivion: The Mystery of the Dead Sea Scrolls* [in Hebrew], 2009. In an interview in March 2009, in the Israeli newspaper *Haaretz*, Professor Elior said, 'Sixty years of research have been wasted trying to find the Essenes in the scrolls. But they didn't exist, they were invented by [Jewish-Roman historian] Josephus. It's a history of errors which is simply nonsense.' *See also* John Ralston Saul, *The Doubter's Companion*, Simon & Schuster, 1994.

2 Professor Lawrence Schiffman in an interview on Israel National Radio referenced in August 2010. Professor Schiffman appears partly to have reverted back to his original view in saying that Qumran 'originated as a group of Sadducee priests who went off to found the Qumran sect'.

3 Reviewing Lawrence Schiffman's book *The Courtyards of the House of the Lord: Studies in the Temple Scroll*, STDJ 75, Brill, 2008, Dwight D. Swanson in *Journal of Hebrew Scriptures*, Vol. 11, 2011.

4 Moshe David Herr, 'A Reevaluation of the Significance of the Recently Published Halakhic Materials from Qumran', The Dead Sea Scrolls – Fifty Years After Their Discovery, International Congress, Jerusalem, 20–25 July 1997. *See also* 12. Josephus, *War 6, Antiquities* 1.10; Philo, Allegorical Interpretation III. 82; Justin, Trypho 19; Tertullian, *Against the Jews*; Jerome, Letter 73; Genesis Rabbah XLIII.

Chapter 13   Akhetaton and the Great Aton Temple

1 The Koran makes a brief mention of the Jerusalem Temple in Sura 17: 'I declare the glory of Him who transported His servant by night from the Masjid al Haram [the Mosque at Mecca] to the Masjid al Aksa [the Further Mosque] at Jerusalem.'

2 Yigael Yadin, *The Temple Scroll: The Hidden Law of the Dead Sea Sect*, Random House, 1985. *See also Temple Scroll Studies*, edited by George J. Brooke, International Symposium on the Temple Scroll, December 1987, Journal for the Study of the Pseudepigrapha, Supplement Series 7. *Literary Sources of the Temple Scroll*, HTR 75, 1985. *See also* Zdzislaw J. Kapera, *A Review of East European Studies on the Temple Scroll*, ibid.

3 From Columns 30–31, as in Florentino García Martínez, *The Dead Sea Scrolls Translated: The Qumran Texts in English*, William B. Eerdmans, 1996.

4   Column 40, ibid.

5   Richey Crapo, an anthropologist at Utah State University, 'Where was the Temple of Herod?', Bibleinterp.com. Crapo discusses Josephus' Prophecy of the Square Temple: War 6.5.4 310–11.

6   Reviewing Lawrence Schiffman's book *The Courtyards of the House of the Lord: Studies in the Temple Scroll*. STDJ 75, Brill, 2008, Dwight D. Swanson, *Journal of Hebrew Scriptures*, Vol. 11, 2011, comments, 'What is notable overall is that the concerns with details of sacrifices in the festivals indicate expectation of these being practices in a real setting. For example, the adaptation of the ordination rites (Ch. 19) making it a permanent annual ceremony, should not be considered merely hypothetical and idealized.'

7   Schulman quoted in J. K. Hoffmeier, *Israel in Egypt: The Evidence for the Authenticity of the Exodus Tradition*, Oxford University Press, 1977.

8   Ancient Egypt Online: www.reshafim.org.il/ad/egypt/timelines/topics/slavery.htm.

9   For example, in the Torah service in synagogue, before the reading from the scroll, the intoned prayer includes: 'For Torah shall come out of Zion | And the word of the Lord from Jerusalem.'

10 Kenneth Kitchen, 'The Joseph Narrative (Genesis 37:39–50)', Associates for Biblical Research, 12 March 2009.

11 Kenneth Kitchen, 'Joseph', *International Standard Bible Encyclopedia*, Vol. 22.

12 Donald Redford, *The Biblical Story of Joseph*, E. J. Brill, 1970.

13 Alan R. Schulman, *Studien zur Altägyptischen Kultur*, 2, 1975.

14 Digital Egypt: www.digitalegypt.ucl.ac.uk.

15 Amé Kuhrt, *The Persian Empire: A Corpus of Sources of the Achaemenid Period*, Routledge, 2007.

16 Cuneiform tablets discovered in 1893 near the ruins of the ancient Babylonian city of Nippur. They describe the business activities of the Marashu family during the 5th century BC and contain words of Semitic origin, and names seen in the biblical books of Ezra and Nehemiah, that had been imported into the language of the region.

17 Ben Zion Wacholder, 'Ezekiel and Ezekielianism as Progenitors of Essenianism', in Devorah Dimant, Uriel Rappaport and Yan Yitshak Ben-Tsevi, eds, *The Dead Sea Scrolls, Forty Years of Research*, Brill Academic Publishers, 1992.

18 Dead Sea Scroll fragment 4Q405. 'The Cherubim praise the vision of the Throne-Chariot', in Michael Morgan (trans.), *The Book of Mysteries*, Scholars Press, Chico, California, 1983.

19 Cyril Aldred, *Akhenaten, King of Egypt*. Despite mentions in the Hebrew scriptures of the thousands of chariots supposedly owned by King David and King Solomon, no remains of such chariots have ever been found in Israel.

20 Zeev Weiss, 'The Sepphoris Synagogue Mosaic', *Biblical Archaeology Review*, September/October 2000.

21 Michael Morgan (trans.), *Sepher haRazim*, Scholars Press, 1983. *See also* F.G. Martínez, 'The Dead Sea Scrolls Translated', Society of Biblical Literature, Text and Translations 25, Pseudepigrapha Series 11, Brill, 1996.

22 Sermon by Rabbi Helen Freeman, West London Synagogue, 9 January 2010.

23 Witold Tyloch, *Aspekty spoleczne gminy z Qumran w swietle rekopisów znad Morza Martwego i tekstów autorów starozytnych*, Warsaw, 1973.

24 BBC News, Middle, East 18 March 2011.

25 N. de G. Davies, *The Rock Tombs of Amarna – Part II*, The Egypt Exploration Society, 1905.

26 Ezekiel 43:13-17: 'These are the measurements of the altar in long cubits, that cubit being a cubit and a handbreadth [approximately 0.5m]. Its gutter is a cubit deep and a cubit wide, with a rim of one span around the edge. And this is the height of the altar. From the gutter on the ground up to the lower edge it is two cubits high and a cubit wide, and from the smaller edge up to the larger edge it is four cubits high and a cubit wide. The altar hearth is four cubits high, and four horns project upwards from the hearth. The altar hearth is square, twelve cubits long and twelve cubits wide. The upper edge is also square, fourteen cubits long and fourteen cubits wide, with a rim of half a cubit and a gutter of a cubit all round. The steps of the altar face east.' City measurements used in the New Jerusalem Scroll are the cubit and the rod, where the rod is 7 cubits (the rod in Ezekiel is 6 cubits). See N. de G. Davies, *The Rock Tombs of El Amarna, Part III – The Tombs of Huya and Ahmes*, The Egypt Exploration Fund, 1905.

27 Lawrence Schiffman, *The Courtyards of the House of the Lord: Studies on the Temple Scroll*, Studies of the Texts of the Desert of Judah, Brill, 2008. Lawrence Schiffman, *Sectarian Law in the Dead Sea Scrolls: Courts, Testimony and the Penal Code*, Brown Judaic Studies 33, 1983.

28 Hans Burgmann, '11QT: The Sadducean Torah', in *Temple Scroll Studies. Papers presented at the International Symposium on the Temple Scroll*, Manchester University, 1987, Sheffield Academic Press, 1989. Hartmut Stegemann and John Maier, *The Library of Qumran*, Eerdmans, 1998.

29 Serge Frolov, '"King's Law" of the Temple Scroll: Mishnaic Aspects', *Journal of Jewish Studies*, 50, No. 2, 1999.

30 Cyril Aldred, *Akhenaten, King of Egypt,* Thames and Hudson, 1988.

31 Ibid.

32 Biblical quotations are taken from *Tanakh – A New Translation of The Holy Scriptures According to the Hebrew Text*, Jewish Publication Society, 1985.

33 Robert H. Eisenman and Michael Wise, *The Dead Sea Scrolls Uncovered: The First Complete Translation and Interpretation of 50 Key Documents withheld for Over 35 Years*, Penguin, 1993.

34 Shlomo Yitzhaki was a French rabbinic scholar better known as Rashi, who lived from 1040 to 1105 AD and was the first person to write a comprehensive commentary on the Hebrew Bible and the Talmud.

35 J. Tyldesley, *Nefertiti: Egypt's Sun Queen*, Penguin, 2005.

36 Daniel A. Machiela, 'The Genesis Apocryphon (1Q20): A Reevaluation of its Texts, Interpretive Character, and Relationship to the Book of Jubilees', Dissertation submitted to the Graduate School of the University of Notre Dame, Indiana, July 2007.

37 Jean-Daniel Stanley, Maria Pia Bernasconi and Thomas F. Jorstad, 'Pelusium, an Ancient Port Fortress on Egypt's Nile Delta Coast: Its Evolving Environmental Setting from Foundation to Demise', *Journal of Coastal Research*, 2008. *See also The Vanishing Capital of the Pharaoh, Ancient Discoveries*, BBC/History Channel.

38 Zoan is mentioned in Numbers 13:22; Psalm 78:12; Isaiah 19:11,13: Ezekiel 30:14.

39 I identify the Hebrew name 'Herqanos' in the Dead Sea Scrolls Genesis Apocryphon

as a Nubian court official of Pharaoh Thutmose III titled 'H'qAn(k AS'. (See Carl Graves, Egyptian Imperialism in Nubia c2009–1191 BC' dissertation submitted to the University of Birmingham, September 2010; and Jeanette Anne Taylor, *Thesaurus Linguae Aegyptiae: An Index of Male Non- Royal Egyptian Titles, Epithets & Phrases of the 18th Dynasty*, Museum Book Publications, 2001.)

40 Andrew M. Wilson and Lawrence Wills, 'Literary Sources of the Temple Scroll', *Harvard Theological Review*, 75, 1985. Hartmut Stegemann, 'Is the Temple Scroll a Sixth Book of the Torah—Lost for 2,500 Years?', *Biblical Archaeology Review*, Nov/ Dec 1987.

41 Michael Chyutin, 'The New Jerusalem Scroll from Qumran – A Comprehensive Reconstruction', *Journal for the Study of the Pseudepigrapha*, Supplement Series, 25, Sheffield Academic Press, 1997.

42 In relation to the scene in Apy's tomb, whilst Michael Chyutin and others assume that the New Jerusalem Scroll description of the Showbread follows the description in Leviticus, I believe it is the other way around, and that this kind of reversal is applicable to many other examples of assumptions of biblical texts as preceding the content of some of the Dead Sea Scrolls material. We see, for example, in the New Jerusalem Scroll details of division of the old bread amongst the priests, which is to take place in the western part of the inner court. Ezekiel and the Temple Scroll confirm this by referring to a place in the western part of the temple where the priests are to eat the excess bread, but only in the New Jerusalem Scroll do we get a description of the ceremony of dividing the bread amongst 84 priests. The bread is given to the elders amongst them first and to an additional group of 14 priests, and the remaining two loaves are given to the high priest and to 'a second who stood apart', possibly the deputy high priest.

43 In the Mishnah tractate *Middot*, Chapter 3, the ramp up to the altar is specified as being 32 cubits long and 16 cubits wide. However, this rabbinic text was written around 100 AD and appears to be referring to the conflagration sacrificial altar, rather than the offering altar of the sanctuary. The *Middot* tractate is clearly describing the Second Temple after the conquest of the land by the Greeks, as it refers to 'the Greek letter Gamma'. Also the authority of the description in Ezekiel, written at a considerably earlier time, must take precedence, as evidenced especially from all the other descriptions of the temple that appear in Ezekiel which testify to his knowledge of the layout of the temple at Akhetaton.

44 Chyutin, 'The New Jerusalem Scroll from Qumran', pp. 126–7.

45 A. M. Blackman, *Preliminary Report on the Excavations at Sesebi, Northern Province, Anglo-Egyptian Sudan, 1936–37*, Egypt Exploration Society, 1937. Columns found in the ruins of the Temple area at Sesebi, discovered by Lepsius in 1849, carried reliefs of Sethis I. These were re-examined by Professor J. H. Breasted in 1907, and he found the reliefs were superimposed on earlier reliefs of Akhenaton. Breasted deduced from this and other evidence that Sesebi had originally been part of Akhenaton's programme of propagating his new religion in the Nubian region of upper Egypt near the 3rd Cataract of the Nile.

46 E. C. B. Maclaurin, 'Date of the foundation of the Jewish Colony at Elephantine', *Journal of Near Eastern Studies*, Vol. 27, Chicago University Press, 1968.

47 Martin Gilbert, *Atlas of Jewish History*, Morrow, 1993.

48 José M. Galán, 'An Apprentice's Board from Dra Abu El-Naga', *Journal of Egyptian Archaeology*, Vol. 93, 2007. The letter mentions King Neferkare ('Beautiful is the soul of Re') and probably refers to a legendary story about a 6th Dynasty king, Pepi II Neferkare, popular in the 18th Dynasty. The opening formula transliterates as: '*s3 dd hr it.f'mrnw.f 'nh wd3 snb . . .*' which translates as: 'It is the servant who says to [his Lord that he (the servant) wishes that he (the Lord) may live, be prosperous] and be healthy for the len[gth of] eternity and forever, as [this (his) humble servant wishes].'

49 Hundreds of rolls of papyrus from the settlement at Elephantine were discovered in the late 19th century, and most of them are now in museums in Berlin, Oxford, and Brooklyn. The Brooklyn collection records the activities of one of the families at Elephantine, mentioning that they worshipped Yahou, the equivalent name for Jehovah, as well as Melqat-ha-Shemayim (Queen of the Heaven). The head of the family, Ananiah, was a priest of the Elephantine temple and bore the title 'Lechen of Yahou the God who is in Elephantine' and was responsible for the god's ritual utensils, garments and jewellery. His wife, Tamut, bore the corresponding feminine title 'the Lechnah of Yahou'. The meaning of these and other priestly titles used at Elephantine is obscure, but appears to relate to the names used for priests in Assyria and Babylon. Other titles included '*koken*', for someone who prepared the sacrifices, and '*kemer*', a title found in the Bible but associated with pagan gods. Another indication of the antiquity of the community comes from Jeremiah, who seems to know of it when, in Chapter 44:7–8, he says: 'And now this is what Jehovah, Lord of Hosts, the God of Israel, has said: "Why are you causing a great calamity to your souls . . . by making sacrificial smoke to other gods in Egypt?"'

50 Apart from the reasons already stated in the chapter, the Hebrew letters Chyutin translates as Passover פסחין ו and פסחא' (Column 12, verses 2 and 3) are rather different from the version that appears in the Hebrew Bible in Exodus 12:11, 27 as פסח. The traditional family Passover takes place in the spring, whereas the Temple ceremony of inauguration takes place in the winter. Also in the usual family Passover it is specified that four glasses of wine must be consumed during the meal, rather than the seven cups mentioned in the New Jerusalem Scroll. The New Jerusalem Scroll ceremony also involves loaves of bread shown every seventh day before God in the temple and is therefore not a once a year ceremony as is the Passover referred to in the Bible. According to the New Jerusalem Scroll the number of priestly shifts in the temple was 26, corresponding with the number of Sabbaths in the Qumran solar calendar and conflicting with the traditional 24 shifts mentioned in the Bible. In addition, a detailed Throne Ceremony, taking place in the temple, is described in the Dead Sea Scrolls, whereas there is no mention whatsoever in the Bible of a throne being present in the Temple of Jerusalem.

Chapter 14 **Christians in the House of Akhenaton!**

1 Howard Jacobson, *The Bible as History*, Channel 4, 24 January 2010.

2 Robert Feather, *The Secret Initiation of Jesus at Qumran*, Baird/Watkins, 2006.

3 Barry Kemp, 'Tell El-Amarna, 2006–7', *Journal of Egyptian Archaeology*, Vol. 93, 2007.

4 N. de G. Davies, *The Rock Tombs of El Amarna, Part II – The Tombs of Panehesy and Meryra II*, The Egypt Exploration Fund, 1905.

5 Early explorers of Amarna and Panehesy's tomb were J. G. Wilkinson (1824), Wilkinson

and G. James Burton (1826), Nestor l'Hôte, Hay and Laver (1833), Richard Lepsius (1843–5). M. Jones, 'The Earliest Christian Sites at Tell el-Amarna and Sheikh Said', *Journal of Egyptian Archaeology*, Vol. 77, 1991.

6 Gillian Pyke, 'Church Wall Paintings from Kom el-Nana', *Egyptian Archaeology*, 22, Spring 2003.

7 E. C. B. Maclaurin, 'Date of the foundation of the Jewish Colony at Elephantine', *Journal of Near Eastern Studies*, Vol. 27, Chicago University Press, 1968.

8 Isaiah 6:2: 'Seraphs [cherubim] stood in attendance on Him. Each of them had six wings: with two he covered his face, with two he covered his legs, and with two he would fly.'

9 The Songs for the Sabbath Sacrifice is a pre-sectarian document that reflects knowledge of Akhetaton. Eight fragmentary pieces were recovered from Qumran and a ninth from Masada, and they have been reconstructed into 13 songs of praise to a divine King of Glory, reflecting a solar year, as followed at Qumran and Akhetaton. The imagery of the text can readily be related to images seen in the tomb of Panehesy at Amarna, and Akhenaton riding his heavenly chariot as seen on the walls of this tomb and elsewhere at Amarna. *See* P. R. Davies, George J. Brooke, Phillip R. Callaway, *The Complete World of the Dead Sea Scrolls*, Thames & Hudson, 2002.

> 'The [cheru]bim prostrate themselves before him and bless. When they rise, a soft divine-sound [is heard], and there is a roar of praise. When they drop their wings, there is a [sof]t divine sound. The cherubim bless the image of the throne-chariot above the firmament . . . there is what appears to be a fiery vision of the most holy spirits.' *(4Q405)*

10 Barry Kemp, Exploration of Kom el-Nan, Amarna www.digitalegypt.ucl.ac.uk/3d/impact.amarna.html.

11 J. Mayo, *A History of Ecclesiastical Dress*, London, 1984.

12 Mamdouh El-Beltagui. *The Holy Family in Egypt*, Egyptian Ministry of Tourism, 1999. According to Coptic traditions, the Holy Family stayed in Egypt for three years and 11 months. Coptic Christians celebrate their journey each year on 1 June (*see* Christian Cannuyer, *L'Egypte Copte*, Gallimard/IMA, 2000).

13 Christ's connections to Qumran are comprehensively discussed in my *Secret Initiation of Jesus at Qumran*.

14 Gillian Pyke, 'Roman Wall Paintings at Kom el-Nana', *Egyptian Archaeology*, No. 37, November, 2010.

Chapter 15 **Clear Solutions to Serious Questions**

1 Dr Esther Eshel of Bar-Ilan University is a world authority on epigraphy and has worked on many of the Dead Sea Scroll translations.

2 The Book of Daniel and the Testament of Levi (4Q212) correlate with the First Book of Enoch 91–93 in describing blocks of weeks for key events in history leading up to the End Days. '[At its close] the chosen ones will be selected as witnesses of the justice from the Plant of [Righteousness] Everlasting Justice; they will be given wisdom and knowledge sevenfold. They shall uproot the foundations of violence and the work of deceit in it in order to carry out [justice]. After this the eighth week will come . . . And after that the tenth week. In its seventh part) there will be an eternal judgement and the moment of the great judgement (and he will carry out revenge in

the midst of the holy ones).' *See also* George Athas, 'In Search of the Seventy "Weeks" of Daniel 9', *Journal of Hebrew Scriptures*, Vol. 9, 2010.

3   Josephus presents a certain amount of confused information. He tells us that between the ages of 16 and 19 he went through the initiation processes of the Pharisees, the Sadducees and the Essenes, but the Essene initiation period alone took several years, and he says he spent three years in the wilderness with Banus. Something does not add up, and we must be cautious about taking his claims without corroboration. For example, in *War* 7, 423–32, Josephus says that Onias III fled from the threat of Antiochus to Egypt and built a temple at Leontopolis, whereas in *Ant.* 20, 236, he states Onias IV built the temple at Leontopolis. Josephus also mixes up his Cleopatras amongst other related confusing statements so that whilst most of his information seems authentic, his facts need to be cross-checked against other sources wherever possible.

4   Jacob Licht, 'Time and Eschatology in Apocalyptic Literature and in Qumran', *Journal of Jewish Studies*, Vol. 16, Nos 3 and 4, 1965; J. Carmignac, 'La Notion d'eschatologie dans la Bible à Qumran', *Revue de Qumran*, December 1969.

5   Emile Puech arrives at a figure of 72 BC. 'Dead Sea Discoveries 3, Developments on the Dead Sea Scrolls', in Julio Trebolle Barrera and Luis Vegas Montaner, eds, *Madrid Qumran Congress: Proceedings of the International Congress on the Dead Sea Scrolls, Madrid, 18–21 March, 1991*, Brill, 1992; as does Hartmut Stegemann, *Die Essayer, Qumran, Jonas der Taufer*, Herder, 1993; and A. Steeled, 'Texts from Qumran', *Reif de Qumran*, 16, 1993. A figure of 60 BC is arrived at by Professor John Collins in *Apocalypticism in the Dead Sea Scrolls*, Routledge, 1997.

6   The Book of Revelation took a contrary stand to the then evolving Christian ideal of finding a personal salvation for the coming End Days through Christ and replaced it with the description of a social apocalypse in which everyone would be victim. Mainly for this reason, it was strongly resisted as a candidate for inclusion in the Christian scriptures. Because it was considered to have been written by St John the Divine, the 'Beloved of Jesus', however, it was finally included. Modern research assigns its composition to a disgruntled early Christian who lived on Patmos, a small rocky island off the coast of Asia Minor. He appears to have inserted elements related to a symbolic vision obtained from a 1st-century AD Jewish work known as the 'Oracle of Hystaspes' (Cana Werman, 'A Messiah in Heaven? A Re-evaluation of Jewish and Christian Apocalyptic Traditions', paper presented at Text, Thought, and Practice in Qumran and Early Christianity, International Symposium, Hebrew University of Jerusalem, 11–13 January 2004).

7   Michael Grant, *The Jews in the Roman World*, Weidenfeld and Nicolson, 1973.

8   Barbara Thiering, *Jesus of the Apocalypse*, Corgi, 1997.

9   The Roman historian Dio Cassius records that no sooner had Emperor Trajan committed Roman troops to a campaign against the Parthians in Mesopotamia than a general call throughout the eastern Mediterranean summoned the Jews to rise up in an attempt to reassert their independence. Revolts flared up in Cyrene, Cyprus, Egypt, Mesopotamia and in the Jewish homeland, commencing in 115 AD and only finally being suppressed in 117 AD, after Hadrian took his seat on the throne of Rome. *See also,* Michael Grant, *The Jews in the Roman World*.

10 M. Cary and H. H. Scullard, *A History of Rome*, Macmillan, 1975; J. Allegro, *The Chosen People*, Hodder and Stoughton, 1971.

11 Various publications give different dates for the end of Akhenaton's reign. I have taken the date as an average figure given by five authoritative Egyptologists as listed in William C. Hayes *The Sceptre of Egypt: A Background for the Study of Ancient Egyptian Antiquities in the Metropolitan Museum of Art*, Metropolitan Museum of Art, 1990. *See also* Robert Feather, 'Egyptian Pharaoh-Ruler Chronology and Probable Scheme of Dates for the Hebrew Patriarchs', in *The Mystery of the Copper Scroll of Qumran*.

12 Even if Barbara Thiering's calculations detailed in her book *Jesus of the Apocalypse* are wrong – and I must admit some reservations about her reasoning – the date of 70 AD deduced from the texts by a number of other eminent scholars as the revised date for the *eschaton* would come almost exactly 1,470 years after the birth, as opposed to the death, of Akhenaton. Either way, the dates are so close to the time of Akhenaton as to be hardly coincidental.

13 For example, Frank Moore Cross, *The Ancient Library of Qumran*, Anchor, 1961 & Sheffield Academic, 1995; Hartmut Stegemann, *The Library of Qumran*, Eerdmans/Brill, 1998.

14 For example John. J. Collins, *Apocalypticism in the Dead Sea Scrolls*, Routledge, 1997; Martin Hengel, *Property and Riches in the Early Church: Aspects of a Social History of Early Christianity*, SCM, 1974.

15 John J. Collins, *Apocalypticism in the Dead Sea Scrolls*, Routledge, 1997.

16 Devorah Dimant takes the period of 390 years given in the Damascus Document as dating from the beginning of Nebuchadnezzar's reign, and therefore places the emergence of the Essenes to nearer 200 BC, even though the scroll clearly talks about the destruction of the Second Temple as the significant date for the start of the 390-year period. Having made this assumption, she then finds that a commonly held view that the Teacher of Righteousness was associated with Jonathan the Maccabee – the so-called Wicked Priest – becomes quite untenable. She cannot suggest anyone as the Teacher of Righteousness who fits her chronology, however, and leaves the matter as 'still an uncharted land waiting to be exploited' (lecture to the Institute of Jewish Studies, University College London, 4 December 2002).

17 H. H. Rowley, *The Zadokite Fragments and the Dead Sea Scrolls*, Oxford University Press, 1952; Frank Moore Cross, *The Ancient Library of Qumran*, Doubleday, 1958.

18 Emil Schürer, Geza Vermes and Fergus Millas, eds., *The History of the Jewish People in the Age of Jesus Christ (175 BC–AD 135)*, T. & T. Clark, 1973. That the Qumran-Essenes could have had a reasonably accurate knowledge of previous chronology is attested to by their writings and by the knowledge in contemporary Jewish circles. For example, in 1 Maccabees, written around the 1st century BC, it is clear the authors, who were antagonistic to the Qumran-Essenes, knew the exact length of the reign of Alexander the Great and dated Antiochus IV Epiphanes (who started his rule in the Holy Land in 175 BC) as coming into office 137 years after the Persians were ousted by the Greeks. Ptolemy, the Greek ruler of Egypt, indeed annexed the Holy Land and drove out the Persians in 312 BC, 137 years before. See P. R. Davies, G. J. Brooke, and P. R. Callaway, *The Complete World of the Dead Sea Scrolls*, Thames and Hudson, 2002.

19 Tel el-Yehoudiah was first described by travellers in the early part of the 19th century; subsequently excavations were undertaken by E. Brugsch Bey, and more extensive work was done by Edouard Naville and F. Griffith commencing in 1887 (*Mound of the Jew and the City of Onias*, Kegan Paul, Trench, Trübner, 1890). It lies some 24km

north of where ancient Heliopolis (now part of modern Cairo) is thought to have been located. Remains from the Middle Kingdom period and from the periods of Seti I, Ramses II and III, and Merneptah found at the site include a representation of the huge temple of On. This shows a double flight of steps leading to the sanctuary level. The steps are guarded by sphinxes and two great pylons flanking the double gate of the sanctuary, and these are fronted by tall masts or flagstaffs. Only one main god, Tum Harmakhis, seems to have been worshipped at the site, which is located north of the supposed location of the Temple of On (Heliopolis). A later-period necropolis, about 2km from the main site, contained *fours à cercueils*-style burials similar to those found in Jewish cemeteries, with tombs inscribed in Greek and Hebrew. The adjoining Jewish settlement is identified as that founded by Onias IV, as described by Josephus. It included a large temple with a tower 60 cubits (30m/98ft) high. The inner furnishings were apparently patterned on those in the Jerusalem Temple, except that the *menorah* was replaced by a golden lamp or orb hanging on a golden chain. The Jewish temple at Leontopolis survived for some 340 years and was eventually closed and destroyed on the instructions of the Roman emperor Vespasian, who knew the settlement as Scence Veteranorum ('Old Establishment') after the destruction of the Second Temple in Jerusalem, probably to prevent it from being used as a rallying point for further revolts.

20 Until recently it was thought that synagogue-style worship did not exist before the destruction of the Second Temple in Jerusalem in 70 AD. In the 1960s, however, an open synagogue area on top of Masada was identified as having been built before 70 AD. In the same period, another synagogue was excavated at Herodian, near Hebron. More recently, in the 1990s, archaeologists from Hebrew University uncovered a synagogue dating to c100 BC beneath the ruins of a palace built by King Herod near Jericho. The synagogue, together with the remainder of a Hasmonean winter palace complex, was destroyed in the earthquake of 31 BC (which also damaged the buildings at Qumran). The excavations have revealed a *genizah* niche cut into a wall like that at the Ben Ezra synagogue in Cairo, probably for the storage of holy texts; a *mikvah* (ritual bath); and a room for ceremonial meals. The synagogue at Jericho is now the oldest known example in Israel, predating by some 30 years the Gamla synagogue, discovered in the Golan Heights (J. Hunting, 'Archaeology Near Jericho', *The Vineyard*, David Press, March 2001). Michael Grant, however, claims that the earliest form of synagogue worship for which there is evidence comes from Schedia, some 24km from Alexandria, dating to circa 225 BC (Grant, *The Jews in the Roman World*).

21 Flavius Josephus, *Jewish Wars* 7 (for example, H. St. J. Thakeray, *Josephus, The Jewish War*, Heinemann, 1957; William Whiston and Paul L. Maier, *The New Complete Works of Josephus*, Kreel, 1999).

22 S. H. Steckoll, 'The Qumran Sect in Relation to the Temple of Leontopolis', *Revue de Qumran*, Vol. 6, No. 21, 1967.

23 S. H. Steckoll, 'Marginal Notes on the Qumran Excavations', *Revue de Qumran*, No. 25, 1969.

24 Robert Feather, *The Copper Scroll Decoded*.

25 In a presentation at Harvard Divinity School in April 1996, Professor F. M. Cross suggested that Simon the son of Boethus, Herod the Great's father-in-law, was the

descendant of the priestly house that served in the Onias Temple near Leontopolis. Simon originated from Alexandria in Egypt. This family line of priests, calling themselves Boethians, continued after the demise of Qumran and could well be the link back, from a separate ancient priestly line of true heirs, to the old high priesthood through to Onias IV. Simon's predecessor, Jesus the son of Phiabi, carries an Egyptian name that was found on a Jewish inscription at Tell el-Yehoudiah. Having a close relative who was part of the Egyptian priestly line that founded the Qumran-Essene establishment would help explain Herod's favourable attitude toward the Essenes, as recorded in Josephus's writings. It would also neatly confirm why Onias IV would have had the historical priestly credentials and learning, as the Teacher of Righteousness, to lead a separatist community into the wilderness of Judaea to Qumran. *See* Israel Knohl,'New Light on the Copper Scroll and 4QMMT', in G. J. Brooke and P. R. Davies, eds., *Copper Scroll Studies,* Sheffield Academic, 2002.

26   *See* Dead Sea Scroll 1QpHab, and also 4QpPsa.

27   Josephus records that Menelaus was executed by Antiochus around 163 BC.

28   1 Maccabees is thought to have been written in Hebrew around 120 BC and 2 Maccabees around 160 BC. The books are not included in the version of the Hebrew Scriptures used by Jews and some Protestants, but the first two of the four known books of the Maccabees are part of the Catholic canon.

29   Pythagoras (580–500 BC) was, in the words of the philosopher Bertrand Russell, 'intellectually one of the most important men that ever lived' (*A History of Western Philosophy,* Allen and Unwin, 1946). He founded a mystic group in the Greek colony of Croton in southern Italy. Josephus in fact equates the Essenes to Pythagoreans (*Jewish Antiquities,* 15.371). The degrees of sympathy to Greek thought and culture in the Jewish communities fell roughly into three categories: traditionalists, exemplified by Joshua ben Sira, author of the Wisdom of ben Sira (Ecclesiasticus), who rejected any Greek assimilations; moderates, who admired the philosophical works of Greek thinkers such as Pythagoras, Socrates, Plato and Aristotle; and extreme Greek sympathizers, exemplified by those who underwent operations to reverse the visible signs of circumcision so they could participate naked in the Greek gymnasium built by Antiochus IV (175–163 BC). Tuvia Fogel, president of the literary agency Caduceo SRL, Milan, has pointed out that there is a tradition that Pythagoras actually met Ezekiel when they were both exiled in Babylonia, and that the influences may have been mutually beneficial. Bearing in mind Professor Ben Zion Wacholder's assertion that Ezekiel was the first Essene, this possible meeting becomes even more pertinent and credible.

30   This sentence comes from the First Letter to the Jews of Egypt mentioned in 2 Maccabees 1 and apparently written in 124 BC, in Raymond E. Brown, Joseph Fitzmyer, Roland E. Murphy, eds., *The New Jerome Biblical Commentary*, Cassell, 1989 p. 441, First Letter 1:1–10a.

31   Christopher Knight and Robert Lomas, in their book *The Second Messiah* (Barnes and Noble, 2000), suggest that the King James version of the Bible classifies the two Books of Maccabees as apochryphal because they were anti-Nasorean, implying there was a link from the Essenes to the Nasoreans through James, the brother of Jesus, that royal interests did not want criticized. This idea ties in with their thesis that Freemasonry can trace its ancestry back through the Stewart kings of Scotland

and the influence of remnants of Templar crusader knights who fled to Scotland in the 14th century, bringing with them Nasorean knowledge and who were thus pro-Essenic. In *The Jews in the Roman World*, Michael Grant suggests that one of the reasons why Judas Maccabeus, for all his heroic triumphs in recovering the Temple at Jerusalem (165–164 BC), is never mentioned in the Mishnah is that he allied with the Romans in his attempts to resist Seleucid influences.

32 The exclusion of the books of Maccabees from the Hebrew scriptures may well be yet another indication that Essenic thinking dominated early rabbinic thinking.

33 James H. Charlesworth, 'Jesus as "Son" and the Righteous Teacher as "Gardener"', in James H. Charlesworth, ed., *Jesus and the Dead Sea Scroll*, Doubleday, 1992.

34 Ibid.

35 André Dupont-Sommer (trans. A. Margaret Rowley), *The Dead Sea Scrolls: A Preliminary Survey*, Oxford/Blackwell, 1952.

36 Classified as Psalm D by A. Dupont-Sommer, and as Hymn 12 of the Thanksgiving Hymns in Geza Vermes, *The Complete Dead Sea Scrolls in English*. Vermes translates Møth-Belial as 'devilish schemes', however.

37 Ian Shaw and Paul Nicholson, *British Museum Dictionary of Ancient Egypt*.

Chapter 16 Melchizedek: Nothing is New under the Sun

1 Descriptions of Melchizedek appear in the Bible in Genesis 14:18–24, where he meets and blesses Abraham; Hebrews 5–8, where Jesus is likened to him; Psalm 110; and in 11QMelch, 4QShirShabb, 1QM of the Dead Sea Scrolls.

2 *Melchizedek in Scripture, Tradition and Liturgy*, Temple Studies Group Conference, 8 November 2008, St Stephen's House, Oxford. Later Jewish commentators maintained that Melchizedek was Shem, the son of Noah, but this appears to be a manoeuvre to downgrade the claims of Jesus to be equivalent to the Righteous King – Melchizedek.

3 Against this interpretation the Genesis Apocryphon says that Abraham was the recipient of the tithe, implying that he was the superior. See my chapter 'Ethereal Melchizedek – and Kabbalah' in *The Secret Initiation of Jesus at Qumran*. Letter to the Hebrews 7:1–4 is discussed in James Davila, 'Melchizedek as a Divine Mediator', International Conference on the Dead Sea Scrolls as Background to Postbiblical Judaism and Early Christianity, University of St Andrews, 26–8 June 2001. Davila says: 'Melchizedek is an Exalted Patriarch who embodies the ideal figure of the Celestial High Priest which is in turn embodied by Jesus.'

4 The Songs of the Sabbath Sacrifices 4Q401, 4Q403; Philo of Alexandria, *Leg. All*. III where Melchizedek is referred to as 'Melchizedek as high priest representing reason and one who rules as a Righteous King'; Josephus (*Ant*. 1.10.2) and the Genesis Apocryphon (Col. 22) paraphrase the passage in Genesis and explicitly identify Salem with Jerusalem; 11th century Genizah fragment K21.95.C in the Taylor-Shechter Library, Cambridge; Pseudo-Eupolemos (*Praep. Evan*. 9.17.6) refers to him briefly as the ruler of a city; in the Talmud, the Youth is referred to as Metatron; Siddur Rabbah, Shuir Qomah 38–42, 'Rabbi Ishmael said to me: Metatron [a rabbinic period name for Melchizedek] the real attendant said this testimony: I testify by Hashem, the God of Israel . . . and the Youth comes and abases himself before H'H; Gnostic texts from the Nag Hammadi collection; Second Book of Jeu a Coptic Gnostic text where Jesus prays to the Father for 'Zorokothpra Melchizedek' in what appears to be a

Mithraic Ritual of a school of Egyptian magicians, who inserted a title which seems to be connected to a magical name 'nomina Barbara', although the title Zorokothpra might relate to Zoroastra; Pistis Sophia Coptic Gnostic text where Melchizedek I is probably being referred to as the 'Celestial High Priest and Divine Warrior'.

5 Margaret Barker, '"The Time is Fulfilled", Jesus and the Jubilees', *Scottish Journal of Theology*, Vol. 53, No. 22, 2000.

6 Two members of Akhenaton's court are listed with the hieroglyphic name which can be enunciated as of Meryre. Meryre I is designated high priest and Meryre 2 superintendent of Queen Nefertiti, and royal scribe.

7 Alan F. Segal, 'The Risen Christ and the Angelic Mediator Figures in Light of Qumran', in James H. Charlesworth, ed., *Jesus and the Dead Sea Scrolls*.

8 Gershom Scholem, *Kabbalah*, Penguin, 1978. James R. Davila, '*The Dead Sea Scrolls and Merkavah Mysticism*', in Timothy H. Lim, ed., *The Dead Sea Scrolls in Their Historical Context*, T. & T. Clark, 2000.

9 See Psalm 82; also Alan F. Segal, 'The Risen Christ and the Angelic Mediator Figures in Light of Qumran', in James H. Charlesworth, ed., *Jesus and the Dead Sea Scrolls*.

10 Two of the same feather-like symbols commence the hieroglyph word for Israel seen in the stela of Pharaoh Merneptah, dated to 1210 BC. This is the first known representation of the name of Israel, in the sense of its being the name of a people rather than a place name. Here, the double *yy* sound of the two symbols, meaning God, almost certainly explains the use of the double *yod* as an abbreviation of the name of God that appears in Hebrew (Messod and Roger Sabbah, *Les Secrets de l'Exode*, Jean-Cyrille Godefroy, 2000).

11 It is not surprising that Merkabah, or 'heavenly chariot', mysticism was strongly condemned by later rabbis, who proscribed discussion on the subject (*m.Hag.* 2.1). The subject led straight back to the heavenly chariot of Pharaoh Akhenaton and a possible eclipsing of Moses. Nevertheless, the tradition of mysticism and heavenly transformation left a strong footprint in both the Hebrew and Christian scriptures, in the latter particularly through the New Testament's continuing concentration on the subject (Rom. 8:29; 1 Cor. 15:49; 2 Cor. 3:18, 4:4; Phil. 3:21).

12 Margaret Barker, 'The Time Is Fulfilled: Jesus and the Jubilee', *Scottish Journal of Theology*, Vol. 53, No. 22, 2000.

13 Joseph A. Fitzmyer, *Responses to 101 Questions on the Dead Sea Scrolls*, Paulist Press, 1992.

14 D. W. Rooke, 'Jesus as Royal Priest: Reflections of the Interpretation of the Melchizedek Tradition in Heb. 7', *Biblica*, 81, 2000.

15 G. W. Buchanan, *To the Hebrews*, Doubleday, 1972; H. Braun, *An die Hebräer*, Tübingen, 1984; H. W. Attridge, *The Epistle to the Hebrews, Hermeneia*, Fortress, 1989.

16 Y. Yadin, 'A Note on Melchizedek and Qumran', *Israel Exploration Journal*, 15, 1965; M de Jonge and A. S. Van der Woude, '11Q Melchizedek and the New Testament', *New Testament Studies*, 12, 1966; J. A. Fitzmyer, 'Further Light on Melchizedek from Qumran Cave 11', *Journal of Biblical Studies*, 86, 1967, 18. In the Epistle to the Hebrews 7:6 ('But he [King Salem] whose descent is *not* counted of them [i.e., who did not come out of the loins of Abraham and was not a Hebrew] received tithes of Abraham, and blessed him'), just as Abraham has to be seen to be associated with the divine figure of Melchizedek (retrospectively in terms of the authors of the Hebrew

scriptures and futuristically in terms of the chronology of Abraham in relation to King Akhenaton and his high priest, Meryre), so Jesus has also to be associated with the kingly priestly figure. As W. L. Lane, 'Hebrews 1–8', *WBC*, 47A, Dallas, 1991, rightly points out, even though Melchizedek united the dual honours of royalty and priesthood, he was unlike the Hebrew kings. This article can also be found in 'Jesus as Royal Priest: Reflections on the Interpretation of the Melchizedek Tradition in Heb. 7', by D. W. Rooke, in *Biblica*, 81, 2000.

17   The Amarna letters are collections of some 400 cuneiform tablets comprising records of correspondence between the Egyptian court and vassal states, composed in the mid-14th century BC. They were discovered at Amarna in 1887. In Amarna letter EA 287, the governor, Abdi-Heba (also translated as Abdi-Khepa), is writing to Pharaoh Akhenaton, setting out his fears for the safety of the city: 'As the king has placed his name in Jerusalem forever, he cannot abandon it – the land of Jerusalem' (*The Amarna Letters*, ed. and trans. William L. Moran, Johns Hopkins University Press, Baltimore and London, 1992). As far as I am aware, this is the first-ever mention of Jerusalem in written texts. Confirmation that the king of Salem, of Genesis, is a holy king comes from Joshua 10:3, where the king is referred to as Adoni-Zedek, relating him to God, as Aton, and high priest.

18   Leonora Leet, *The Secret Doctrine of the Kabbalah*, Inner Traditions, 1999.

19   Cyril Aldred, *Akhenaten, King of Egypt*.

20   N. de G. Davies, *The Rock Tombs of Amarna, Part I: The tomb of Meryra*, London, 1903.

21   Cairo-Damascus, Community Rule and Messianic Rule documents of the Dead Sea Scrolls. *See*, for example, translations in Geza Vermes, *The Complete Dead Sea Scrolls in English*.

22   The Dead Sea Scroll of Blessing (1QSb) has a long description of a kingly messiah who is fierce and can kill the sinner.

23   Cairo-Damascus and Community Rule documents of the Dead Sea Scrolls and the Cairo-Genizah collection. According to Richard Elliott Friedman in his *Who Wrote the Bible?*, HarperSanFrancisco, 1989, there was a clear distinction between the family of Moses (priests in the north of Israel) and the family of Aaron (Zadokite priests based at Hebron in the south).

24   Jeremiah 22; Ezekiel 34; Micah 3; 1 and 2 Chronicles; 1 and 2 Kings.

25   1 Chronicles 21:14–17; 2 Samuel 11.

26   2 Samuel 12. Intriguingly, Nathan's condemnation of David recounts that the Lord will deal with him publicly, 'before all Israel, and before the sun'. Appending this to the Lord's judgment against King David makes little sense unless 'the sun' has some profound value. I argue elsewhere that, although there may well have been aberrational pagan worship of the sun in Israel, authentic references to it by such God-fearing Jews as King Hezekiah and King Josiah are almost certainly Egyptian-inspired imagery related to Akhenaton's vision of God, alluded to in the form of a sun disc. In 1 Samuel 19:12–14, there is further evidence that David was not an ideal character to perceive as a messiah. In the section where he is being pursued by King Saul, who seeks to kill him, his wife, Michal, helps him escape and then wraps the household idol in a goatskin cloth.

27   Joseph A. Fitzmyer, *The Dead Sea Scrolls and Christian Origins*, Eerdmans, 2000.

28   Daniel I. Block, 'My Servant David: Ancient Israel's Vision of the Messiah', in Richard

S. Hess and M. Daniel Carroll, *Israel's Messiah in the Bible and the Dead Sea Scrolls*, Baker Academic, 2003. In a chapter in the same work, 'If He Looks Like a Prophet and Talks Like a Prophet Then He Must Be . . . ', J. Daniel Hays finds it difficult to substantiate the idea that Moses or even David could be the messianic figure behind Isaiah's suffering servant. In 'The Imagery of the Substitute King Ritual in Isaiah's Fourth Servant Song', *Journal of Biblical Literature*, 122 (4), 2003, John H. Walton has no doubt that the suffering servant messianic figure has royal connotations.

29 Robert L. Webb, 'John the Baptizer and Prophet: A Socio-Historical Study', *Journal for the Study of the New Testament*, Suppl. Series 62, Sheffield Academic, 1991. Interestingly, in the Masoretic text of Zechariah 6:12–13, the prophet is told to make 'crowns' and set them on the head of Joshua, the high priest. This can only be an allusion to a practice unique to Egypt, in which enthronement involved two crowns representing the 'Two Lands' of Upper and Lower Egypt. *See also* Frank Moore Cross, *The Ancient Library of Qumran*.

30 C. D. Elledge, 'The Prince of the Congregation: Qumran "Messianism" in the Context of Milhama', *Journal of Hebrew Scriptures*, Vol. 9, 2009, opposes much recent scholarship that views the 'Prince' in Qumran literature as a Davidic messiah. Elledge concludes that this figure should be considered a 'quasi- or proto-messianic' figure.

For example, in Ezekiel 34, 37, and 40–8, the prophet carefully avoids naming David as the founder of the lineage of a new order. And, as discussed above, Ezekiel also carefully avoids mentioning Jerusalem as the place where a reconstituted Temple will be built at the time of the coming of the messiah, but refers to it as a place in which 'the Lord is there'.

31 Robert L. Webb, 'John the Baptizer and Prophet: A Socio-Historical Study'.

32 K. Pomykala, *The Davidic Dynasty Tradition in Early Judaism*, Scholars Press, 1995. *See also* Richard S. Hess and M. Daniel Carroll, *Israel's Messiah in the Bible and in the Dead Sea Scrolls*.

33 Marilyn Lundberg, 'The Misbegotten Messiah: A Re-Examination of a Disputed Reading in 1QS^a (1Q28^a)', The Dead Sea Scrolls – Fifty Years After Their Discovery, International Congress, Jerusalem, 20–25 July 1997.

34 Geza Vermes, *The Complete Dead Sea Scrolls in English*. It should be noted that Isaiah 10 and 11 do not specifically mention King David, and the Hebrew text in the scroll mentions a "branch of David" and not King David himself. According to Professor Hartmut Stegemann, lecturing at University College London on 23 November 1998, the Qumran-Essenes awaited figures from the 'Hebrew Scriptures who would be anointed through God's holy spirit'. Stegemann described Psalms 17 and 18 as the only pre-Dead Sea Scrolls references to a 'future messiah – a royal messiah'. The priestly messiah who will atone for sins, he said, has nothing to do with Jesus; the function was the traditional role of the high priest.

35 Writers on this theme include: Lawrence Schiffman, 'Messianic Figures and Ideas in the Qumran Scrolls', in *The Messiahs: Developments in Earliest Judaism and Christianity*, Fortress, 1992; García Martínez, 'Messianische Erwartungen in den Qumranschriften', *Journal of Biblical Theology*, 1993; J. VanderKam, *Messianism in the Scrolls: The Community of the Renewed Covenant*, Notre Dame University, 1994; E. Puech, *Messianism, Resurrection, and Eschatology at Qumran and in the New Testament*, Notre Dame University, 1994; W. M. Schniedewind, 'King and Priest in the Book of

Chronicles and the Duality of Qumran Messianism', *Journal for the Study of Judaism*, 45; (1994); J. J. Collins, *The Scepter and the Star: The Messiahs of the Dead Sea Scrolls and Other Ancient Jewish Literature*, Doubleday, 1995; Jean Duhaime, 'Recent Studies on Messianism in the Dead Sea Scrolls', Dead Sea Scrolls – Fifty Years After Their Discovery, International Congress, Jerusalem, 20–25 July 1997.

36 Geza Vermes, *The Complete Dead Sea Scrolls in English*. It has been suggested – for example, by Charles Fritsch (*The Qumran Community: Its History and Scrolls,* Macmillan, 1956) – that 'the Star' refers to the leader who took the Qumran community off to Damascus when they came under threat from King Herod the Great, only to return after the king's death in 4 BC. *See also* 4Q175, known as 4QTestimonia.

37 Barbara Thiering, *The Gospels and Qumran*, Sydney Theological Explorations, 1981.

38 Barbara Thiering, *Jesus of the Apocalypse*, Corgi, 1997.

39 This reference to Seth is, I believe, to the same Seth who appears in the Nag Hammadi texts, significantly in a codex known as the Gospel of the Egyptians (*see* Chapter 14). It is surely not a reference to Adam's third son, briefly mentioned in Genesis, or to the 'Sons of Sheth' mentioned in Numbers 24:17 (who have been identified with a nomadic tribe living to the north of Canaan), which unconvincing conventional explanations propose.

40 John J. Collins, *Apocalypticism in the Dead Sea Scrolls*.

41 James VanderKam, *Calendars in the Dead Sea Scrolls,* Routledge, 1998. Devorah Dimant, 'The Scrolls and the Study of Early Judaism', in *The Dead Sea Scrolls at Fifty: Proceedings of the 1997 Society of Biblical Literature, Qumran Section Meetings*, Scholars Press, 1999; Devorah Dimant, 'The History of the Dead Sea Scrolls Ascetic Community: What Is New', paper presented at the Institute of Jewish Studies, University College London, 4 December 2002. Professor Dimant's views of the origins of the solar calendar used at Qumran are refuted by evidence from the Dead Sea Scrolls. The Jubilees scroll, for example, asserts that the 364-day year had been recorded in the 'heavenly tablets' going back to the time of Moses. This conclusion was initially arrived at by A. Jaubert (*La Date de al Cene*, Sorbonne, Paris, 1957.) It was also noted by Ben Zion Wacholder and it has been accepted by many scholars (IV Kongress der International Organization for Qumran Studies, Basel, 5–7 August 2001).

42 A full discussion of the significance of this relief, which Psalm 104 of the Bible effectively paraphrases, is given in Robert Feather, *The Mystery of the Copper Scroll of Qumran*. See also *The Pharaoh's Holy Treasure*, BBC2 TV, 31 March 2002.

43 There is a difference of rabbinic opinion about whether the *lulav* should comprise one or three types of leaf. A modern commentary states: 'The Hebrew word for fronds or branches "*Kappot*" is written defectively, without the letter "*vav*", so that the word could also be read in the singular rather than the plural. Hence the traditional view that a single palm frond was to be held by each worshipper.' (*Prayers for the Pilgrim Festivals,* Reform Synagogues of Great Britain, 1995) This seems to be confirmed by the single palm seen being waved in a relief in the Metropolitan Museum of Art, New York, dated to 1353-1336 BC.

44 Joseph A. Fitzmyer, *The Dead Sea Scrolls and Christian Origins*, Eerdmans, 2000. Although it has been argued that there are messianic portents of a royal figure in earlier parts of the Hebrew scriptures, they are not crystallized until the time of the Qumran-Essenes and their writings. There is no messianism before 500 BC, and any

reference to *moshiah* (messiah) is applied to a historical figure, never to expected or eschatological figures (John Collins, *The Scepter and the Star: The Messiahs of the Dead Sea Scrolls and Other Ancient Literature,* Doubleday, 1995). Modern Jewish scholars, like H. L. Ginsberg and David Flusser (*Encyclopaedia Judaica,* Keter, 1971), see Jewish messianism as emerging only in the Roman Second Temple period.

45 Józef T. Milik, *Ten Years of Discovery in the Wilderness of Judaea,* SCM, 1959. Milik noted that, in 4Q Testimonia (Florilegium), three biblical passages relating to the future messiahs are immediately followed by a section from the Psalms of Joshua that alludes to past events connected with the persecutors of the Hebrews: 'When Josh[ua] fini[sh] ed off[ering prai]se in [his] thanksgivings, [he said]: c[ursed be m]an who rebui[l] ds [this cit]y!' *(4Q175)* The essence of these connected texts is that the original exemplars for the three messiahs predated the exodus, as the pseudepigraphical Psalms of Joshua allude to past events connected with persecutors of the sect.

Chapter 17 Signposts from Amarna to Qumran

1 Recent DNA analysis of members of the Cohanim (Jews thought to have descended from the priestly Levite class, who through the ages have traditionally intermarried only with other Cohanim) shows that they carry distinctive hereditary patterns. These markers differentiate them from other Jews, but it appears that the biological event that caused the marker occurred at least 29,000 years ago! Other websites give a figure of 11,375 years ago for the differentiating event: www.familytreedna.com/ nature97385.html and www.bsu.edu/classes/fears/relst251/dna.html. In other words, the line of priestly Cohanim existed aeons before they were apparently separated out for appointment as priests in the time even of Jacob, let alone Moses (K. Skorecki, S. Selig, S. Blazer, et al., 'Y Chromosomes of Jewish Priests', *Nature,* 385, 2 January 1997).

2 Jan Assmann, *Moses the Egyptian: The Memory of Egypt in Western Monotheism,* Harvard University Press, 1998.

3 Peter van der Veen, Christoffer Theis, Manfred Görg, 'Israel in Canaan (Long) Before Pharaoh Merenptah? A Fresh Look at Berlin Statue Pedestal Relief 21687', *Journal of Ancient Egyptian Interconnections,* Vol. 2, No. 4, 2010.

Chapter 18 Isaiah Knew about Akhenaton

1 Isaiah 2:7. 'And its land is full of silver and gold, And there is no end to its treasures, And its land is full of horses, And there is no end to its chariots, And its land is full of idols; They bow down to the work of their hands . . .'

2 Among her books are: *Studies in Egyptology Presented to Miriam Lichtheim,* Eisenbrauns, 1990; *Egyptological Studies,* Humanities Press, 1983; *Non-verbal sentence patterns in Late Egyptian,* Griffith Institute, Oxford University Press, 1967.

3 Sarah Israelit Groll, 'The Egyptian Background to Isaiah 19:18', Colloquium on Isaiah 18–19 – A Meeting of Cultures: Israelite, Egyptian, Assyrian, Hebrew University, 5 April 1995.

Reference to the Aton in the form of *hwt-p3-jtn* at Memphis, is documented into the time of Seti I (c1280 BC) – W. Spiegelberg, *Rechnungen aus der Zeit Setis I.,* Strasbourg, 1896.

Professor Groll cites a number of other researchers who contributed to her conclusion that Akhenaton's name and religion continued on after his death. 'Akhenaton's successors indeed abandoned his religious center and he was certainly hated in certain circles (in the inscription of Mes [line S 14] he is referred to as *p3-hrw n 3h.t-itn* "the enemy from El-Amarna"), but I do not believe that they succeeded in completely extinguishing all memory of him and of his religious theories from the Egyptian consciousness. From the Nineteenth to the Twenty-Fifth Dynasty, that is, to the time of Isaiah, one finds numerous references to *p3-itn* "the deity Aton". As opposed to *-itn*, "the solar disc". [Professor Groll correctly differentiates the pagan solar disc and monotheistic Aton logo as two separate ideas, unlike many who confuse the two and see Akhenaton worshipping the sun rather than an invisible force merely visualized as the sun with rays projecting from it.] In particular, *p3-itn* is often associated with the rising sun. The proper name Loukianos Naphenaton (M. Chaîne, *Le manuscrit de la version copte en dialecte sahidque des 'Apophthegmata Patrum'*, L'institut français d'archéologie orientale, Cairo, 1960, No. 36), which may be analyzed as Loukianos of *ahe(3h.t)-n-p(p3)-aton(itn)* "the Horizon of Aton" with metatesis of the *p*, suggests that memory of the site of Akhenaton's religious center may have survived even into Coptic times.'

See also J. Allen, *Genesis in Egypt: The Philosophy of Ancient Egyptian Creation Accounts*, Yale University Press, 1989; J. Assmann, 'Die "Häresie" des Echnaton von Amarna: Aspekte der Amarna-Religion', *Saeculum*, 23, 1972; J. Assmann, 'Egyptian Solar Religion in the New Kingdom: Re, Amun and the Crisis of Polytheism', *Studies in Egyptology*, London and New York, 1995; H. Brunner, 'Echnaton und sein Versuch einer religiösen Reform', *Universitas*, 17, 1962; G. Fecht, 'Zur Frühform der Amarna-Theologie; Neubearbeitung der Stele der Architekten Suti und Hor', *ZÄS*, 94, 1867; E. Hornung, *Der Eine und die Vielen: Ägyptische Gottesvorstellungen*, Wissenschaftliche Buchgesellschaft, Darmstadt, 1971; O. Keel, ed., 'Monotheismus im Alten Israel und seiner Umwelt', *BBB*, 14, Kegan Paul International, 1980; D. Redford, *Akhenaten, the Heretic King*, Princeton University Press, 1984.

4 Douglas M. Gropp, 'The Wadi Daliyeh Documents Compared to the Elephantine Documents', The Dead Sea Scrolls – Fifty Years After Their Discovery, International Congress, Jerusalem, 20–25 July 1997. Gropp demonstrates that many of the features and beliefs of the aberrational community, often referred to as a Jewish colony, at Elephantine Island, have a much earlier ancestry than is usually assumed. Although, as I argue above, this community was connected to Amarna, it was not on the direct line that also linked Amarna to Qumran. One would therefore expect to find differences in their customs from conventional Judaic practice existing at the time of their assumed departure from Israel to Egypt. This is exactly the case. An analysis of the Elephantine schema of deeds of conveyance, seen in the Elephantine papyri, written in Official Aramaic, which are thought to derive from the Persian period, has confirmed that these are radically different to later Judaic schemes in Israel, and relate to fundamentally different legal systems. In the case of the Judaean formulary, for example recovered from Wadi Daliyeh, near Qumran, the content is modelled on cuneiform of the late Neo-Babylonian period of Darius I, whereas the Elephantine schema is closer to a Neo-Assyrian tradition of the late 9th or early 8th century BC, demonstrating that the Yeb community dated to a much earlier period than is generally assumed.

5 V. Taylor, *The Gospel according to St Mark,* Macmillan, 1966. *See also* Daniel B. Wallace, 'Mark 2:26 and the Problem of Abiathar', Evangelical Theological Society, Southwest Regional Meeting, Dallas Theological Seminary, 13 March 2004.

Chapter 19 And Along Came Kabbalah

1 The third revolt against Roman occupation of what had been a Jewish state was led by a charismatic figure called Bar Kochba or Bar Kosiba. He was hailed as the Messiah by some of his supporters after he led a successful uprising which wrested control of the country from Rome and established a Jewish state for a period of nearly three years, 132–5 AD.

2 Reports also appeared in the *Jewish Chronicle*, and the story was picked up the by BBC and many news services around the world. Unfortunately, many of the stories were based on quite erroneous information.

3 Johann Scheibel, *trans., The Seventh Book of Moses*, Stuttgart, 1849.

4 The blessing at Akhetaton is recorded on the wall of the tomb of Meryre, and was published in N. de G. Davies. *The Rock Tombs of El Amarna: Part 1. The Tomb of Meryra.*

Chapter 20 The Controversial 'Son of God' Fragment

1 Józef Milik was assigned publication of 4Q246 in 1958 and, although he eventually gave a lecture on it in 1972 at Harvard University, it was not published until 1996. Emile Puech, '246. 4QApocryphe de Daniel', in G. Brooke et al., eds., *Qumran Cave 4: XVII – Parabiblical Texts, Part 3*, Clarendon, 1996. *See also* Kapera and Feather, *Doyen of the Dead Sea Scrolls.*

2 Geza Vermes, *The Complete Dead Sea Scrolls in English.*

3 Carsten Peter Thiede, *The Dead Sea Scrolls and the Jewish Origins of Christianity*, Lion, 2000.

4 Lecture by Józef Milik at Harvard University, reported by J. A. Fitzmyer in *New Testament Studies,* 20, 1973–4.

5 Martínez and Tigchelaar, *The Dead Sea Scrolls Study Edition*; Florentino García Martínez and Julio Trebolle Barrera, eds., *The People of the Dead Sea Scrolls*, E. J. Brill, Leiden, 1995.

6 John J. Collins, 'The Nature of Messianism in the Light of the Dead Sea Scrolls', in T. Lim, ed., *The Dead Sea Scrolls in Their Historical Context*, T. & T. Clark, 2000. Collins lifts his eyes to the far horizons of the Mediterranean and does not ignore Egypt: 'There is also evidence for the anointing of non-royal officials in Egypt and of Egyptian vassals in Syria'; 'The sonship in question is generally recognized as adoptive, and does not imply the degree of divinization that we find, for example, in Egypt.' *See also* Robert Feather, *The Mystery of the Copper Scroll of Qumran.*

7 A similar logic can be applied to another controversial fragment, 4Q369 (4QPEnosh?), which talks of a prince, glory of the light, a crowned ruler.

8 Nicholas Weeks, *Egypt's False Prophet Akhenaten,* Thames and Hudson, 2001.

9 Scrolls 4Q252, 4Q285, 4Q161, 4QSa and 1QSb.

10 N. de G. Davies, *The Rock Tombs of El Amarna: Part II, The Tombs of Panehesy and Meryra II*, Egypt Exploration Fund, 1905.

11 From the Damascus Document. A. Dupont-Sommer (*The Dead Sea Scrolls: A Preliminary Survey*, Blackwell, 1952) points out that the sect was led by a Mebhakker,

who was over the priests. He had supreme control of administration, as well as having a spiritual role. I equate this title, in sounding and role, to the name of Meryra or Meryre, Akhenaton's high priest at Akhetaton. *See also* Florentino García Martínez, 'Qumran Messianism', *Revue de Qumran* 73, 1999. CD 1QSb.

12 1QM (War Scroll).

13 For 4Q285 (4QSefer ha-Milhamar), the so-called Pierced Messiah fragment which mentions the Prince of the Congregation, *see* Chapter 16.

14 C. D. Elledge, 'The Prince of the Congregation: Qumran "Messianism" in the Context of the Milhama', in M. T. Davis and B. A. Strawn, eds., *Qumran Studies: New Approaches, New Questions*, William B. Erdmann, 2007.

15 The early Egyptian god Horus was Osiris's 'son' of renewed incarnation, and this title 'Son of God' became applied to the pharaoh of Egypt.

Chapter 21 A Chance Meeting: The Elephant on the Move

1 D. Barthélemy and J. T. Milik, *Qumran Cave 1*, Discoveries in the Judaean Desert. I; Oxford: Clarendon, 1955.

2 Michael Baigent and Richard Leigh, *The Dead Sea Scrolls Deception*, Touchstone, 1991.

3 Weston W. Fields, *The Dead Sea Scrolls: A Full History. Vol.* 1, Brill, 2009. In his review Father Jerome Murphy-O'Connor betrays a bias towards Jordanian interests, already seen from other Catholic scholars on the Dead Sea Scrolls campus, and tries to defuse any implication that Jewish scholars had been discriminated against in the scrolls team.

Talking about the composition of the original translation team, Murphy-O'Connor comments: 'On rather slender evidence Fields concludes that "it is virtually certain that Jewish scholars would have been invited to join the Cave 4 team had Jerusalem not been divided in 1953".' If this was the case, it hardly explains why Jewish scholars were still not invited on to the team after Jerusalem was united in 1967. A main thrust of Fields's work seems to be to promote lack of funds and disruption of the team after 1960 as the main reasons for delays in publication and to refute suggestions of anti-Semitism being a possible reason.

4 The London conference on 40th anniversary of discovery of the scrolls was convened by Professor Geza Vermes, and it called for the *immediate* publication of all Roland de Vaux's original notes and photographs without transcription, commentary, or editorial notes. All the members of the team working on the official publications were invited, as well as those remaining former members who were still alive.

5 Ancient Near East-2 website, February 2009.

6 Weston W. Fields, *The Dead Sea Scrolls: A Full History.*

7 Review in *Biblical Archaeology Review* www.bib-arch.org/reviews/review-dead-sea-scrolls-full-history-b.asp.

8 Michael Baigent and Richard Leigh, *The Dead Sea Scrolls Deception*, Touchstone, 1991.

9 A translation appears in Appendix 2.

10 New York Dead Sea Scrolls Conference, 14–17 December 1992, Blood Center, New York.

11 Robert Eisenman and Michael Wise, *The Dead Sea Scrolls Uncovered: The First Complete Translation of 50 Key Documents Withheld for Over 35 Years,* Element Books, 1992.

12 'New Accusations Erupt Over the Dead Sea Scrolls', *New York Times*, 18 December 1992.

13 Hershel Shanks, 'A Plea for Civility', *Biblical Archaeology Review*, Jan/Feb, 1992.

14 Joseph Zias, 'The Cemeteries of Qumran and Celibacy, "Confusion Laid to Rest?"', *Dead Sea Discoveries*, 7, 2, 2000.

15 Robert Feather, *The Secret Initiation of Jesus at Qumran.*

16 Another indication of the mindset of the Ecole team was their frequent reference, by Rolande de Vaux, John Allegro and others, to the Qumran site as a 'monastery', implying it was a Christian institution and that the Church had more right to pronounce on its relevance that other denominations

17 Interviews by David Pryce-Jones at www.bibliotecapleyades.net/scrolls_deadsea/ deadsea_scrollsdeception/scrollsdeception.htm#contents.

18 Interview with John Strugnell by Hershel Shanks, 'Ousted chief scroll editor makes his case', *Biblical Archaeology Review*, July/August 1994.

19 Kapera and Feather, *Doyen of the Dead Sea Scrolls.*

20 John Marco Allegro, *Sacred Mushroom and the Cross*, Sphere, 1973. John Marco Allegro, *Dead Sea Scrolls and the Christian Myth*, Sphere, 1981.

21 John Marco Allegro, *The Chosen People*, Panther, 1971.

Chapter 22 **Beyond Reasonable Doubt: The Elephant Appears**

1 Niels Peter Lemche, 'The Old Testament – A Hellenistic Book?', *SJOT*, 7, 1993.

2 Hans Barstad, *History and the Hebrew Bible: Studies in Ancient Israelite and Ancient Near Eastern Historiography*, FAT, 61: Tübingen: Mohr Siebeck, 2008.

3 Jens Bruun Kofoed, *Text and History; Historiography and the Biblical Text*, Eisenbrauns, 2005. *See also*: Jim West, 'The Copenhagen Boomerang: Deadly Weapon or the Retrieval of a Forgotten Truth', www.bibleinterp.com, April 2005.

4 William G. Dever, 'Contra Davies', www.bibleinterp.com, January 2003.

5 Donald Redford, *An Egyptological Perspective on the Exodus Narrative, Egypt, Canaan and Israel: Archaeological and Historical Relationships in the Biblical Period*, Tel Aviv University, 1987. Redford adds that Ramses II, for example, in his recording of the battle against the Hittites at Kadesh, used liberal amounts of mythic language to describe a verifiable historical event that not even the most radical minimalist would deny.

6 The fellows of the Westar Institute include scholars with advanced degrees in biblical studies, religion or related fields and, by special invitation only, published authors who are recognized authorities in the field of religion. Since its inception, more than 200 fellows have participated in the Jesus Seminar. Other Westar seminars are also at work, including one on The Acts of the Apostles, which began deliberations in 1999, and will evaluate and report on the historical authenticity of the Acts in much the same way as the Jesus Seminar has reviewed the sayings and events in the gospels.

7 Florentino García Martínez and Julio Trebolle Barrera, *The People of the Dead Sea Scrolls*, Brill, 1995.

8 Weston W. Fields, *The Dead Sea Scrolls: A Full History. Vol. 1.*

9 'Dead Sea Scroll Concordance Now Available for Use by Scholars', *Biblical Archaeology Review*, March/April 1990.

10 Wacholder and Abegg published their results as *A Preliminary Edition of the Unpublished Dead Sea Scrolls,* Biblical Archaeology Society, 1991.

Appendix A

Scholars' Ideas about Qumran

The positions held by various scholars on what was going on at Qumran during the period of Essenic presence of approximately 200 years to 68 AD.

Qumran was a communal religious centre:
Roland de Vaux, Józef Milik, Dominique Barthélemy, Pierre Benoit, John Allegro, John Strugnell, Claus-Hunno Hunzinger, Patrick Skehan, Frank Cross, Maurice Baillet, Jean Starcky, Lankester Harding, Godfrey Driver, Yigael Yadin, Eleazar Sukenik, Ernst-Marie Laperrousaz, James Sanders, William Brownlee, John Trever, Johannes van der Ploeg, Adam van der Woude, Raymond Brown, Joseph Fitzmyer, David Freeman, Eugene Ulrich, Elisha Qimron, Geza Vermes, Hershel Shanks, Carol Newsom, Eileen Schuller, Lawrence Schiffman, Jodi Magness, Magen Broshi, Ben Zion Wacholder, Witold Tyloch, Martin Abegg, Edward Cook, Peter Flint, Greenfield, Michael Wise, Torleif Elgvin, Minna and Kenneth Lonnqvist, Jonas Greenfield, Israel Knohl, Armin Lange, Manfred Lehmann, Timothy Lim, Sarianna Metso, Donald Parry, Joseph Baumgarten, Shemaryehu Talmon, Hanan Eshel, Esther Eshel, Michel Stone, Ronny Reich, Annette Steudal, Richard Freund, Robert Eisenman, García Martínez, Eibert Tigchelaar, Emile Puech, Philip Alexander, John Collins, Esther Chazon, Sidnie White Crawford, Devorah Dimant, Stephen Pfann, Charelsworth, James Robinson, J. C. Charlesworth, James VanderKam, Ada Yardeni, Jacob Sussman, Charlotte Hempel, Jacob Neusner, Martin Goodman, Greg Doudna, Michael Chyutin, Judah Lefkovits, Kyle McCarter, Johann Maier, John Kampen, Stephen Goranson, Hartmut Stegemann, Joe Zias, Adolfo Roitman, Emanuel Tov, George Brooke, Philip Davies, Phillip Callaway, Devorah Dimant, Susan Guise Sheridan, Olav Röhrer Ertl, Harold Ellens, Robert Feather, Stephen Goranson, Dennis Mizzi,[1] Edna Ullmann-Margalit,[2] etc.

Qumran was not a communal religious centre but a:

Military fortress	Norman Golb (Raphael Golb)
Farmstead / manor house	K. H. Rengstorf, Yizhar Hirschfeld
Pottery-making facility	Yuval Peleg and Yitzhak Magen[3]
Commercial centre	Alan Crown and Lena Cansdale
Health spa	Gloria Moss
Villa / palace	Jean-Baptiste Humbert
Villa rustica	Pauline and Robert Donceel-Voûte,[4]
	Zdzislaw Kapera[5]
Winter villa	Michael Le Morvan
Perfume facility	Joseph Patrice
Essenes were not there	Rachel Elior, Albert Baumgarten

Most of the Dead Sea Scrolls were written / copied at **Qumran:**

Roland de Vaux, Józef Milik, Dominique Barthélemy, Pierre Benoit, John Allegro, John Strugnell, Claus-Hunno Hunzinger, Patrick Skehan, Frank Cross, Maurice Baillet, Jean Starcky, Lankester Harding, Godfrey Driver, Yigael Yadin, Eleazar Suknik, James Sanders, William Brownlee, John Trever, Johannes van der Ploeg, Adam van der Woude, Raymond Brown, Joseph Fitzmyer, David Freeman, Eugene Ulrich, Elisha Qimron, Geza Vermes, Hershel Shanks, Carol Newsom, Eileen Schuller, Lawrence Schiffman, Jodi Magness, Magen Broshi, Ben Zion Wacholder, Martin Abegg, Edward Cook, Peter Flint, Greenfield, Michael Wise, Torleif Elgvin, Minna and Kenneth Lonnqvist, Jonas Greenfield, Israel Knohl, Armin Lange, Manfred Lehmannm, Abraham Ruderman, Timothy Lim, Sarianna Metso, Donald Parry, Joseph Baumgarten, Shemaryehu Talmon, Hanan Eshel, Esther Eshel, Michel Stone, Ronny Reich, Annette Steudal, Richard Freund, Robert Eisenmann, García Martínez, Eibert Tigchelaar, Emile Puech, Philip Alexander, John Collins, Esther Chazon, Sidnie White Crawford, Stephen Pfann, James Charlesworth, James Robinson, James VanderKam, Ada Yardeni, Jacob Sussman, Charlotte Hempel, Jacob Neusner, Martin Goodman, Greg Doudna, Michael Chyutin, Judah Lefkovits, Kyle McCarter, Johann Maier, John Kampen, Stephen Goranson, Hartmut Stegemann, Joe Zias, Joseph Patrice, Adolfo Roitman, Emanuel Tov, George Brooke, Philip Davies, Phillip Callaway, Devorah Dimant, Susan Guise Sheridan, Olav Röhrer Ertl, Harold Ellens, Robert

Feather, Stephen Goranson, Edna Ullmann-Margalit, Dennis Mizzi, etc.

The Dead Sea Scrolls were not written/copied at Qumran but came from Jerusalem:

Norman Golb, Yuval Peleg and Yitzhak Magen, Yizhar Hirschfeld, Alan Crown and Lena Cansdale,[6] Jean-Baptiste Humbert, Pauline Donceel-Voûte and Robert Donceel, Rachel Elior, G. R. Driver,[7] D. Winton-Thomas.

Notes to Appendix A

1 Dennis Mizzi, Oriental Institute, University of Oxford, believes 20–30 Qumranites lived on site at Qumran and that they deposited the scrolls in various caves that had seasonally been occupied by Bedouin, who left cylindrical jars they had used for storing food in the caves.

2 Albert Baumgarten believed Qumran was not a religious centre largely because of the possibility that a latrine was found on the site, but is hesitant to explain his own view as to its function.

3 Magen and Peleg assume that Qumran was a forward observation post for the Hasmoneans, before becoming a pottery factory. Early on, Yitzhak Magen had proposed, together with General Amir Drori, that Qumran was first a Hasmonean farmstead and then became a military outpost.

4 Pauline and Robert Donceel-Voûte. Dr Donceel-Voûte (of the Département d'Archéologie et d'Histoire de l'Art, College Erasme, Louvain, Belgium) seems to have changed her mind as in 1993 she initially claimed the site was a perfume factory producing balsam. In communications between the author and the Donceels in July 1999, Mme Donceel-Voûte, mentioned that she thought the occupants of Qumran had too many expensive goods and were engaged in the manufacture of perfume.

5 Zdzislaw Kapera calls the site 'a kind of Jewish *villa rustica*'.

6 A. D. Crown and L. Cansdale, 'Qumran, Was It an Essene Settlement?', *Biblical Archaeology Review*, 20, 1994. L. Cansdale, 'Qumran and the Essene: A Re-Evaluation of the Evidence', *Texte und Studien zum antiken Judentum*, 60, Tübingen, 1997.

7 Professor Driver thought the manuscripts were of Zealot origin.

Appendix B

Email Correspondence Relating to Norman Golb

From: Carlo Gadda [mailto:carlogadda@yahoo.com]
Sent: Tuesday, June 19, 2007 10:59 AM
To: Meg Sullivan
Subject: Your article on the "Virtual Qumran" film
Importance: High

Dear Ms. Sullivan,

I have read your article on the 'Virtual Qumran' film, and I regret to inform you that it gives a seriously misleading impression to anyone who might not be familiar with the current state of scholarship on Qumran.

(1) To begin with, Norman Golb did not publish an 'article' in 1996; he published a 400-page book entitled 'Who Wrote the Dead Sea Scrolls?'

(2) Your sources (no doubt Cargill and Schniedewind themselves) failed to inform you that the thesis they are defending has been rejected not only by Golb, but by an entire series of major archaeologists since 1990. These include most notably the Donceel team (officially appointed by the Ecole Biblique to review and finish de Vaux's work); Yizhar Hirschfeld (see his book Qumran in Context); and the officially appointed Israel Antiquities Authority team led by Yizhak Magen and Yuval Peleg, who, after ten seasons of digs at Qumran, have published their conclusions that the site was never inhabited by any sect and that the Dead Sea Scrolls are the remnants of libraries from the Jerusalem region.

These facts are well known to Qumran scholars, and your article gives a distinctly misleading impression to the reader by not mentioning them. Dr. Schniedewind is known to be a radical defender of the disputed Qumran-Essene theory, and he has a right to defend his views, but it

259

was highly inappropriate of him to use $100,000 in grants to mislead the public in this film by failing to mention the conclusions of the Magen and Peleg team, and it was inappropriate for you to advertise the film without informing people of the actual facts.

(3) Your article also fails to mention that the film has already been subjected to biting criticism by Norman Golb (see his article 'Fact and Fiction in Current Exhibitions of the Dead Sea Scrolls – A Critical Notebook for Viewers', available on the University of Chicago website at http://oi.uchicago.edu/research/projects/scr/). In the wake of Golb's criticism, one commentator has suggested that 'the goal of this film is simply to indoctrinate visitors, before they see the rest of the [San Diego Scrolls] exhibit, into believing in the old, Qumran-Essene theory, despite the fact that it has now been rejected by virtually all of the major archaeologists in the field.'

I have left aside the clear manipulation of evidence in the film itself, e.g., the way it argues that Qumran was inhabited by a group of male Essenes, despite the fact that the remains of women were found in the cemetery – since Pliny states that the Essenes of the Dead Sea were celibate, the makers of the film were obliged to distort, ignore or explain away the actual evidence to support their view. And so on and so forth with the other claims they make.

In the hope these observations will have given you fruit for thought, I am

Yours sincerely,
Charles Gadda

Note: The closing paragraph of this email from ' 'Charles Gadda' ends with the unpunctuated words I am followed by a closing and a signature line. Note the resemblance to letters signed by Norman Golb to the UCLA Provost and by 'Robert Dworkin' to a SDNHM board member. Note too the use of double hyphens [--] as a dash. This is similar to the signed letter written by Norman Golb to the San Diego Natural History Museum.

Email 1 from alias Emily Kaufman to Elizabeth Carter
On Sun, Feb 8, 2009 at 7:55 PM, Emily Kaufman <kaufman.emily1@ gmail.com> wrote:

Dear Professor Carter,

A student in your department, who prepared a film being shown in Dead Sea Scrolls exhibits, is now involved in deleting information about the controversy surrounding those exhibits from wikipedia articles. He uses the pen-name 'XKV8R' to this end – see his user-page at: http://en.wikipedia.orghttp://en.wikipedia.org/wiki/User:IsraelXKV8R, and compare his edits and statements at http://en.wikipedia.org/w/index.php?title=Dead_Sea_scrolls&action=history   <http://en.wikipedia.org/w/index.php?title=Dead_Sea_scrolls&action=history>

This activity is inappropriate for a Ph.D. candidate at UCLA. It is also inappropriate for the student in question, because he has a conflict of interest, having been personally involved in preparation of material used in the exhibits.

I hope you will take measures to stop 'XKV8R' from inappropriately interfering in the contributions I and other authors have been making to the wikipedia article on the Dead Sea Scrolls. It is annoying to us to see our work suddenly disappear under one pretext or another, simply because 'XKV8R' is trying to suppress any discussion of a controversy surrounding exhibits in whose preparation he has played a role.

Yours sincerely,

Emily Kaufman

Email from alias Steve Frankel to Elizabeth Carter

From: Steve Frankel [mailto:steve.frankel2@gmail.com]

Sent: Tuesday, January 22, 2008 3:56 PM

To: Bakhos, Carol; Banani, Amin (Bol Fwd); Band, Arnold; Bodrogligeti, Andras; Boustan, Ra'anan; Buccellati, Giorgio (FWD); Burke, Aaron; Cooperson, Michael; Cowe, Peter; Davidson, Herbert A.; Dieleman, Jacco; Englund, Dr. Robert; Ezer, Nancy; Fishbein, Michael; fitz@ucla.edu; Hagigi, Latifeh (FWD); Hakak, Lev; Hirsch, David G.; Jaeckel, Ralph; Keshishian, Anahid;Poonawala, Ismail; Sabar, Yona; Schmidt, Hanns Peter; Shayegan, Rahim; Slyomovics, Susan; Wendrich, Willeke; Pirnazar, Nahid; Ziai, Hossein

Subject: The recent conduct of Bill Schniedewind and his student Robert Cargill

Gentlemen,

A short while ago, I mailed the following to the chairman of your department from a friend's email address, with a blind copy to all of you. Please address any correspondence to me at the above email. Now we will see if Dr. Carter takes any action on this matter or hushes it up.

Best,

S. Frankel

Dear Professor Carter,

As an alumnus of UCLA, I write to you concerning an important, but delicate matter.

It has come to my attention that Robert Cargill, a graduate student of Dr. William Schniedewind in your department, recently produced a 'virtual reality' film on Khirbet Qumran, which was shown to some 450,000 visitors attending the San Diego Natural History Museum's controversial exhibit of the Dead Sea Scrolls.

According to published accounts, this film (funded with $100,000 from Stephen Spielberg's Holocaust fund) presents Dr. Schniedewind's views on Qumran, and in doing so distorts the current state of research in this field of studies, making many demonstrably false claims, treating disputed interpretations as facts and defending an old, and widely disputed, theory of Dead Sea Scroll origins without informing the public of the reasons why an entire series of major researchers, including the officially appointed Israel Antiquities Authority team led by Drs. Yitzhak Magen and Yuval Peleg, have now rejected that theory. This becomes abundantly clear in a review of the film by University of Chicago historian Norman Golb, published on the Oriental Institute website (see http://oi.uchicago.edu/pdf/san_diego_virtual_reality_2007.pdf).

My concern is as follows. I have scoured the internet in vain for any response by Dr. Schniedewind or Mr. Cargill to this detailed critique of their film. But I have read that the preparation of the film has been a key focal point of Mr. Cargill's work towards his Ph.D. The accumulation of transparently erroneous and mendacious statements made throughout the film, documented in Dr. Golb's article and clearly designed to mislead the public, can hardly be called an example of ethical conduct on the part of a doctoral candidate. If it were merely a question of Dr. Schniedewind failing to answer criticisms of his views, one could write it off as another example of a typical academic dispute, but in this case we are dealing with a graduate student, and with basic standards of scholarship that obviously must be met; questions that those who adhere to such standards would rightly expect to be raised at a dissertation defense; etc.

For example, in marginal correspondence that is apparently part of his unpublished film script, Mr. Cargill refers to a 'reason' justifying one of his statements that he is careful 'never to write down' (see Dr. Golb's article for details). One cannot but wonder whether those attending Mr. Cargill's dissertation defense will carefully question him as to precisely what this reason is that, in violation of all canons of scholarship, he never writes down.

Ultimately, I feel that I have no choice but to ask: What is UCLA going to do to ensure that Mr. Cargill provides a candid explanation of his behavior with respect to this film? Will steps will be taken to ensure that he responds to Dr. Golb's criticisms, corrects his false statements and issues a public apology for having misled 450,000 people? Will Mr. Cargill be allowed to receive a Ph.D. for work of this quality, in the face of an unanswered refutation published for all to see by an influential historian teaching at the University of Chicago?

I conclude that we appear to be dealing with a serious issue here that should be dealt with forcefully and responsibly, to avoid the risk of its being raised by various parties at Mr. Cargill's dissertation defense, as well as the even more upsetting likelihood of hearing that it has been raised with the university administration and local newspapers.

With best regards,
Steve Frankel

Appendix C

Letter from Father Benoit, Jerusalem, 9 November 1972

To: Professors M. Baillet, F. M. Cross, J. T. Milik, P. W. Skehan, J. Starcky, J Strugnell.

Several amongst you have expressed the wish that I visit the Jordanian authorities in order to put in place the method which we think should be pursued to progress publication of *DJD*. Mr Cordy, of Clarendon Press, has also asked me for exact details on the subject.

I therefore returned to Amman, shortly after my return from France and Rome, that is to say on 25–26 October. I had a long conversation with Yusuf Ben Alami, Director of Antiquities. The next day he took me to the Ministry of Tourism and Antiquities. Mr Baravet apologized for not being able to receive me, as he had an obligation to attend a conference at the University of Amman. Mr Battaineh, under-secretary at the ministry, received me in his place.

I explained to those present the extent of the problem and how I wanted to find a solution which enabled a resumption of the publication of *DJD* and took maximum account of the legitimate sensibilities of the Jordanians. I was not able to accord them a formal superiority, which would be equivalent to an official recognition of the authority of the Rockefeller Museum by the Israelis. I said to them that I could not meet their request for this impossible gesture, but only asked them to understand that the solution adopted was the only possible one, if one wished to avoid other unacceptable solutions: not to publish anything more, or to let the Israelis take control of the editions. In short I assured them that our 'team' were sympathetic to their claims to take all possible measures not to hurt their rights in pursuit of publication in the interest of scientific requirements.

It seems to me that the personalities encountered were very aware of the required courtesy and understood the problems. The conversation with Yusef Alami was long and very cordial. It was particularly satisfying through the note that Biran authorized me to write in the Preface, where I explained the change of title and said clearly that it did not imply on our part any official recognition of the actual political situation. Mr. Batteineh was less informed – the meeting with him was briefer. He welcomed the proposal which he would convey to his officials. He authorized me to say that we could continue the collection 'as it was before'. When I remarked that there would be a subtle change in the presentation, he replied that he was well aware but he was authorized to tell me that. Once again, the Jordanians were not able to give an official endorsement which would amount to taking a political position. The essential thing is that they have understood our problem, understood our loyalties and that they are acquainted with our action. I think now that they will not raise any difficulties when the new volumes appear.

This is what I am writing to Mr Cordy for assurance.

The new development is in effect to establish that Clarendon Press accept the recommencement of the collection, and in particular the content of the volume is interesting but not too large that we are only in a position of the offer for the moment. I will keep you informed of the progress of their response and developments.

[Paragraph on technical translation matters]

Thank you and until soon,

Pierre Benoit

[Translation from French by Robert Feather]

Glossary

Ain Feshka Essene settlement 3km south of Qumran, from where fresh water was available. Evidence of parchment manufacture and crop cultivation indicates that it was a source of materials, food and potable water for the Qumran-Essenes.

Akhenaton Revolutionary pharaoh who helped initiate a belief in one all-powerful, omnipresent, omniscient God he knew by the name of Aton or Adon.

Akhetaten Modern day El-Amarna located in Middle Egypt on the east bank of the Nile.

Akkadian A Semitic language originating in the Tigris–Euphrates region in the 3rd millennium BC. In use at the time of Akhenaton in Egypt, and as the diplomatic language of the Levant, until superseded by Aramaic.

Ankh A symbol shaped like a cross with a circular loop shape at the top, it was originally an Egyptian symbol but has been adopted into Christianity as a form of the Cross. In the Amarna period, the ankh sign was to the fore as one of the most important symbols. It represented the 'Sign of Life' or 'Breath of Life' and was the ancient hieroglyph sign for 'life'. In inscriptions it is often seen close to the nostrils of humans and appeared on the ends of the rays in the solar depiction of God as the Aton.

Apocrypha Or 'hidden' (from the Greek *apokryphos*). Sacred Jewish texts, written in the Second Temple period and up to 135 AD, which are additional to the 39 books accepted by all Christians as part of the Old Testament. They are known from the Greek Septuagint version of the Old Testament and are accepted as scriptural by the Catholic Church, but were excluded from the canon by many Protestant churches at the time of the Reformation. They include the books of Judith, Tobit, the Wisdom of Solomon and Ecclesiasticus. (Not to be confused with Ecclesiastes which is part of the Catholic, Protestant, and Jewish scripture.) *See also* Pseudepigrapha.

266

Aramaic A Semitic language dating back to 900 BC, the *lingua franca* of the Persian Empire and used extensively by the Jews after they returned from the Babylonian exile. The cursive script replaced ancient paleo-Hebrew for secular writing and holy scriptures.

Assyrians Semitic tribes of ancient west Asia who dominated the Middle East in the 8th century BC and into the late 7th century. They conquered the Northern Kingdom of Israel around 722 BC and laid siege to Jerusalem, in the Southern Kingdom, in 701 BC.

Aton or Aten Name given to the concept of God in the Amarna period of the 14th century BC in Egypt. Depicted as a solar disc with rays emanating down ending in hands, hands holding ankh signs, or mattocks.

Babylonians *See* Mesopotamia.

Boethians A group named after Boethius, the father-in-law of Herod the Great. Boethius' son, Simon, was an Egyptian priest from Alexandria and appears to have been buried in the Hebrew cemetery at Leontopolis, the site of a temple built by Onias IV. The likelihood that Onias IV was the Teacher of Righteousness of the Qumran-Essenes would help to explain an apparent connection between an on-going movement known as the Boethians, who are referred to by later rabbinic sources, and the Essene movement.

Elephantine Island A small island (approximately 1,200m x 400m) located in the Nile opposite Aswan in Upper Egypt. It was known as Ab and Yeb in early ancient Egyptian history and is probably referred to in Isaiah as Cush. After the conquests of the Greeks in the 4th century BC it was known as Elephantine Island, probably from the shape of coastal bolder formations which resemble the outline of elephants. A triad of gods, Khnum, Satis and Anuket were worshipped on the island, but the dominant god was Khnum – a ram-headed god believed to control the waters of the Nile – who had a temple built in his honour in the 3rd Dynasty. Various pharaohs built on the island including Amenhotep III, Akhenaten's father, and there are remains of his work and of Tuthmosis III. Excavations commenced in the 19th century and still ongoing, mainly by German archaeologists, have revealed evidence of a pseudo-Hebrew colony, with its own temple, which was founded at least as early as 800 BC and could date to the time of the expulsion of Hebrews from Akhetaton. Knowledge of the layout of the town and the temple are derived from excavations and a large collection of Aramaic papyri, discovered in the late 19th century that describe the activities and beliefs of the religious settlement occupants.

Essenes   A name applied by contemporary historians like Josephus to a religious group, centred at Qumran, Judaea, on the Dead Sea at the time of the Second Temple. They practised an abstemious lifestyle with their own versions of ritual washing, a solar calendar, religious outlook, and philosophy. Those who did not wander the country evangelizing devoted themselves to prayer and writing, including many works now considered as part of the Dead Sea Scrolls.

Freud, Sigmund   (1856–1939) As well as being the father of psycho-analysis, Freud had an abiding interest in studying ancient religions and archaeology, particularly Egyptian. In 1931 he wrote a study on the origins of Moses entitled *Moses and Monotheism*, which attracted considerable criticism and reprobation, largely because he portrayed a first Moses as having been murdered by the Hebrews and the arrival of a second Moses. The work was heavily influenced by his own 'angst' in dealing with his Jewish parentage and feelings of guilt over his own non-conformity.

Genizah Collection   Vast cache of mainly Jewish religious and secular texts discovered in 1896 in the Ben Ezra synagogue in Old Cairo, Egypt, by two Scottish travellers – Agnes Lewis and Margaret Gibson. Most were written between the 10th and 12th centuries AD, but some Karaite writings date back to the 6th century AD. Significantly, some of the texts were of Qumranic-Essene origin. Some 140,000 fragments (75% of the total known to exist) are now housed in the Taylor-Schechter Library, University of Cambridge, England.

Hellenism   Greek influences in language, literature, philosophy, art, and design which spread across the Middle East after the conquests of Alexander the Great in the 4th century BC.

Hippolytus   (c170–222 AD) Christian writer, who became Presbyter in Rome and possibly the 'anti-Pope' to Callistus from 217–22 AD. He mentions the Essenes and their daily routines of 'girding themselves with linen girdles ... taken their seats [for breakfast] in order and in silence ... conversing quietly (for supper)'. (Hippolytus, *Refutation of All Heresies*, G. Vermes and M. Goodman (eds.), *The Essenes According to the Classical Sources*, Sheffield, 1989).

Jewish scriptures   These are usually understood to comprise the Torah (Five Books of Moses), Neviim (Books of the Prophets), Ketuvim (The Writings, including the Psalms and Proverbs). In addition, there are oral laws and discussion codified in the Talmud.

Josephus, Flavius (37–100 AD) Jewish historian who became a Roman citizen and wrote extensively, *inter alia*, about the Essene community and their settlement on the Dead Sea, and about Pontius Pilate. Born into a wealthy priestly family, he spent the first half of his life in Jerusalem. As a general commanding the Galilee area during the Jewish uprising of 66 AD he fought against the Romans, but after being captured gained favour with the Romans by correctly predicting that the commander of the Roman army, Vespasian, would become Emperor. After 70 AD he settled in Rome, continuing his friendship with the new emperor and subsequently his successor Titus. He wrote extensively on Roman–Jewish history, including his *Jewish War* describing the period 175 BC to 74 AD and *Jewish Antiquities* covering the period from the creation of the world to 66 AD. He mentions the Essenes, John the Baptist, Caiaphas the High Priest, Pontius Pilate, James the brother of Jesus, and Jesus – although this latter reference is thought to have been augmented by later copyists.

Kabbalah Jewish religious belief based on hidden revelations. Kabbalah was codified by Shimon bar Yohai, in the *Zohar* in the 13th century AD, in Spain. It claims to give the true meaning behind the Torah in two forms – one basic and the other secret. Its teaching was prohibited until the 16th century AD, but parts of its doctrine, of mystical piety and concentration on the presence of God, were absorbed into Hasidism (a branch of Orthodox Jewry) around the 18th century AD.

There are some similarities in its teachings with Buddhism, Confucianism and Indian religious ideas of inner awareness, in the ten levels of attainment before one-ness with God can be achieved. There are also overtones of Egyptian mythology in the visible and invisible aspects of God, the judgment of the soul after death and allocation to paradise or hell, or transmigration into animal or other human form where restitution may be sought.

Mysticism, magic, divination and sorcery were, and are today, severely frowned on in rabbinic teaching. Nevertheless, after the exodus, residual beliefs lingered on in superstition and folklore and eventually found expression in the form of 'Kabbalah' - which can be traced back as far as ancient Egypt. Akhenaton, however, shunned Egyptian magic and mysticism, and it was also strongly resisted in ancient Judaism, and is still looked on with reservations by many rabbis.

Karaites Jewish movement established by a Persian Jew named Anan ben

David, c750 AD. He advocated a return to strict Old Testament Judaism, with the exclusion of other rabbinic teachings, like the Talmud and Mishnah. One of the main surviving works of the Karaites is the Cairo Codex. Written in Tiberius, in 895 AD, by Moses ben Asher, it contains the books of the prophets written in Hebrew, and as such, prior to the finding of the Dead Sea Scrolls, contained the oldest Hebrew version of the Old Testament. It is now kept in the Russian State Library, St Petersburg. The Asher family also compiled the Aleppo Codex, an 11th-century version of the Old Testament, found at Aleppo in Syria, in the 14th century AD. It is incomplete, having suffered fire damage, and is now kept in the Shrine of the Book, Jerusalem. Karaite historians believe that the movement looked to the Essenes for spiritual inspiration and was familiar with the Damascus Document amongst other Dead Sea Scroll texts.

Maccabees   Jewish priestly family whose head was High Priest Mattathias and whose son Judah led a successful revolt against the Greek Seleucid leader, Antiochus Epiphanes, in 167 BC and re-occupied Jerusalem in 164 BC. His re-dedication of the Second Temple at Jerusalem is now remembered by celebrating the Festival of Chanukah.

Masoretic text   Hebrew Bible based on the Aleppo codex and compiled over several centuries by a group known as the Masoretes, based in Tiberius, Jerusalem and Iraq. It was written down on parchment by Salomon, son of Wia, in about 935 AD. During rioting in Syria in 1947, it was badly damaged in a fire before being brought back to Jerusalem in 1958. Together with the Leningrad Codex, which dates to c1010 AD and is housed in the National Library of Russia in St Petersburg, it forms the basis of the modern Tanakh or Hebrew Bible. The Leningrad Codex is the most complete extant version of the Masoretes' work, but has many variants from the Septuagint and Dead Sea Scrolls versions of the Hebrew Bible which date to more than 1,000 years earlier.

Mesopotamia, Sumeria and Babylonia   Sumeria was composed of city states which emerged about 3400 BC, in the region of the Tigris and Euphrates rivers, modern Iraq, generally referred to as early Mesopotamia. Babylonia was a kingdom in the southern portion of Mesopotamia formed under Hammurabi around 1790 BC. Its capital, Babylon, was about 80km south of today's city of Baghdad.

Midrash   See Torah.

Mishnah   See Torah.

Orthography   Form, style and content of words giving an indication of when and where they were composed.

Ostracon   Ceramic medium used early on in history for writing inscriptions or images.

Palaeography   Form, style and shape of the letters and symbols used in writing.

Papyrus   Writing media made from papyrus plant found growing mainly in the delta marshes of the Nile, in Egypt. Earliest examples date back to 3035 BC.

Parchment   Animal skin, usually goat or sheep, specially prepared and used for writing. Used in Egypt from 2000 BC and Judaea from about 200 BC.

Pentateuch   The first five books of the Hebrew scriptures: Genesis, Exodus, Leviticus, Numbers and Deuteronomy.

Persians   People from the area of modern-day Iran who drove out the Babylonians from the Holy Land and conquered Egypt c525 BC under King Cyrus, and dominated the Middle East for about 200 years. They allowed Jews exiled by the Babylonians to return to the Holy Land and generally acted benignly towards them. The Biblical story of Esther is generally thought to have been enacted in Persia.

Philo, Judáeus   (c20 BC–c40 AD) – Jewish-Egyptian philosopher and Greek scholar, born in Alexandria. He worked at Alexandria on Bible commentary and law, and mentions the Qumran-Essenes in his writings.

Pliny the Elder   (23–79 AD) – Gaius Plinius Secundus was born in Como, Italy, of an aristocratic Roman family. After a term in the Roman army he later devoted himself to writing historical treatises on, for example, oration, and the history of Rome. A friend of Emperor Vespasian, he died during the volcanic eruption of Mount Vesuvius in 79 AD. He wrote about the Essene community by the Dead Sea.

Pliny the Younger   (c62–113 AD) – Nephew and adopted son of Pliny the Elder, he was born in Novum Comum and became a renowned orator and Roman author. In correspondence with Tarjan he recorded the denigrating attitude of early Romans toward Christians and how the Christians 'sing a hymn to Christ as to a god'.

Pseudepigrapha   Biblical-related texts whose authorship is unclear, but is often wrongly attributed by the author(s) to figures of the past. Jewish pseudepigrapha were generally written between 200 BC and 200 AD. They are not regarded as having full scriptural authority by either Jews or most Christians.

Ptolemies   Greek rulers of Egypt who followed the 'Greek Macedonian' period of rule by Alexander the Great, his half brother, and his son, from 332–310 BC. The Ptolemaic period of Egypt lasted from 305 BC until the demise of Cleopatra VII in 30 BC.

Ris   A measurement of length of 350 cubits. It was based on the length of the side of the Great Pyramid of Cheops at Giza of 440 royal cubits, which equated to 1.25 *stadia*. The perimeter of the base of the Great pyramid was reported to be 5 stadia. The *stadion* is called a *ris* in the Mishnah, and appears to be the same measurement used in the New Jerusalem Scroll.

Romans   Dominant power in the Middle East and Mediterranean area from the middle of the 1st century BC to the 4th Century AD. The Romans conquered the Holy Land c44 BC and, Octavian Augustus appointed himself pharaoh of Egypt in 30 BC.

St Jerome   Previously known as Eusebius Hieronymus (c342–420 AD). Born in Stridon, Dalmatia, he studied in Rome and, after being baptized a Christian, became a priest at Antioch, travelled to Rome where he became secretary to Pope Damasus. In 386 AD he settled in Bethlehem, where he made an important Latin translation of the Bible from the Hebrew, later known as the Vulgate. This, in corrected editions, is regarded as authoritative by the Roman Catholic Church.

Talatat Prefabricated building blocks, developed in the Amarna period to facilitate faster and more effective construction of buildings and structures. They were generally made of sandstone and measured 1 cubit (52 cm) x 0.5 cubit x 0.5 cubit.

Tannaitic period   Rabbinic period from about 10 AD, through the destruction of the Second Temple in Jerusalem in 72 AD lasting to about up to 200AD. The rabbis of this period were responsible for fixing the content of the Hebrew bible as the Tanakh.

Teffilin   Phylacteries, or small leather containers with leather straps, strapped on the left arm and on the forehead during daily prayer recital by pious Orthodox Jews. Today they usually contain a piece of leather inscribed with a section of Deuteronomy (6:4–9 and 11:13–21) and Exodus (13:1–10 and 13:11–16). The forehead tefillin contain the same Biblical citations, but are written on four separate leather rolls secreted in four separate compartments. Tefillin found at Qumran also contained the Ten Commandments and their context of Deuteronomy 5:1–6, 9, and an extended passage relating to 'circumcision of the heart' (Deuteronomy 10:12–11:21). Some 30 phylacteries were found in various Qumran caves, most containing biblical texts which varied from the normal now found in modern teffilin.

Torah The Torah, in its narrowest sense, comprises the Five Books of Moses as in the Pentateuch of the Christian Old Testament. In its wider sense, it encompasses the whole of Jewish teaching. In addition, there are oral laws, traditional stories and stories of moral instruction comprising the Mishnah (developed in the 1st and 2nd centuries AD), which, when combined with the Gemorah (discussions on the Mishnah developed between 200 and 500 AD), are known as Talmud (either deriving from Palestrina or Babylonia). Midrash are homilies and interpretations on the Jewish scriptures, developed in the 13th century AD.

Yahad Literally means 'together' in Hebrew and is a term used ·by the community at Khirbet Qumran to refer to themselves, as in their sectarian texts, such as the Community Rule (4QSd).

Index